Problems with History and Current Events:

Reflections on Historical Narratives from an American Who Lived in Paris

Bradley O' Cat

Contents

Dedication i

Acknowledgements ii

About the Author iii

Introduction 4

Paris - An Architectural and Historical Marvel 12

Section 1 – Historical Narratives 23

Chapter 1: The Romans 26

Chapter 2: The Age of Faith 37

Chapter 3: Societal Organization after the Roman Empire
.... 47

Chapter 4: The Awakening of the West 56

Chapter 5: The Beginnings of the Modern Nation-State .. 64

Chapter 6: Luther: The Man and his Imperfections 68

Chapter 7: The Thirty Years War and the Westphalian
System 73

Chapter 8: The Negative Impacts of the Industrial
Revolution 77

Chapter 9: The Narrative of Liberal Democracy 80

Chapter 10: Societal Organization in the West and how it
Relates to the EU 83

Chapter 11: Progression toward Superstates - The EU 90

Chapter 12: The United Nations 96

Section 2 – Current Political Landscape 108

Chapter 1: The Trump Presidency 111

Chapter 2: Comparisons of American Social Problems with
the UK and France 114

Chapter 3: The Narrative of Race Relations 145

Chapter 4: Disrupting the Narrative of the Presidency ... 153

Chapter 5: Trump Paraphernalia 158

Chapter 6: Donald Trump and His Lies 162

Chapter 7: The Media Climate Today Enables Trump's
Lying 170

Chapter 8: Trump's Coddling Of Dictators 176

Chapter 9: American Isolationism 185

Chapter 10: Trump and the Emoluments Clause 203

Chapter 11: American Soft Power Is Important 224

Chapter 12: Trump's Tactless Manner of Speaking 230

Chapter 13: Trump's Antics and Behavior 233

Chapter 14: Trump and Social Media 236

Chapter 15: The Electoral College and the Party
Conventions 239

Chapter 16: Soundbites and Simple Solutions to Complex
Problems 248

Chapter 17: Racism and Racist Attitudes Debunked 259

Chapter 18: Trump and Hypocrisy 270

Chapter 19: Trump Continues To Have a Stranglehold on
the Party 274

Chapter 20: Concluding Thoughts 281

Section 3 – Narratives and their Flaws 292

Chapter 1: The Superior Western Narrative 292

Chapter 2: The Communist Narrative 296

Chapter 3: Muslim Narrative 302

Chapter 4: The Japanese Narrative 306

Chapter 5: The Chinese Narrative................................. 312

Chapter 6: The Jewish Narrative 319

Chapter 7: The Nazi Narrative 324

Chapter 8: Anti-Semitism in General in Connection With

Nazism 329

Chapter 9: Napoleonic Narrative 334

Chapter 10: The Narrative of the Conquered and Colonized

Peoples 342

Chapter 11: Bumps in the Road with Narratives 361

Chapter 12: Narratives and Their Flaws 377

Epilogue 390

Index 396

Dedication

Dedicated to my maternal grandparents and my mom.

Acknowledgements

To my maternal grandfather, who taught me a lot about different subject matters and the value of reading. Also, to my maternal grandmother, who lived with me, took care of me, and just recently passed away.

About the Author

The author was born in New York but grew up in Quezon City, Philippines. He moved to the US permanently at the age of 12. In the US, the author has lived in New Orleans, the San Francisco Bay Area, Saint Paul, Minnesota, and Los Angeles. He has spent a year in the UK, and has lived for several years in Paris. He attended Jesuit High School in New Orleans, has a Bachelor of Arts in Political Science from the University of San Francisco, a Juris Doctor from Hamline School of Law, a Master of Laws in International Law with International Relations from the University of Kent at Canterbury, and a Master of Arts in Global Communications from the American University of Paris.

Introduction

The times we live in have definitely been tumultuous ones in American politics and world events. The division of the world into two camps, the communist world and the non-communist world, which was the way the world was during the Cold War, no longer exists. I will refrain from using the term "Free World" since there were many states in the non-communist camp that were hardly free as they were ruled by tyrannical despots aligned and supported by the US. This Cold War division of the world into two camps has been replaced by a more complex and uncertain world with various states and regions vying for their place in the world order. Biden, in his first trip abroad as president, gave a message of unity in the West to counter Russia and China, which gives an inkling of the world we live in three decades after the end of the Cold War. Biden talked admiringly about democracy and how it is a positive force that, despite its challenges, will in all certainty prevail in the long run.[1] No other belief states the Western narrative and worldview more clearly than Biden's proclamations to his European counterparts. These past few years, from 2016 to 2020, have witnessed a US president unlike any other to navigate the

---

[1] Briefing Room. (2021, February 19). Speeches and Remarks. https://www.whitehouse.gov/briefing-room/speeches-remarks/2021/02/19/remarks-by-president-biden-at-the-2021-virtual-munich-security-conference/

country through these uncertain times. Trump has changed the presidency after his four years in office for better or for worse. Who would have thought there would be a US elected president who would act the way he does? I could never imagine that one day a US elected president would behave the way he did. His outrageousness knows no bounds. He flouted every norm and every expectation of how a president should act. Marine General John Kelly, the former White House chief of staff, described Trump as "the most flawed person" he has ever come across.[2] This is obvious as he was always promoting himself and always preferred what was good for him over the national interest. He continued to promote the big lie that he won the election, and his actions caused social tension, which can never be in the best interests of the US. Kelly observed first-hand his shockingly dishonest nature. Trump, in all honesty, had no reverence for the office which he held. Basically, he had no intention of lifting himself up to the level of the office. Instead, he dragged the office down to his level. In any case, the historical narratives of various societies and times are not always perfect and have underlying problems that cause major flaws in the narrative. Trump is just one of the worst,

---

[2] CNN. (2020, October 16). Former White House chief of staff tells friends that Trump 'is the most flawed person' he's ever met. https://edition.cnn.com/2020/10/16/politics/donald-trump-criticism-from-former-administrationofficials/index.html

if not the worst, at destroying narratives, but this has happened time and again throughout history. To be fair, Trump did not create all the racism that he fuelled. Just like how Hitler and the Nazis did not invent anti-Semitism, Trump did not start all the racism that was just underneath the surface among certain elements in the population. He just gave those elements a voice they needed by saying the outrageous, politically incorrect things that he said and the way in which he said them. These are times that we need to look back to the founding fathers as they seem to know a lot about the nature of democracy and how it should be run. The Jeffersonians believed that citizens should be enlightened and virtuous, which meant education holds central importance in a democracy. Thomas Jefferson actually called for a "crusade against ignorance."[3] This was one of the arguments in favour of a public school system. It makes sense as uneducated and ignorant people are not going to make the best decisions, and they can be easily manipulated by someone with ill intent and someone who does not have the best interests of the country in mind. Trump, during his campaign and speeches, for the most part, was demeaning and attacking his opponents to the detriment of actually talking about the issues, which his opponents Hillary Clinton

---

[3] Brinkley, A., Current, R. N., Freidel, F. Williams, T. H. (1991). American History: A Survey Eighth Edition. McGraw-Hill, Inc.

in 2016 and Joe Biden in 2020, would actually do. For someone to get away with this, who is running for the highest office nonetheless, shows major flaws in the educational system. And indeed, there have been major criticisms and flaws of American public education for a long time. In any event, a fully functioning democracy is one where candidates discuss, argue, and debate the issues rather than engaging in more attention-grabbing antics than the others. It does not serve the electorate when the nation's problems are not discussed and debated.

Since I was in Paris during the Trump presidency, I had a feel for where things were headed in the US by watching the news. And the news made it seem like things were spiralling out of control with racists coming out in the open and everything ugly in society rearing its odious head. This also included the anti-Asian attacks that started at the end of the Trump presidency, at the height of COVID and continued into the Biden administration. And it seemed like everything that was wrong was outrageously encouraged by an overtly outspoken, tactless, crude, and bombastic commander in chief. I would ask people online on social media who were in the US about the situation in the US and what it was like and was told that anti-Asian incidents were mostly in New York and California and predominantly in certain areas of cities. In any case, whether the media was sensationalizing things or not, the image that they painted was a dire one, with the fabric of social cohesion in society tearing apart at the seams. Whatever the case might be, it was obvious that things were not good by any stretch of the imagination. There was no doubt that there were problems. This, along with other incidents like the racist taunts black Capitol Police officers received during the insurrection, made it really seem like racists were now out in full force with the encouragement and backing of a president who shared their views. Trump's refusal to speak out and condemn right-wing fanaticism was an affirmation to those individuals that they could continue with their racial assaults with impunity. It was as though Trump was a volume-enhancing device like a microphone or a megaphone for these extreme voices in society. In the past, they were at the extreme edges of the social and political spectrum, but Trump's divisive and racist rhetoric gave them a sense of legitimacy and, to a certain extent, made their voices mainstream.

In any event, I was fortunate enough to live through these events across the pond in Paris. And it is in this great and majestic city that I have decided to write this book. Even while gallivanting the streets of this urban marvel, enjoying the cuisine that this city has to offer, watching the rain pour down on the rooftops of buildings, and sometimes having a seat and watching the day pass away at the Jardin des Tuilleries, I still kept up to date as to the news and current events in the US and the world in general. From my apartment in the seventeenth arrondissement of Paris with a marvellous view of La Defense in the distance and then later from a suburb of Paris, I watched the news every day. Keeping abreast of current events over these years has made me think of the times we live in now in contrast to the context of the narrative of World History, particularly by the dominant Western narrative and the American narrative. It also allowed me to observe and study the problems within these narratives as opposed to other narratives outside the dominant Western and American narratives. The Trump presidency and events around the world need to be discussed and explained in context and its place in Western and world history. The election of Donald Trump is a perfect example of the flaws of democracy and the Western narrative. Winston Churchill once said, *"Many forms of Government have been tried, and will be tried in this world of sin and woe. No one pretends that democracy is perfect or all-wise. Indeed it has been said that democracy is the worst form of Government except for all those other forms that have been tried from time to time."* This shows that politics, in every state and society, no matter what form it takes, is difficult as the government needs to satisfy society at large and all the factions within it with its competing interests, whether it is a democracy or not. Some groups or individuals have interests that are against the interests of other groups, which means no matter what form a government takes, be it a democracy, monarchy, dictatorship etc., the duty of governing is not easy and is sometimes a thankless endeavour. Trump has definitely proven Churchill right. A substantial number of Trump voters were a part of society that felt like they were not being heard, and Trump gave them a voice. However, Trump's presidency has disrupted the narrative of the presidency and how presidents behave. A reason for this is that it was someone like Trump that the forefathers did not want to occupy the office. This will be discussed in detail later in the book. Basically, it is demagogues like Trump that the forefathers feared, which is why they tried to create a filter between the passions of the masses and the direct election of the president by creating a body known as the Electoral College, which in reality is the body that votes for the president. This body has been diluted and stripped of its powers over the years compared to what it was when the nation was founded, which is how a disruptor of the American historical narrative in major and crucial ways was elected. The US and the West have always tried to impose their ways, in other words, their narrative or parts of it, on the rest of the world through colonization or otherwise. This has happened throughout the last several centuries. It has been taught, and the West acts like their narrative is the way the rest of the world should develop, whether it is through Western-style industrialization or democratic government. But as will be discussed further, there are always problems with narratives. Likewise, there are setbacks and disruptions with narratives even in the West and the US. Their narratives of economic and political progress have always been portrayed to be improving over time to a better and better state and that the rest of the world should emulate it. And if Western states are having problems with their narrative, we can imagine far greater problems that it can create in Non-Western societies where the Western narrative is being imposed in one form or another.

Paris - An Architectural and Historical Marvel

The American social psychologist Jonathan Haidt suggests: "Human mind is a story processor, not a logic processor." So when it comes to global politics, one word, in particular, that keeps popping up in political conversations is narrative. While politics worldwide has evolved into a social activity that has become central to human life, political narratives and even their analysis rely a great deal on geopolitical factors and historical and cultural context. There is a need to understand the background and stage from where any political commentary is being delivered in understanding and dissecting political discourse. This background allows readers to distinguish between the sub-genres of political text and see the political landscape from a different lens. It is within this framework of understanding that compels me to write this book that can offer you some context in the interpretation of political utterances around the world as well as my analysis of the different political narratives.

The place you live in tends to mould you as a political actor or analyst. And the city from where I write this book is of note in this context as a city of consequential significance and defining history. Paris has been home to poets, artists, writers, eccentrics and a myriad of others who have made a mark for themselves as illustrious members of humanity. These people, along with many other visitors and local Parisians, have breathed the air of this timeless city. Promenading along the streets and boulevards of this city that is not just an architectural wonder but has also been rich in culture and history for several years now has made me think of all the great figures who have walked these same streets and patronized the numerous cafes that dot this urban marvel. I have experienced this city in all its moods, during the heat of the summer and under the relentless rain in the fall and winter. If nothing else, Paris is all about the rain, probably just as much if not more so than London. But besides myself and the countless others who will remain nameless to posterity, many famous and historical figures have visited its storied streets and world-renowned architecture and have called the city home at one time or another. I have come to believe that Paris needs to be lived and not just seen. Such is the allure of this legendary French capital. Il faut vivre à Paris et respirer son air et découvrez la grandeur de la ville lumière.

In fact, several of the United States founding fathers have also called Paris home a couple of times in history. During the War of Independence, several of them went to France in order to gain the French alliance and assistance and had spent a lot of time in the Court at Versailles. Individuals like

John Adams, Thomas Jefferson, and Benjamin Franklin liked French life and culture and even learned French. Benjamin Franklin knew how to play the game at Court in Versailles and wined and dined with important court figures late into the night in complete contradiction with his advocacy of the proverb "Early to bed and early to rise makes a man healthy wealthy and wise," as written in the Poor Richard's Almanack. He was doing none of this at Versailles and was more like a party animal to the complete shock of his colleague John Adams. Franklin, the consummate diplomat, on his part, knew how to be a diplomat and realized this was how one gets things done.[4] Jefferson loved France and even assisted in writing the Declaration of the Rights of Man. He would also buy products from France to be brought back to his home in Monticello.[5] He even famously had his slave, Sally Hemings, with him in Paris, with whom he had relations and bore children. Sally was a free woman in France, but she would be a slave again had she returned with Jefferson to Virginia. Sally agreed to return to Virginia only on the condition that her children would be freed when they came of age.

---

[4] Myers & Monroe. (n.d.) Founding Fathers and French Furniture. https://www.myersandmonroe.com/founding-fathers
[5] Minister to France. https://www.monticello.org/research-education/thomasjefferson-encyclopedia/minister-france/

It can be argued that the United States would not have gained independence if not for the assistance of the French and the actions of these founding fathers in this great European capital. The independence of the United States and the influence that people like Jefferson had on the French scene could arguably have had an influence in sparking the French Revolution.

Being an American of Filipino ancestry, I also learned about how Filipino historical figures who played a significant role during the fight for the independence of the Philippines spent time in Paris. Jose Rizal, the national hero of the Philippines, spent some time in the City of Light along with the Luna brothers Juan and Antonio. The former was a famous Filipino painter, while the latter was a scientist and Filipino general during the revolutionary war against Spain and the subsequent Philippine-American War.

Antonio Luna was a researcher who published a scientific treatise that was received in a good light by his peers in the scientific community. He was even an assistant to doctors at the Pasteur Institute. The Spanish government recognized his abilities and commissioned him to study tropical and communicable diseases. Upon his return to the Philippines, he worked with the Municipal Laboratory of

Manila.[6] He later fought in the War against Spain and the US in the Philippines and was known to have a fiery temper which resulted in his assassination by his own troops.

Antonio's brother, Juan, was a painter who was the creator of some of the famous artworks in Philippine history like Spoliarium, The Blood Compact, Las Damas Romanas, and The Parisian Life or Interior d'un Café. The last of these works is one of his most notable art pieces. This last piece was painted during his time in Paris. It shows a scene inside a Parisian café of a woman who was probably a courtesan. He has portrayed the woman in a position where she is in the middle of standing up to her feet. She overshadows three men in the far corner of the painting.

These men happened to be himself, José Rizal and one of his colleagues. An important element of the subject of the painting is the belief among some art scholars that the form of this Western, Parisian woman represented the entire Philippine archipelago.[7] As talented as an artist that he was, he was also mired in scandal and controversy. He killed his wife and mother-in-law in a crime of passion as he believed

---

[6] Vallejo Jr., B. (2010, August 12). General Antonio Luna: Scientist, soldier and revolutionary. https://www.philstar.com/business/science-andenvironment/2010/08/12/601469/general-antonio-luna-scientist-soldier-and-revolutionary
[7] Arcangel, Jr., Rey T. (2013, November 11). Mysteries behind Luna's 'The Parisian Life,' revealed. https://tawidnewsmag.com/cache-juan-luna-parisian-life/

her to be having an affair with a Frenchman. The media sensationalized this love triangle killing at the time as "Le Drame de la Rue Pergolèse" (The Drama of Pergolèse Street).[8] He was acquitted by a court of law and afterwards left for the Philippines with his son.

Even his son was a Filipino of note with connections to Paris. Born in Paris, he left as a child for the Philippines along with his father. He then returned to Paris and studied at the École des Beaux-Arts. Upon returning to the Philippines, he was appointed as the architect of Manila.[9]

Of all these prominent Filipino statesmen and revolutionaries who called Paris home at some point in their lives, none was more prominent than the Philippine national hero, José Rizal. In Europe he wrote Noli me Tangere and El Filibusterismo which highlighted the avarice and excesses of the Spanish friars in the Philippines. He spent about eight years of his life in Europe in various European countries such as Spain, France, Germany, and the United Kingdom. Not content with the quality of education in the Philippines, he wanted to pursue his studies in Europe, specifically in Spain. Eventually, he pursued his medical studies and trained in other countries such as France and Germany. He

[8] McCoy, Alfred W. (2009). An Anarchy of Families: State and Family in the Philippines. University of Wisconsin Press.
[9] Andres Luna de San Pedro. (2022, July 30). In Wikipedia. https://en.wikipedia.org/wiki/Andrés_Luna_de_San_Pedro

even did research in the United Kingdom. It was in Paris where he spent time with his friends, including the Luna brothers. He stayed at various hotels in Paris, such as the Hotel de Paris and one currently where the Hotel Aramis is now. He also did a portion of his ophthalmology training in Paris for several months.[10] He was also one of the prominent world-renowned figures among many who glared at the marvels of the famous 1889 World's Fair. One only need to gaze at the plaque against the wall on 37 Rue De Maubeuge where he once stayed and walked through Place José Rizal to know that this national hero of an island archipelago in Asia had once enjoyed the glitz and entertainment that The City of Light offered in the years during the "Belle Époque". Together these three individuals, Rizal and Juan and Antonio Luna, were active in the movement that advocated reforms to Spanish rule in the Philippines, particularly regarding the Church's behaviour towards native Filipinos, which forever engraved their name in the annals of Philippine history.[11]

Many other important figures around the world have passed through these magnificently lighted and gilded boulevards. Two of the most famous Spanish artists, Pablo Picasso and Salvador Dali, were once Parisians who strolled

---

[10] Embassy of the Philippines. Paris, France. (n.d.). FILIPINOS TRACE RIZAL'S FOOTSTEPS. https://parispe.dfa.gov.ph/2013/75-filipinos-trace-rizal-s-footseps
[11] Wikipedia. (n.d.). José Rizal. https://en.wikipedia.org/wiki/José_Rizal

the boulevards and enjoyed the cafés of this most beautiful of cities. Picasso made his first trip to Paris as a young man during the Fin de Siècle at the height of the Belle Epoque. There are not many who know that he was a suspect in the theft of the Mona Lisa from the Louvre in 1911 when it was taken by an Italian worker of the museum.[12] He lived in Paris through the German occupation of WWII, finally dying in the south of France in the early 1970s.

Salvador Dali, though not born in Paris, spent the majority of his life roaming this marvellous city. As an artist, Montparnasse was where he was in his element. Dali left such an impression in the city that there are places named after him all over the city. There is even a Dali Museum dedicated to his works.

There were many other notable figures who made this city home. Ernest Hemingway (Ernesto to the Spanish speakers who knew him) moved to the city in the 1920s after getting married. On a side note, not many people know he was on the D-Day landings, albeit on the seventh wave when the beaches were already secured and where there was virtually no chance of him even getting wounded.[13]

---

[12] Wisdom Land. (2020, January 28). Stealing the Mona Lisa-Art Theft of the Century. [Video]. Youtube.
https://www.youtube.com/watch?v=uYsPSL5XkV4
[13] LA TIMES ARCHIVE. (1994, May 31). D-DAY INVASION / June 6, 1944: THE INVASION OF NORMANDY: BY THE NUMBERS.

Other renowned figures also called Paris home at the time with whom Hemingway was acquainted; Gertrude Stein, Ezra Pound, James Joyce, and Max Eastman. They would be among those of the "Lost Generation".

Even Karl Marx moved to Paris, where he met Engels in person, which produced one of the greatest and historic friendships in history. He was even forced to leave Paris to move to Brussels due to the pressure from the Prussian government, who wanted him extradited. He was eventually stripped of his citizenship by Prussia, and he ended up in London as a stateless refugee, where he died. Though he was a wanderer moving from one country to another, he lived in Paris during an important period of his life.

Many other foreign notables, closer to our present-day, called Paris home, including Kenzo and Karl Lagerfeld from the fashion industry. The famous photographer Helmut Newton also took many of his famous photographs in Paris while living there (whose eroticism shows in his photographs as he could not seem to get sex out of his mind). Even the US Secretary of state, Antony Blinken, spent his adolescent years in Paris.

Moreover, an infamous personality, Carlos the Jackal, who initially became notorious due to murdering a couple of

https://www.latimes.com/archives/la-xpm-1994-05-31-wr-64227-story.html

police officers at an apartment at 9 Rue Toullier in the Quartier Latin during the 1970s, had a lot of his terrorist and criminal activities connected with Paris.[14] He was finally caught by French agents in Khartoum in the mid-1990s and brought back to France to face trial for his crimes, as many were committed in Paris.

There were some rather mysterious events as well, such as the mysterious disappearance of Mehdi Ben Barka. He was probably kidnapped in Paris and subsequently disappeared without a trace. Another one was the death of Jim Morrison in a Paris hotel under mysterious circumstances. One could even go back centuries and ask, "Who was the man in the iron mask?" One of the more fantastic theories of his identity was that he was the twin brother of King Louis XIV. However, some of the more plausible candidates for the man behind the mask were Eustache Dauger and Ercole Matthiole.[15] Some of the most prominent works of literature like Les Miserables and The Hunchback of Notre Dame by Victor Hugo had Paris as a setting. And the Phantom of the Opera of course by Gaston Leroux was set in the Paris Opera. All these works were not

---

[14] Peter David. (2018, June 8). History's Mysteries - Carlos the Jackal (History Channel Documentary) [Video]. Youtube. https://www.youtube.com/watch?v=0po_ss6K6Og
[15] The Editors of Encyclopedia Britannica. (2022, May 31). the man in the iron mask. https://www.britannica.com/biography/the-man-in-the-iron-mask-Frenchconvict

just set in Paris, but it could also be argued that Paris itself was an important character in these novels.

This list is in no way exhaustive, and one can write an entire book about all those notable figures who called Paris home. The ones that have been mentioned are just some examples of some of the notable historical figures who have lived in Paris and became part of the history during their stay in the city. And for this reason and more, I take great pride in being a part of this incredible city. I was born in New York, raised in Manila, then moved to the US permanently at the age of twelve and subsequently lived in several parts of the US, followed by one year in the UK. For several years now, I have been living in Paris, where I have written this book. I also have three graduate degrees on top of my college degree, including a law degree, a master of laws, and a Master of Arts in Global Communications. With this backdrop, I, too, wanted to do something of note while living in this most magnificent of cities, which is a reason that inspired me to write this book. So maybe in this way, I can somehow make a mark of my own, however small, in this city that I have called home "depuis plusieurs années déjà".

Section 1 – Historical Narratives

History has been used as an important tool for understanding how the world around us has taken shape. Not only does it help understand how the current world has become what it is by the process of constant change, but it also lends insight into envisioning the future. Like most long-running interdisciplinary relationships, political narratives and history has taken significant turns. And in that sense, history has always remained a core feature of political analysis and narratives. That said, it is also important to remember that both political analysts and historians are often interested in history to use it as a tool for supporting or discrediting theoretical hypotheses and political narratives.

Therefore, thinking of history as knowledge of the past and possibly of nothing else can help us make sense of the current world without buying into flawed narratives. This is important because analysis of political narratives might remain incomplete without a full perspective of history and the past political landscape. So, before discussing different types of narratives and their flaws, let us first examine the historical background that shaped different political narratives.

For instance, the western historical narrative can be seen as a progression as the West went through the Dark Ages then grew out of its dark slumber into the Middle Ages. This progression gave way to a beginning of interactions with the Muslim East through the Crusades and then with the Renaissance and Enlightenment on to the French Revolution and various other revolutions that swept Europe during the nineteenth century. Then there was major technological advancement in the Industrial Revolution where the modes of production within society became more efficient and mechanized as opposed to the agricultural society of the past. With the Industrial Revolution, a large and robust middle class was born who demanded more political rights, and so one sees here not only a technological progression in the West but a political one as well. And now, in the 'Fourth Industrial Revolution,' which is all about the internet, and social media, the world is now firmly in the Information Age. This Industrial Revolution is much cleaner than its predecessor. And more people in the world now are living under democracies than at any time in history.

Similarly, one can also observe a progression in Western history and development from that of society being predominantly ignorant and superstitious to the people of today being rational.

Through this narrative of cultural, intellectual, and technological progress throughout the centuries, there has always been an underlying dark side to the narrative that often gets overlooked or swept under the rug in each historical period as it does not jive with how these historical époques should be seen or are sometimes thought to be inconsequential to the major themes and developments of these particular historical periods.

History makes significant contributions to our political knowledge by shedding light on new facts and giving perspective and intention to current political relations and developments. The study of past political movements, developments, occurrences is incredibly important to understand different political narratives. The knowledge of historical background can help us to formulate the right political objectives and conclusions.

Chapter 1: The Romans

One thing that has remained common throughout the two thousand years of Western history, from the Greeks and Roman Empire to the United States today, the world's number one power, is their superiority complex. The Romans and Greeks believed they were superior to all the civilizations around them at the time. They regarded the various tribes and peoples outside their jurisdiction as barbarians only because they spoke in languages that were not understood by the Romans and Greeks. Since the Greeks came up with the concept of democracy, it was natural that they thought it superior because now all men were free and responsible citizens in the polis, which guided it in how it should run its affairs. All other societies they engaged with or had political relations with practised some sort of authoritarian rule where not everybody was represented in the running of social affairs. Consequently, this made the Greeks perceive themselves as superior to the groups around them. This is especially true of the Persians with whom they engaged in several wars. Greek society also gave birth to prominent thinkers and philosophers like Plato and Socrates. This was another realm that enabled the Greek narrative to thrive as it further advanced the idea of how men ought to behave and aspire to embody. They were indeed successful in not only fending off their foes that allowed their thoughts and beliefs to survive up until the Romans came along and conquered them but also in leaving a legacy of their culture and beliefs that were later adopted by Romans. As a result, this further advanced the belief and strength of the narrative of what all societies would eventually evolve to become. The Romans continued this belief that theirs was the model all other barbarians should mould themselves to emulate. A notable example of this was how the Romans and a barbarian group would have an exchange of one of their children to grow up with the other side to see how they lived and learn about their ways.[16] The primary objective of this exchange was that the Romans believed that an outsider who would live and grow up among them would be able to witness that their civilization was indeed impressive and would then embody the characteristics and traits of what it is to be a Roman. Another benefit of this exchange was that the barbarian tribes would ally themselves to Rome so that these barbarians would eventually take on the traits of the Roman civilization.

Of course, this was not perfect and had its own problems, proving that the narrative did not always work the way the Romans wanted it. A good example of this was Arminius, who was of barbarian origin, but his tribe was allied with

---

[16] Dyck, Ludwig Heinrich. (2016, October 19). World History Encyclopedia, Arminius. https://www.worldhistory.org/Arminius/

Rome. So, he learned to speak Latin and joined the Roman military. His moulding into a proper Roman came to a crashing end in the Battle of the Teutoburg Forest, where an entire Roman Legion was ambushed and wiped out in a single battle. One reason for the disaster was the fact that Arminius had learned Roman tactics, so he knew their strengths and weaknesses pretty well. He knew that the Romans were at their weakest when they were not into a formation, and that opportunity came when they were making their way through the forest. The Romans needed an open field to be able to use their tactics and manoeuvrability in order to outsmart their opponents. These tactics, which the Romas believed to be superior, were taught to Arminius in his training, who then used them against the Romans to outplay them.[17] The Romans miscalculated as they overestimated their ability to mould or brainwash others into their way of thinking. He was not exactly completely brainwashed and indoctrinated into the Roman worldview as he changed loyalties and united the tribes against Roman rule. This was an example where someone who was in the Roman army and learned Latin did not completely buy into the fact that Roman civilization was the end-all and the best of all societies conceived by mankind, thus putting a

---

[17] Stay a while and listen. (2018, September 7). The Germanic Revolt Against Rome: Arminius [Video]. Youtube.
https://www.youtube.com/watch?v=AF4HJdsF3i0

defining dent into the western narrative. He was still loyal in the end to his native people, and a statue stands to this day in Germany in memory of him.

Contrary to Roman beliefs, the Roman Empire had its ups and downs and was not always progressing to a better and better state through its one thousand years of existence. For one, the greatness of the Roman Empire was built on the backs of slaves. This is the evident dark side of the narrative of Roman greatness. The Romans would conquer other tribes and nations and would take those that they captured into slavery. Slaves were used as gladiators in the arena or for hard manual labour. The number of slaves was astounding, and they were oppressed to the degree that a slave rebellion under Spartacus eventually achieved a certain amount of success until finally it was defeated.

Spartacus achieved some initial successes due to the fact that the Romans underestimated his abilities. This is especially an important aspect when we talk of the ugly side of Roman society. They used the labour and entertainment that they needed and wanted by means of exploitation of the slave labour. These slaves came primarily from the people they had conquered, which was even more humiliating for those enslaved and, as a result, continued to build up the animosity against the Romans. They had lived as free people before their tribe was defeated by the Romans. Not only did they suffer the humiliation of defeat in battle or war, but they then had to further suffer by becoming slaves. These supposedly most civilized Romans then behaved very brutally against those whom they saw were not equal to their status.

The Romans also had some major military defeats even though they were perceived as the best military force at that time. The Romans fought major wars against the Carthaginians, and they suffered major defeats against them during the Second Punic Wars under the Carthaginian General Hannibal. The Roman bogeyman had Roman civilization teetering on the edge of defeat and being conquered at one point. Some defeats were in the Italian Peninsula itself, and in one battle, the Romans lost fifty thousand men. Hannibal gave the Romans a lot of sleepless nights until he was finally defeated by Scipio. This defeat finally set the Roman Republic on its course of empire as it got control of vast territories that they otherwise would not have controlled had they not fought the Punic Wars, much less if they were defeated by the Carthaginians.

The Romans also saw their Republic end with the imposition of the empire by Augustus Caesar after a bloody civil war fought against Mark Antony and Cleopatra that ended with the Battle of Actium. This shows that no matter how strong the Roman military was and how large their empire had grown, there was always internal instability where various individuals tried to usurp power. Later on, the unity of the world's most powerful empire was fractured into as much as four territories. Eventually, the division of the empire settled into two separate regions. This shows that no matter how proud they were of the size of their empire, it was just too big to manage from one centre. Thus, it was divided into two parts to better administer both wings. We see here that the narrative of unity and size of their empire did not always hold sway due to internal political conflicts that gave way to a civil war that ended their republic and the difficulty of administration in later centuries that fractured their empire into the east and west wings. This was beneficial later on because what we think of as the "Fall of Rome" was the end of the Western Empire. The Eastern Empire centred in Constantinople lasted for another thousand years.

The Romans also have themselves to blame for treating the barbarians as groups of people that could be used and abused. Evidence of this is seen with the various barbarian groups that were allowed to enter and settle within the borders of the empire. These immigrant barbarians were taxed heavily, and their children were taken to be trained into the Roman army. They would also abuse their barbarian allies by positioning them on the front lines, who, therefore, had to take the brunt of the enemy attack, and they would thus suffer more casualties. These actions sowed distrust among the barbarians of their Roman overlords. This was a major reason for the Sack of Rome in 410 by Alaric and the Visigoths. By this time, the Germanic tribes had undergone massive changes due to their interactions with the Romans. As a result, they were slowly but surely closing the gap between themselves and the Romans. But because of the way the Romans saw these barbarians, they were not treated favourably by the Romans, which led to the Sack of Rome at various times during the late Roman Empire. This demonstrates how the Romans were not living up to their potential as civilized people acting in a benevolent manner towards their barbarian subjects, and were treating people within their empire who were loyal to them and were their allies as their inferiors, which led to disastrous results. Slowly but surely, as the Roman Empire neared its end, barbarian groups from all over were pillaging and encroaching into Roman territory. One of these barbarians who caused nightmares for the Romans was Attila (the scourge of God). He caused a lot of mayhem and destruction to the western part of the empire. It got so bad that he was getting paid in treasure in order not to sack and pillage Roman lands. This was how some believed the pope was able to convince Attila not to sack Rome after meeting him when Attila was approaching Rome. These barbarian incursions into the peninsula, for instance, was a reason for the founding of Venice.

Ever wondered why Venice has the flood problems that it has and why it is sinking? Yes, there is an interesting history to it and one that is relevant to our discussion about narratives. Venice is not the ideal place to build a city, and it was built out of desperation by people fleeing from the mainland who were in the swath of Attila's path of destruction. Refugees from the continent wanted to escape the wrath of Attila, so they went to the coast to build Venice among other islands on a lagoon as they had gauged that the barbarians would not bother them there. Not only was it surrounded by water, but the water level was constantly rising, which meant that Venice would continue to slowly sink. It was never an ideal place to build a city by any stretch of the imagination, but because of an emergency of people fleeing in peril, they had no choice but to build a city there. The foundations of the city are the thick wooden poles underneath the structures that have petrified over the centuries.[18] Thus, the foundations of the city that enable it to survive are man-made and not natural. If you were an academic and you studied the paintings of Canaletto from several centuries ago, you would notice the difference in

[18] Science Channel. (2014, February 24). The Surprising Foundations of Venice | Strip the City [Video]. Youtube.
https://www.youtube.com/watch?v=B3INp81NimE

water levels from those times compared to the water levels in Venice today.[19] Regularly the water rises and floods Venice, known as the High Water or Acqua Alta. Slowly but surely, the city is sinking, which is why scientists are trying to find solutions to this problem. The point is the problems that Venice is facing can be traced all the way back in history to the barbarian invasions toward the end of the Roman Empire and is testimony to the decline of the Roman Empire and their inability to protect their own borders from menacing threats.

In any event, these numerous barbarian incursions from different barbarian groups along with the decadence of the Roman Empire through their corruption and increasing dependence on their barbarian allies eventually led to their downfall in the last quarter of the fifth century. Even to this day, people tend to think of these barbarians as savages who had nothing to contribute to humanity. On the contrary, they had their own rich culture, art, etc., that can be traced back to that time even today.[20] This totally debunks the narrative that the Romans were the only ones who had a civilization worthy of note, while the barbarians who were living in their

---

[19] The climate change clues hidden in the work of Canaletto. (n.d.). Royal Museums Greenwich. https://www.rmg.co.uk/stories/topics/climate-change-clues-hiddencanalettos-paintings-venice
[20] Perspective. (2020, April 30). What The Barbarians Did For Art: The Huns, Vandals and Goths (Waldemar Januszczak)| Perspective [Video]. Youtube. https://www.youtube.com/watch?v=7qPA3Y38asM

midst were brutal savages who had nothing worthwhile to contribute to the patrimony of mankind. Again this shows that narratives are not always what they seem to be.

Another example of the Roman narrative is the superiority of their military. Through superior technology, tactics, and discipline, they believed that they were invincible against any foe. The problem arose in the last centuries of the empire as more and more barbarians were being incorporated into the Roman Army, and as a result, their tactics and equipment became diluted. They no longer carried the heavy weaponry of the past but were looking more and more like their barbarian allies. Their shields, for instance, became smaller and no longer the rectangular shields of the past that covered their entire body practically.[21] So instead of making the barbarians more Roman, in this instance, the Romans were becoming more like the barbarians. This shows how the Roman narrative, in this case, manifested by Roman propaganda, was chopped down to size by their supposed inferiors - the barbarians living in their midst. Thus, this is a dent in the narrative of Roman progress. The Romans always believed themselves to be the most technologically advanced society. But in the last few centuries before the end of the empire, the Roman

---

[21] Weapons and Warfare. (2015, September 20). Weapons and Warfare; History and Hardware of Warfare.
https://weaponsandwarfare.com/2015/09/20/late-roman-armor/

army was just a shadow of its former self at the height of the empire.

The fall of the Roman Empire is an example of where a narrative does not always progress in a linear fashion to a better society as the West was plunged into the Dark Ages through Rome's decadence, stupidity, and corruption in the latter period of their empire. It also shows the ugly underbelly of their great society, which was built on the shallow foundation of violence, slavery and maltreatment of outside groups, which would eventually become their undoing.

Chapter 2: The Age of Faith

The Age of Faith, which coincided with the Dark Ages, is regarded by a vast majority of European citizens as an age of ignorance and superstitions. It was the monks secluded in their monasteries that kept the flame of knowledge burning through writing books and manuscripts and keeping the light of education constantly lit. Most of those outside the monastery walls were illiterate and superstitious or, at best, less educated than the monks inside the monasteries. Other higher church officials tended to be educated and literate as well, such as bishops and archbishops. Literacy was, thus, typically the realm of the churchmen. Even noblemen in the early Dark Ages tended to be illiterate as they were mostly warriors, which was their primary duty in society. Fighting was their life, and learning was neither considered necessary for them nor were they expected to acquire knowledge as it was not essential to them in doing their job. As an example, Charlemagne learned to read later in life as it was not considered important to him being a ruler, and he was busy ruling his realm and defeating enemy tribes.[22] Education was just not seen as important. Due to the fact that monks and other churchmen were educated and literate, this gave them

---

[22] Vision Video. (2020, November 9). How Should We Then Live | Season 1 | Episode 2 |. The Middle Ages | Francis Schaeffer [Video]. Youtube. https://www.youtube.com/watch?v=QgtaKXX5OL4

a lot of power and skills needed to fill important and functional roles in society. Keeping records and writing histories are some examples of these roles. A major practice in the Age of Faith included the veneration of objects connected with Jesus and the saints. In order to get a fair idea of this aspect of history, all one needs to do is go into the European cathedrals all over the continent to find objects connected to the saints or even to Jesus like a piece of the true cross. It was widely believed by the people of those times that these objects had miraculous power since they had connections with the saints. These objects would be venerated since they were believed to endow their believers with healing powers. These relics were so important that relic boxes were made wherein to place the relics. These were beautifully crafted and ornately adorned with jewels. There was a saint for some aspect of everyday life which was connected to how those saints lived their lives or how they died. Thus, the sale of holy relics was big business in those days as there was always a market of believers willing to pay top price for them. The church would also exploit the masses' superstitious faith with tithes, indulgences and the fear of hell to keep them in line. Kings would consider it worthwhile to collect holy relics to be part of the church's collections. Holy relics were so important that when the Venetians somehow got their hands on the relics of Saint Mark in the Near East, they brought them back to Venice and placed them in Saint Mark's Cathedral. William, the Conqueror who also kept saints' relics in high regard, took Harold Godwinson's oath as binding when Harold swore on holy relics in Normandy that he would support William's claim to the throne of England as the legitimate successor to Edward the Confessor. Such are examples of the high premium that was placed on holy relics during this time in human history.

There were many downsides to this narrative during the Age of Faith. Yes, it was marked by excessive piety, but it also came at a price. And that price was violence if necessary. This violence was especially witnessed when it came to heretics. The Catholic Church had a monopoly on religion during these times, and Church and state were inseparable and worked closely together, so when people were considered heretics, it was considered so serious as if they were violating their loyalty to the state itself. And it was the state which enforced the punishment as that was not the Church's role even though the Inquisition comprised of religious figures who would decide on the punishment. And the means employed in order to maintain one faith throughout the Christian lands were violent if necessary for those who deviated grievously from the orthodoxy of Catholicism. The Inquisition, as an institution, was so strong that it lasted several hundred years up to the mid to latter half of the nineteenth century. Even Napoleon, who tried to eradicate it as he viewed it as archaic and not in accordance with the principles of the French Revolution for which he was fighting, was still not able to eradicate it completely.[23] As a result, it still lasted several decades after he was in power. In any case, the Inquisition had its roots in the Age of Faith primarily to stamp out heresy.

One example of a major heresy during those times was Catharism. This heretical movement emerged from the southern part of France in the Languedoc. They were characterized by identifying themselves as Bons Hommes, Bons Femmes, or Bons Chrétiens (Good men, Good women, and Good Christians). They believed in a dualistic doctrine. Everything physical in the world was evil, and God was a spirit that was uncorrupted by the physical world. And for the most part, they rejected the beliefs of Catholicism altogether. The Church started a systematic campaign against them.

They were burned if they refused to repent. Eventually, a crusade was launched against them, similar in stature to the crusades launched against the infidels in the Holy Land. The Crusaders took the towns in the region where there were

[23] Piper, G. (2021, July 17). Napoleon Ended A Three Century Reign of Terror In Spain, The end of the Spanish Inquisition. Exploring History. https://medium.com/exploring-history/napoleon-ended-a-three-century-reign-of-terror-b2e61a811919

numerous Cathars one by one, which included a Massacre at Béziers. The other towns were put under siege and were taken as well. Once military operations were done, the Inquisition was established to root out the Albegensians within their towns. Punishments were varied, with the harshest being burning at the stake if the heretic absolutely refused to repent.

The crusades were arguably the most important events during the Age of Faith. The First Crusade was called by Pope Urban II, inspiring Christians to free the Holy Land from Muslims. The crusaders were told that they would be expunged from their sins committed while on Crusade, whatever they may be, due to the righteousness of their cause. This led to the egregious excesses of the crusades, like the massacre of Jews and Muslims in Jerusalem at the culmination of the First Crusade when the Crusaders finally overran Jerusalem in 1099 after besieging the city. This was yet another example of how blood was shed in the name of the one true faith. Richard the Lionheart also showed his ruthlessness during the Third Crusade when he had thousands of Muslim prisoners executed after the fall of Acre. These are just some of the shocking excesses of violence committed during the four major crusades and the countless others that followed that shed real light on the excesses committed in the name of the religion founded by Jesus.

Another case where the force of the state was made to bear was what happened with the Knights Templar. The Knights Templar were an instrumental force in the Holy Land during the times of the crusades. They protected pilgrims who were travelling to the Holy Land from Europe from bandits who may want to rob them. They also came up with a system where pilgrims could deposit their money with a Templar office in Europe and get the same amount once they went to a Templar office in the Holy Land, thus creating the modern banking system.[24] They were also given the Temple Mount in Jerusalem as a base which they excavated, and whatever they were able to find is all but left to conjecture and lost to history.[25] They were also used in battles for the purpose of turning the tide of battle if needed. They were the special forces of their time, without a doubt.

After the crusades were over, they had lost their purpose for existing, but they still had amassed a lot of wealth, especially land. Philip the Fair, king of France, was in debt to them, and he also desired their lands. He needed to

---

[24] Jeremy Small. (2020, November 3). National Geographic Knights Templar Warriors of God. [Video]. Youtube. https://www.youtube.com/watch?v=HJyl6CiA6-4
[25] Jeremy Small. (2020, November 3). National Geographic Knights Templar Warriors of God. [Video]. Youtube. https://www.youtube.com/watch?v=HJyl6CiA6-4

concoct something in order to erase his debt to them and also acquire their wealth. But to do this, he needed the approval of the Church in the form of the Pope. He came up with the plan to accuse them of heresy which they allegedly practised during their initiation ceremonies. The Church investigated but found no evidence of heresy, but the Pope reluctantly agreed with Philip the Fair, which resulted in the Templars' arrest on Friday the thirteenth, a day which has ominous repercussions to this day. The leaders of the Templars, Jacques de Molay and Geoffrey de Charney, were burned at stake for their alleged heretical practices. Here is another example of the underlying narrative of violence used by the state during the Middle Ages in the name of the one true faith (Catholicism).

There were many other problems as well during that age when people were supposedly so pious. The Church was so embroiled in politics that it tried to control the behaviour of monarchs to a certain extent. On the other hand, the Pope as well became a plaything of the kings. The Avignon Papacy or the Babylonian Captivity, as it is referred to, is proof of how the Church was so embroiled in worldly affairs. During this period, the Pope resided in Avignon instead of Rome. There was no other reason for the move than politics, and so the Pope and Church would be under the influence of the French monarchy. Then eventually, after several popes in

Avignon, the Pope moved back to Rome. But then, due to more politics, the second line of popes was started at Avignon, known as antipopes, as opposed to the Popes who were in Rome, so there was a time in history when there were two different groups of popes. All this happened due to worldly monarchs trying to exert influence on the Pope and making the Church their sort of pawn on the chessboard. The popes, at other times, would try to exert their power and influence over the monarchs of Europe to get them to behave the way they wanted them to behave since the representative of Christ on earth was supposed to be higher authoritatively than the worldly kings. A good example where kings and the popes would try to exert leverage of their power, for instance, was the appointment of church officials like bishops. The popes would also exert their power and influence by getting the nobles of Europe to go on Crusade to kill for Christ, whether in the Holy Land or against heretics domestically. These instances give one a more earthly perspective on the Age of Faith and show that it had its worldly problems just like any other age, with selfish players trying to play the game in order to advance their worldly influence even though it was historically an era marked by piety as evidenced by all the cathedrals built during that time period.

The Inquisition would also be used against converted Jews and later on during the Protestant Reformation to enforce orthodoxy. And it would also be used against individuals who made scientific discoveries that were contrary to orthodox teachings. For example, when Copernicus discovered that the sun was the centre of the universe, the Catholic Church held firm that the earth was the centre. So the Inquisition would continue on and become more prevalent and ruthless at the dawn of the Reformation and Enlightenment due to the fact that the Catholic Church could no longer control what people thought due to the scientific advancements and the more critical nature of how people thought about things. Modern inventions like the printing press made literature widely available to a larger audience which means that the church had less and less control over what was being diffused throughout society. In times past, with books being expensive, handwritten by monks, and difficult to obtain, the few books that existed were copied meticulously by hand by monks inside monasteries that allowed the Church to easily impose orthodox thinking with the information being disseminated contained in these books. This is why the Church had to be more ruthless in the form of the Inquisition during the Reformation and Catholic Counter-Reformation, as the Catholic Church no longer had control over orthodox thinking that was being diffused. The Inquisition survived well into the nineteenth century in certain parts of Europe like Spain and the Papal States. De Goya was called in front of the Inquisition, for instance, for painting a nude woman, so in some sense, it veered away from imposing orthodoxy instead evolving into a sort of censorship committee. But make no mistake about it, this violent institution had its origins in the Age of Faith. The reason for the Inquisition was to save souls, but the Church also made a lot of money from its believers in the form of taxes, tithes, and services that needed a local priest. If people were lost to the faith, it meant not just a loss of souls to the one true faith but a loss of income from all these individuals who strayed and no longer believed. Money had a big part to play in the Age of Faith.

Today when one visits Cathedrals all throughout Europe, one can admire the architecture of these structures and the priceless holy artefacts found inside. These are all testimony to that great Age of Faith that Europe lived through for several centuries after the Fall of Rome. Tourists and believers alike can visit these places and admire the works and relics inside. But if one were to delve deeper into the history of this era, one would learn all the violence that was perpetrated in the name of Jesus and the one true faith, which places a worldly and real perspective of what happened during this era.

Chapter 3: Societal Organization after the Roman Empire

The Dark Ages after the fall of Rome were a huge step back as a society. The lands of the former Roman Empire were now more rural and regional. Communal or societal interests, by this time, had also shrunk onto a rural scale. One can see here a regression in the narrative of Western Civilization from that of a civilized Roman world to rather less civilized dark times in Western history. This is where one cannot see history as progressing toward the betterment of mankind. It is also important to note that the progress of societies is never linear as there are always regressions and setbacks. The progress of any type of political narrative can be more akin to a soap opera or professional wrestling with their twisted plotlines without any firm resolution in the end, like a movie with a happy ending. A perfect example of this is societies like Iran and Afghanistan.

Back in the 60s and 70s, the elites in these societies had Western lifestyles, with people going to nightclubs and women wearing skirts rather than veils. But now, due to the harsh Islamic rule that they are under, that way of life is gone and is replaced by a conservative brand of Islam and, in the case of the Taliban, an extreme form of Islamic rule. This is an example of how a society or culture face a setback or goes through a regression. This was no different for the West during the Dark Ages after the fall of Rome.

During the Dark Ages, people were illiterate, superstitious, and ignorant. From the vastness of the empire with, for the most part, a homogeneous administration, Western society devolved into very local administrations, with rulers now ruling small geographical areas within what was left of the former empire. An example of this was in 476 when with the fall of Rome, Odoacer deposed the final emperor and became the King of Italy. So administration was now local to the Italian Peninsula instead of a larger empire it once was. Yet Rome's fall did not happen overnight. It was neither abrupt nor unexpected. The fall of Rome was long and gradual, and the Dark Ages could be foreseen long before the empire collapsed. Just like Rome was not built in a day, Rome did not fall in a day either. Odoacer deposing the emperor and making himself the ruler was simply symbolic of what was already an established societal fact since the barbarians already had the power and were ruling behind the scenes. The Roman emperor, by this point, was just nominal, and his strings were being pulled by the barbarians. Rome as a civilization had been declining for quite some time after experiencing centuries of greatness, and that decline continued onto the Dark Ages after the ultimate fall of the empire. So if we can assume that the

Roman narrative peaked at probably the time of the Caesars when their power was greatest, it wouldn't be wrong to say that it declined in the last century or so before the fall, and it was obvious that the empire would not last for several generations more. Barbarians were just penetrating through the empire whether by force or through lawful means, and their numbers were just too high for the Romans to do anything about it. Romans couldn't control them anymore, and this meant that they did not live up to their values of absorbing different people to see what they could contribute to Rome. This also meant that they couldn't exploit the barbarians within their territories, whether through taxation or through drafting their youth into the Roman military.[26] However, in the wake of the end of their narrative, they influenced other cultures in Europe and other parts of the world that incorporated wholesale and many of the things the Romans were known for. The Eastern Empire, though, managed to last another thousand years until the fall of Constantinople in 1453. The West was now weaker as there were various rulers with their own armies that could now turn on the other rulers if it best suited their interests, unlike the unified empire of the past. This new form of administration was a step back from the more advanced form

---

[26] Searles, H. (2016, June 28). The Fall of Rome Began with the Abuse of Refugees. Fee Stories. https://fee.org/articles/the-fall-of-rome-began-with-the-abuse-of-refugees/

of society and administration that the Roman Empire offered. And even though there were attempts from Constantinople under Justinian to reconquer the West, it was forever lost to the local, regional administrations that eventually formed the modern nation-states of Europe that we know today. The devolution of power from a central Roman administration to regional rulers set up Europe for disaster against various invaders like the Muslims in the eighth century. After taking over almost all of present-day Spain, the Muslims were finally halted in their progression of attempting to conquer the rest of Europe in the south of France in Tours by Charles Martel.

Then after the Muslims, continental Europe had to deal with the Vikings, who were raiders. Vikings preferred quick raids instead of conquests, which allowed them to gather up instant wealth that they could readily take away with them. They would raid all over Europe using the rivers as their highways. They built boats that were conducive to navigating these waterways. With powers now localized as opposed to former times under the Roman Empire, it was easier for invaders like the Vikings to raid up and down the rivers. It wasn't until Charlemagne's rise to power and his coronation in 800 as emperor by the Pope that there would be an empire once more that could rival Constantinople and try to recreate once again the Western Roman Empire. The

Holy Roman Empire, though not Holy, not Roman, and not an empire was a huge leap forward from the way Western rulers organized themselves. Finally, there was an emperor who was competent and powerful and who admired Rome and the power of the Roman Empire and styled himself like a new Roman emperor. Though a step forward, it was still nowhere near the form of an organization like the nation-state or the superstate like the EU that we know today. The coronation of Charlemagne by the Pope also marked the close collaboration of church and state in the administration of society, and so religion could now mix with politics for a momentous chunk of Western history up until the Thirty Years War.

During this time, the notion of the modern nation-state was still far off in its development as the primary organization of society during these times was feudalism. Lords would swear fealty to a monarch who would then grant these lords or nobles land in exchange for their loyalty and unchecked power. This ruling class was responsible for fighting while the church also held a lot of influence and controlled the society hand in hand with the ruling classes, making the distinction between church and state almost negligible. The church would ordain and sanction the monarch's power as long as its actions did not overstep the church's principles. If the Pope did not like a monarch's action, the Pope had the power of ex-communication. The power between the Holy Roman Emperor and the Pope played out in the Northern Italian city-states, which was the chessboard in which the Pope and Holy Roman Emperor vied for the advancement of their power on the Italian Peninsula. The Italian city-states, though nominally independent of external powers as they ran their own affairs, were nonetheless exploited by the Pope and Emperor for their own interests and for advancing their power vis a vis their opponent. The city-states were classified as either Guelphs or Ghibellines, depending on whether they supported the Pope or Emperor.

The cities based their alliance on their interests, depending on who was more of a threat to them. The Pope was very much an important player in the power politics of his time. The conflict between the emperor and the Pope, embodied in the conflict between the Guelphs and Ghibellines, was based on who had the power to choose and install bishops. It was this world, for instance, that Dante was born into. Dante was a native of Florence who experienced banishment from his own city during his lifetime. He knew the politics of the society in which he lived. His writings show a vivid description of hell with its nine layers filled with sinners, each lower level replete with more grievous sinners than in the levels above. And at the ninth and lowest level are found the traitors of history, Judas, Brutus, and Cassius, who are being chewed on by the devil for their sins.[27] His writings offer us a vivid depiction of what was going on in his mind and how he viewed the world of his time with all the politics and intrigue.

Some of the few places where feudalism did not hold sway were the Italian City-states which had a strong merchant class that would later fuel the Renaissance. For the most part, though, the way societies organized themselves was through feudalism. Religion and politics would mix seamlessly for a long time, largely until the Thirty Years' War. The Thirty Years' War was a remarkable turning point in the development of the nation-state because it was during this war that it was realized that the interests of the state do not necessarily have to align with religion. This feudal system would slowly decline after the Black Death when there was a shortage of labour due to the high death toll caused by the plague, and so the peasants had more bargaining power when it came to offering their services.

Thus, one can see here a progression when societies started in a rigid class structure with strong religious overtones but, of course, with the exception of the Italian city-states where feudalism did not take hold. One can add

---

[27] Dante, A., Must, M., & Powers, R. M. (1971). Dante's Inferno. Bloomington: Indiana University Press.

to the mix the Papal States, the strip of land across the centre of Italy, where the Pope held power both temporal and spiritual. We can thus see in the Europe of the time a hodgepodge of ways in which societies organized themselves, depending on what suited their needs. This new way was far removed from the strong centralized government that the Roman Empire exercised at the height of its power. Thus, this is an example in the Western historical narrative where human progress encountered a major setback. On the other hand, it is also true that we cannot expect society to always evolve into a better state as time goes on, as history has its fair share of ups and downs and is not always improving for the betterment of humanity. In layman's terms, there are always bumps in the road.

During these times, as there was no semblance of the modern nation-state, the land changed hands every so often after a victory or defeat in a war. Alliances would also be forged through marriage when a princess of a certain geographical area would marry a prince of another region, forging an alliance with a key player in the European political arena.

For the most part, up until these times, the state structure was very regional. Powerful local princes and barons held much of the power within their own territories, and the monarchs, to a certain extent, were dependent on them for political support. This naturally meant that the monarch had to keep them happy, which was a constant give and take that we see in the very embodiment of the feudal structure.

Chapter 4: The Awakening of the West

When one considers the organization of societies, there is an enduring belief that societies gain more and more wealth as society progresses and citizens become more educated by learning more about the world around them. In the West, during the Dark Ages, the feudal system was the predominant structure of society throughout much of Europe. There were a few exceptions where feudalism did not get a foothold like the Italian city-states, but for the most part, it was the dominant way in European societies or Christendom, which is how they identified themselves. This system was distinctly recognizable by the fact that the monarch was the supreme head of the state and derived his powers from God himself. This meant that his proclamations and decrees could not be questioned. Along with this, the noble class that he belonged to, which was a small segment of the population, held much of the land and much of the power along with the church, and the vast majority of peasants had little power vis a vis the aforementioned two classes. The noble classes' role in the social order was to fight, the church to pray, and the peasants to toil. Feudalism would slowly but surely go on the decline, starting with the Black Death and the enormous toll it took on the population of Europe. After the Black Death had passed and Europe lost a big chunk of its population, labour was in scarce supply, which gave peasants more bargaining power, thus increasing their standard of living as their services were now in demand. There was also the rise of the Italian city-states that feudalism did not even touch as these polities were the stronghold of merchants who had a lot of disposable wealth that they could then use for luxury products like works of art, which is why the Renaissance was born in Florence. Conjecture as to the identity of the Mona Lisa, for example, was that she was a merchant's wife.[28] The merchants were the movers and shakers of the northern Italian city-states, which is why they could afford to pay the most talented painters like Leonardo Da Vinci to paint something for them. The Medicis were wealthy bankers who could pay the best artists like Michelangelo, and these artists could experiment with their art, and so the Renaissance entered the world stage. The subject of art during the Renaissance also changed to non-religious subjects as opposed to the purely religious subjects of the past. With religious subjects, the work itself was important, and so, therefore, many of the artists of those works were unknown. But during the Renaissance, when subjects became more worldly, and the painter and sculptor were seen as the artist that he was instead of blue-collar workers that did not have any special skills, artists became

[28] Lisa del Giacondo. (2022, June 9). In Wikipedia. https://en.wikipedia.org/wiki/Lisa_del_Giocondo

household names like Michelangelo and Leonardo Da Vinci. In short, the artists of known repute attained celebrity status as opposed to the craftsmen status of their professional forebears. A big reason for this was the knowledge aspect when it came to art which involved mathematics and anatomy. It was also during the Renaissance, for instance, when art rediscovered perspective. Now art could be visualized in three dimensions. Perspective was known to the Romans but was lost after the fall of Rome during the Dark Ages. In Pompei, one can see the three-dimensional art on the wall among the ruins. This is a testament to the fact that Romans knew how to represent three dimensions on a two-dimensional canvass. Double-entry bookkeeping also began to be practised during the same age, which helped merchants and businessmen enormously when keeping accounts of their profits and debts.[29] What started with art would flow into other things like politics, science, religion etc. Needless to say, the Renaissance was just that - a rebirth. The West rediscovered the knowledge that was once known centuries ago but was subsequently lost and was applying this lost knowledge from antiquity once more in the various fields of human endeavour. It was a time bursting with

[29] Devlin, K. (2019, May 1). How Double-Entry Bookkeeping Changed the World. Mathematical Association of America.
https://www.mathvalues.org/masterblog/2019/4/26/how-double-entry-bookkeeping-changed-the-world

energy and creativity in science, mathematics, art etc. It was a time when humans felt closer to God by virtue of the fact that they possessed more knowledge about the world he created, unlike their medieval ancestors, who were superstitious and ignorant. The people who lived before the Renaissance were so ignorant of the world and its laws that God to them seemed a distant and mysterious being whose wisdom was infinitely superior to theirs and their poor grasp of the world around them. In essence, the humanities were now at the forefront.

But even this narrative, where Western civilization was taking a step forward with the Renaissance in the Italian city-states, had a downside. The flip side to the narrative was that there was a lot of violence underneath the surface of the great things that the Renaissance was producing. It was in this atmosphere that Machiavelli wrote "The Prince" as a sort of guidebook on 'realpolitik' since he wanted to teach princes of his day to be practical and see the world for what it was and rule accordingly without any lofty ideals and false hopes of trying to create a paradise on earth, a utopia, to be more precise.[30]

Machiavelli knew that if princes or rulers were naïve or idealistic in nature and outlook, they would be taken

---

[30] Machiavelli, Niccolò, 1469-1527. The Prince. Harmondsworth, Eng.; New York, N.Y. :Penguin Books, 1981.

advantage of or even ousted from power. And the Italy of Machiavelli's time was definitely a ruthless and cunning society with the various powerful families of the various city-states vying for power vis a vis their adversaries. These Italian city-states had a lot of rivalry between their prominent families. For instance, San Gimignano was considered the Manhattan of the Middle Ages due to its many medieval towers. The reason for this was that families who were prominent in society would build a tower as a status symbol that told the fellow townsfolk that they were a prominent family.[31] The way these families interacted with each other was very competitive and, in many instances, violent. Romeo and Juliet may have been a work of fiction, but the societal problems it presented with rival families constantly intriguing against each other was very real during the Renaissance in Italy. This could be seen with the two prominent rival families in Florence: the Medicis and Pazzis. The history between the two families was long and complex, but basically, when one family would gain power, the other family would be exiled and vice versa. And the violence between them could be evidenced by the murder of Lorenzo the Magnificent's brother, Giuliano, as he was assassinated

---

[31] To Tuscany. (n.d.). San Gimignano-medieval Manhattan. https://www.to-tuscany.com/travel-guide/townsvillages/florence-chianti/panzano/top-ten-things-to-do/san-gimignano-medieval-manhattan/

in church on Easter, which signified the start of the Pazzi Conspiracy.

There were also wars between the various Italian city-states, which they fought to a certain extent with mercenary forces. These mercenary soldiers, who could be English and German (or whoever else was looking for work as a soldier for that matter), would come down to Italy because that is where they could find work as mercenary soldiers. They would hire themselves out to certain cities and would sign contracts laying out the rights of the employers (the cities) and the employees (the mercenary soldiers). The contract would lay out when the armies could fight, the seasons, for example, how long they would fight, and if the contract was over, how and when they could offer their services to another city. There were also clauses as to who would be responsible for weapons, horses etc. Sometimes these armies would be problematic because they would not fight if conditions were horrible.[32] So their loyalty had limits. None was a more perfect exemplar of this than the Englishman, John Hawkwood (Giovanni to Italians). He made a living on hiring himself out to Italian cities that were willing to hire him. He died and was buried in Florence, the city that hired him, and he is buried there in the Duomo with a portrait of

---

[32] Saunders, Frances Stonor. Hawkwood: The Diabolical Englishman. Faber, 2004.

him by Paolo Uccello. This shows that there are always different layers to the narrative. Though the West was waking up from its long slumber with the Renaissance and its improvement in diverse fields of learning like the Arts, it was propagated by an ugly layer underneath, as can be seen with family rivalries and inter-city violence. Not to mention these Northern Italian city-states were the chessboard in which the Holy Roman Emperor and the Pope fought their wars against each other in the twelfth and thirteenth centuries in the era of Medieval Italy right before the Renaissance. This shows that inter-city warfare has always been present and a part of Italian city-state 'realpolitik' and was not a mutation of a particular time in an otherwise peaceful region. Nowhere are the contrasts in narratives present than in the persons of Pope Julius II and Michelangelo, who was hired by the former to paint the Sistene Chapel even though Michelangelo resented the job. Michelangelo was, of course, one of the poster boys of the Renaissance, and when people think of the Renaissance, they associate it with Michelangelo and his painting of the Sistene Chapel, among his numerous other works. However, his employer Pope Julius II represented the other side of the narrative as he was a warrior Pope who led his own army into battles and was even successful in expelling the French to the other side of the Alps with the aid of allies.

The narrative is not always perfect. We today know about the works of art produced during the Renaissance and the genius artists of that time. But we don't usually know or discuss the warfare that was prevalent between the various city-states during the same time period. This shows that there are always parts of the narrative that are imperfect and loopholes that are turned a blind eye to, no matter how marvellous we make the Renaissance out to be.

Chapter 5: The Beginnings of the Modern Nation-State

When we study political history, around the middle of the second millennium, we see the stirrings and beginnings of the modern nation-state, which shows the progress in the organization of how states organized themselves. A very good example is Spain with the forging of the modern nation-state as a result of the "Reconquista". After the Muslim conquest of most of the Iberian Peninsula, the Christians were left in control of only a small portion of the entire Peninsula where their power formerly rested. Slowly but surely, throughout the centuries, the Christian princes reconquered various regions of the Iberian Peninsula until the only geographical area under Muslim control was Granada.

During these centuries, there were many professional warriors like El Cid who would hire himself out to both Christian and Muslim princes before becoming, in the end, the Christian hero he is known to be, as portrayed in the movie by Charleton Heston. When Grenada finally fell to Ferdinand and Isabella, Spain was united, and the modern nation-state was born as power was now with the monarchs and no longer with the local princes.

In France, the monarchy overcame the powerful local princes over time, and they established total sovereignty over France in the 16th century, which was a result of several factors. One of the key factors was the laws of primogeniture which meant that the firstborn would inherit everything as opposed to the inheritance being shared equally among various heirs. Another was recognition of the superiority and illustriousness of the Capetian line as opposed to their other noble rivals.[33] And there was also the support of the church for the Capetian Dynasty, which would bode well for a strong central government in France. A reason for this strong alliance with the church and the French monarch can be traced back to the First Crusade, which was composed predominantly of Franks.

In England, too, the modern nation-state was formed during the Middle Ages.

After the defeat of the Vikings by King Alfred the Great, subsequent rulers defeated local and Welsh rulers, thus consolidating power in a central monarchy. More defeats of other political rivals on the British Isles subsequently ended the rule of local rulers in favour of a central monarch, thus making it a nation-state in the modern sense.

Thus, these were some of the first nation-states that were developed. It was a leap forward in the structure and organization of societies in which power was now

[33] Britannica. (n.d.). Capetian Dynasty.
https://www.britannica.com/biography/Henry-I-king-of-France

centralized in a central government. This government had the power to craft laws, defend their land and impose taxes. This was a more efficient system than what was predominant in Europe in the past, where local lords and princes held power within their territory with the power of coinage, defence, laws etc. That former system was less efficient since constant taxation of goods would increase their prices. An example of this could be seen in the Rhine River, where one sees to this day castles at certain intervals throughout the river that were built by the local lords and barons of those areas to charge taxes and tolls on goods as they were making their way through the river.

The system of defence before the modern nation-state system was also less efficient because, during the feudal period, the monarch was, to a certain extent, reliant on its vassal lords for armies to fight wars. And the modern nation-state was also a step forward in a way that it had the power of coinage throughout the realm. There were only different currencies once someone left a territory and entered another.

One sees in the formation of the modern nation-states the monopolization and centralization of power that was lost during the years after the Fall of Rome. Thus the social organization was slowly creeping back to a semblance of top-down efficiency that societies severely lacked since the downfall of the Roman Empire.

The modern nation-state, though an improvement in the way societies organized themselves when compared to the way societies were organized previously, still has its problems with regards to the narrative of societal organization. In the past, nation-states were organized in the way that they ruled over a territory, and its people and problems also came with it. Gradually, over time nation-states were organized with the way they waged wars vis a vis other nation-states. Evidence of this can be seen in the likes of conscription of people to fight wars and the alliances they can enter into with other nation-states to fight against their enemy states. For instance, the Levée en Masse, which started during the French Revolution, was used by Napoleon to raise troops in France and among the occupied states against armies with larger numbers which made Napoleonic battles numerically sizable compared to battles up to that point which just multiplied the carnage on the battlefield thanks to the organizational abilities of states to raise ever-larger numbers of troops. The destructive power in the wars that nation-states can wreak culminated in the two world wars of the twentieth century. Thus, the way governments of nation-states organize for wars is a noteable problem in the narrative of nation-states.

Chapter 6: Luther: The Man and his Imperfections

The primary cause of the Thirty Years' War was the rivalries and power struggles of the princes of the Holy Roman Empire that stemmed from religion. The Holy Roman Emperor and his allies - the Catholic princes, fought against the Lutheran princes of the realm. Lutheranism was one of the largest branches of Protestantism that believed in the theology of Martin Luther, a 16th-century German monk and reformer. It was Luther's efforts to reform the theology and practice of the Roman Catholic Church that launched the Protestant Reformation.

Thus, Protestantism, in the form of Lutheranism, finds its origins in the early sixteenth century when a Catholic monk expressed his many grievances against the Catholic Church of his time by posting them on the door of the local church. Foremost among these was the sale of indulgences. Luther wanted to discuss and debate the issues that he observed. He found the way the Church was running its affairs problematic and something that required reformation. The Pope, with the Holy Roman Emperor on his side, demanded a recantation of Luther's beliefs. When Luther wouldn't budge from his new ideas, he was excommunicated from the Roman Church. He was then sent into exile into

Wartburg Castle, where he translated the New Testament from Greek into German, among other things.

However, in the decades that followed his death, his beliefs spread like wildfire, primarily due to the Printing Press that allowed his teachings to reach the masses like never before. In the years after his death, his followers eventually multiplied to enormous numbers, which also included princes, rendering the Lutheran reform movement legitimacy as it was not just relegated to the common folk anymore. This demonstrates that though there is a technological progression in the human narrative with the improvement in the means of communication via the printing press, it came at a cause which was that of causing social upheaval as well as the fracturing of a common creed into rival confessions. We observe this again later with the creation of the internet and social media, which has opened up multiple channels of communication and has caused extreme marginal voices to find an outlet and a way to magnify the scope of their ideologies to show that they are a potent societal force. The bottom line is because technology has given voice to everyone in society, even the marginalized, the advancement in technology inevitably causes a fracturing in the fabric of the social mantel.

Similarly, Luther himself and his narrative are not free from faults. Though he is historically seen as a pious, devout, and reform-minded Christian trying to reign in the excesses of the Roman church, the truth is he was not perfect either.

This is especially evident with his eventual support of the princes in the German Peasant's War when the princes brutally suppressed the uprising. Luther, though understanding the plight of the peasants, did eventually lay the hammer down hard against them as their rebellion was causing social upheaval even though they were airing out their grievances, albeit violently, through rebellion due to the fact that they thought Lutheranism lent credence to their plight.[34] Luther argued that though oppressed, the peasant's duty on earth was to work. This was the typical worldview of many people of his time. In order for there not to be any social upheavals, people were taught and believed that the nobles and the peasants were born into their circumstances by God's divine will. And to make it even worse, they believed that it should not be questioned and to violently overthrow the social order would be trying to tamper with the divine order of things on earth. Another flaw to point out is that Luther supported the princes against the peasants because he was dependent on their protection against the powers in the Holy Roman Empire and in Rome, who wanted him to be done away with permanently. One must

---

[34] German Peasants' War. (2022, July 14). In Wikipedia. https://en.wikipedia.org/wiki/German_Peasants%27_War

remember that Luther was excommunicated by the Pope and was declared a heretic and an outlaw by the Holy Roman Emperor, which meant he had enemies, so he needed protection, and that protection could be provided by the princes. In this way, Luther's narrative falls apart in that though he was historically a devout Christian who was only trying to reform the excesses of Rome or, as some would say, the "Whore of Babylon", he also wanted to survive and had his smart street wits about him by realizing who could protect him against his enemies. Though the peasants had some real grievances, he knew the ones who could benefit him were not peasants but the princes.

Luther was also fiercely anti-semitic like many other notable personalities of his time, which will be a stain on his historical reputation. He wrote an anti-semitic treatise against them called "On Jews and their Lies". In the treatise, he advocated many anti-semitic policies. For instance, he denounced the religion and supported its persecution. He also advocated burning and destroying their synagogues and homes. He also wanted their sacred books to be taken from them. He wanted their rabbis to be forbidden to teach and that safe-conduct not be given to them on the roads. He also wanted usury prohibited, which was only prohibited to

Christians but were allowed to Jews.[35] This is evidence that he was also a product of the anti-semitic environment of his time. Thus underneath the surface of this historical movement and figure lies an ugly dark side that tends to be often overlooked by his followers and the world in general as the narrative is that of a man who helped break away from Rome to start a purer form of Christianity free from the shackles of Roman corruption and debauchery.

---

[35] Paras, E. (n.d.). The Darker Side of Martin Luther. IWU. https://www.iwu.edu/history/constructingthepastvol9/Paras.pdf

Chapter 7: The Thirty Years War and the Westphalian System

The Thirty Years' War was a series of wars that took place among European nations for various reasons. It erupted in 1618 over an attempt by the King of Bohemia, who became the future Holy Roman Emperor Ferdinand II, to impose Catholicism throughout regions that fell into his territory. Protestant nobles rebelled, and as a result, by the 1630s, most of continental Europe was at war.

The Thirty Years' War itself had several phases, and it dominated the first half of the seventeenth century. In the aftermath of its destruction, Europe was to never be the same as European politics became much different afterwards. During the years leading up to the Thirty Years' War, with the increasing numbers of Protestants, there were constant disputes between them and Catholics. The politics were even further complicated with the rise and growth of another Protestant group, the Calvinists. These tensions became so much worse that finally, they led to war in 1618. Though the war was predominantly fought within the Holy Roman Empire, it also involved outside powers that were allied with one side or another in accordance with their economic and political self-interests outside of religion. One sees this with France allying with Protestants. And since they aligned based on their self-interests, including religious interests, these outside powers allied themselves with those who did not share their religion, like France allying with the Protestant powers like Sweden against the Habsburgs. This was all thanks to Cardinal Richelieu, probably the greatest politician of his era. His main objective was to advance French interests and make France the greatest power in Europe, and the Habsburgs stood in the way of French dominance. Richelieu's cunning was exhibited in The Three Musketeers as he was the novel's principal antagonist. There were different phases of the war, as mentioned earlier, that led to different involved powers intervening with one side or another based on political and economic interests during the war that started as one of Catholics against Protestants. And since they aligned based on their self-interests, including religious interests, these outside powers allied themselves with those who did not share their religion, like France allying with the Protestant powers like Sweden against the Habsburgs.

The subsequent Peace of Westphalia was regarded by many historians and scholars within the field of international relations as the birth of the precepts and concepts of international relations that is even reflected in current-day politics and international relations. Included in it was the primary principle that borders are inviolable and that external states cannot interfere in the sovereign affairs of other states. This was a huge step up in the creation of rights and powers of the modern nation state that were not recognized before. This is still practised today and states cry foul when other states try to intervene in their internal affairs, typically when Western states complain of the human rights practices of other states. This is yet another rupturing of the narrative. Even today, despite the principles of the Westphalian System in place, some states use their power and influence to interfere in the sovereign affairs of other states. If it is not chastising a state for egregious violations of human rights, some states may use its influence in the form of aid, for example, so the state receiving aid will pursue laws and policies favourable to the state giving the aid. Today one can see proof of this in the Middle East, with many on the Arab streets complaining that the US government gives aid to Arab governments with many strings attached. In other cases, some also blame the US government for aiding governments that are brutal to their own people but friendly to the US.

The most recent example of the violation of state sovereignty is perhaps the Russian invasion of Ukraine. Russia invaded Ukraine based on lies that Ukraine was being run by Nazis. But in reality, Putin does not want Ukraine to join NATO or be within the "Western sphere of influence," which is what Ukraine wants in accordance with its right to self-determination. Putin, instead, wants Ukraine to be within its sphere of influence or perhaps a neutral state like Austria, Finland, or Sweden. But who knows what Putin wants? In my opinion, Putin, too, is exercising Russia's self-interest in that case as he wants protected borders in Europe. NATO is getting closer and closer to the Russian border, and Russia does not have the buffer of Communist Eastern Europe anymore that the Soviet Union had. It can also be said Putin is paranoid of invasion as Russia and the Soviet Union had to deal with Napoleon and Hitler, both of whom laid waste to huge swaths of their homeland. But Putin's assertion of Russian self-interest is at the cost of Ukraine's sovereign right to determine its own destiny. And Ukraine inclines more toward Europe than Russia when it comes to the country's self-interests. Here we see again the breakdown in the narrative of state sovereignty and self-determination, which was a bedrock principle of the Westphalian System.

Nevertheless, the biggest scoring point of the Treaty of Westphalia was the principle of state sovereignty, and it serves as the basis for the modern system of nation-states.

Chapter 8: The Negative Impacts of the Industrial Revolution

With the enlightenment thinkers, feudalism was now walking on its last legs. The peasants were no longer tied to the land as surfs, had more rights and owned their own small plots as independent peasant farmers. It was around this time that one of the most significant events in human history and one that had a profound effect on many nations throughout the world took place, today known as the Industrial Revolution. While the revolution first began in England in the 18th century and then in the rest of Europe, it took place throughout the centuries that followed. The impacts of the Industrial Revolution can still be seen in our lives today. When it first started, these peasant farmers started going to the cities to seek jobs in factories. The peasants were uprooted from the peaceful way of life that they knew in the small towns and villages of the countryside. They moved to big cities like London and Liverpool, where they could only get factory jobs at minimum wage while being savagely exploited with dangerous work conditions. Moreover, there was also the risk of getting injured or losing a limb to the dangers of the machines with which they were working. The Industrial Revolution was, though, a step forward, as means of production were now mechanized, and output was thus multiplied many times over; it was, in fact, at the cost of the exploitation of the working class in inhuman conditions where their life was always in danger from pollution and injuries due to the operating of dangerous machinery in the factories. In the big cities, the bad air from the smoke being belched from factory chimneys could be seen, which caused an ever-present smog in industrial cities. This was the ugly side to the narrative of progress that is claimed to be the direct outcome of the Industrial Revolution. The problems of the early days of industrialization in the Western World can still be seen in China with its current phase of industrialization. For instance, the air quality is now at dangerous levels in Chinese cities throughout the country. The comfortable lives we live today in the Western World came at a price when the Industrial Revolution was in its infancy generations ago. The narrative of technological and lifestyle progress had a price that was paid by our ancestors, and in a way, it is still being paid today due to the environmental problems we are dealing with to this day, like Global Warming and species extinction, among others. The West colonized other regions of the world and imposed their way of life on the natives, who were more in tune with the natural environment than Westerners were with their narrative of progress.

While it is true that the Industrial Revolution led to great economic growth and offered new opportunities, the other side of the story is that this progress came with significant downsides. From damage to the environment and health and safety hazards to poor living conditions for workers and their families, there are a lot of negative effects of the Industrial Revolution that are often overlooked. The southern states of the US, for example, in the period before the Civil War, argued that living conditions in factories in the north were exploitative of their workers whenever the north criticized the slaveholding south for having slaves.[36] It could also be argued that Ebenezer Scrooge in a Christmas Carol, which was written in 1843 at the height of the Industrial Revolution, was also representative of the greedy capitalist who was out to maximize profits at the expense of his employees further down the chain which highlighted the stark differences in Victorian England between the haves (the industrialists who owned the factories) and the have nots who had to work in these factories in miserable conditions.

---

[36] U.S. History. (n.d.). The Southern Argument for Slavery. https://www.ushistory.org/us/27f.asp

Chapter 9: The Narrative of Liberal Democracy

People in the United States, in particular, and to a lesser extent, the West, in general, have a belief that all societies are progressing toward an end goal of becoming liberal democracies that believe in free trade. In some circles, one can add the one true faith to that narrative as well. Although Christianity becoming known and accepted all over the world is more of a marginal belief than the former, where all the countries will have liberal democracies, it is still regarded as the end goal in some schools of thought. The spread of the Western narrative and way of development has been the belief throughout 2000 years of Western Civilization that has been promoted by the powers in that civilization, from the Roman Empire on to the crusades and on to the Colonial and Imperial period and to the US of today - the world's preeminent Super Power since World War II. The rest of the world is catching up to American power, especially China though there is no doubt at this point that American power still reigns supreme, which means the US still has better control over the narrative of how a society should progress. We see this in the way they bully or cajole other countries into 'behaving' properly or in a Western fashion. We see this when the US tries to influence China into behaving more like a Western democracy in regards to respecting human rights. This behaviour on the part of the United States has been evidenced through a number of administrations through the years, some with more emphasis than others.

The problem with this way of looking at the world through the lenses of western democracies is that it is a dream at best because, in reality, this is not the natural trajectory of societies. The Communists and Marxists also had their own narrative and vision of the world where they believed all workers of the world would revolt and unite and end the rule of the oppressive bourgeois classes. They even believed this revolution would happen first among the industrialized nations. This was so because they believed capitalism was the highest form a society could achieve before making the transition to communism. Their dreams of a socialist or communist utopia did not come to fruition as the major communist powers self-destructed at the beginning of the last decade of the twentieth century, thus ending the Cold War and the competition between two competing narratives of the world. The communist narrative was annihilated on its face. Today there are only a handful of communist states in the world. Thus, the Western narrative is still in the game with its view of the world on what all nation-states should aspire to become. However, events throughout two millennia of Western history and especially events of the last few years have shown this not to be the case. All societies are different with their own societal, cultural, economic and political evolutions, which are unique to each state. In that sense, the Western model is not the 'one size fits all' that states and societies will eventually end up becoming. History has a lot of bumps and bruises that all societies go through. Some progress while others regress. Some might be set back a bit while others go through a roller coaster ride. The Western narrative of history is the dominant strain that westerners themselves believe in and expect that can and will be imposed on all societies in the future.

Chapter 10: Societal Organization in the West and how it Relates to the EU

Another important thread that needs to be discussed with regards to the negating of the Western narrative is the way Putin has behaved toward the West and how he has tried to divide the West among themselves. Putin did this by invading Ukraine in the hopes of dividing the NATO alliance by exacerbating each of their own state interests, especially their dependence on Russian gas. It is also important to understand how he has also tried to divide factions of societies within a nation-state as he has within the US exacerbating the differences between conservatives and liberals through interference in the 2016 US elections. Thus, a full understanding of where we are now and how we organize ourselves in society now compared to how societies organized themselves in the past can give us a better perspective on what Putin is trying to achieve. Putin does not like the creation of these superstates like the EU or even these alliances like NATO. He wants to go back to a time when states were pursuing their own self interests. Putin knows when Europe is not united, then it is easier for him to pursue his interests at the expense of Europe because if Europe is united, then its economic and military leverage is much greater than that of Russia's. But a divided Europe will be easier prey for the fox that wants to invade the hen house since there will be no unity of response to an outside threat like Russia. Evidence of this can be seen with the various responses of European states regarding sanctions toward Russia.

We need to go back and see the progression of the organization of societies through time to understand the nation-state today and also the beginnings of superstates like the European Union.

Societies were not always organized as they are now, that is, nation-states with defined borders with the right to defend their borders and the sovereign right to establish the laws within their states. Since the years after the Second World War, we have started seeing the formations of 'super states' like the European Union with laws applicable throughout the Union and the adoption of a common currency as well as the ease of travelling between various European states. It took time, centuries, even millennia of wars, to get to this point in human history.

More than two thousand or more years ago, the focal point of power in the European continent was the Greek city-states. They were autonomous and could trade and interact with one another with ease. Some were dominant and would have their way against their neighbours, like Athens, which was also the city of the great thinkers of Western history that we know of today. One of their rivals was the Spartans, who lived in a war-like society. Whenever there were outside enemies threatening their existence, they tended to work together to protect themselves from getting conquered. These outside enemies were typically the Persians, who organized themselves in a completely different way than the Greeks. They did not enjoy the freedoms that the Greeks did and were living under the rule of a tyrannical king. The Greeks, in the end, were successful in defending their existence against the Persians and winning the Battle of Salamis. The power of the Greeks eventually waned in favour of the Romans. On the other hand, the Romans started out as a Republic and then later transformed into an empire during their one thousand years of existence. Even an empire as mighty as the Roman Empire was too huge to administer and, therefore, had to be divided into two between the East, centred in Constantinople and the West, centred in Rome and even up to four divisions at one point, with a subsection for North Africa and the far western part of the empire. This gave a major setback to the administration as there were now numerous emperors who were responsible for their portion of the empire and did not necessarily answer to their co-emperors. This was actually a step back in administration from one administration for the entire empire. Moreover, it was burdensome due to the vastness and diversity of the land and its people for several administrations who were responsible for their own portion of the empire. It even made it less efficient as they did not have to coordinate with the other emperors. This diffusion of powers and responsibilities became one of the reasons for it being fodder for the marauding tribes that devoured the lands of the Roman Empire during the later period of the empire. When the Roman Empire was still intact, these external tribes pitted themselves against the Romans and had a different form of organization from them. Though the Romans, in their empire, had roughly defined borders where their laws applied, and they were loyal to a 'Roman way of life' that they needed to defend, similar to how we think of our nation-states today, the barbarians were organized in a completely different fashion. They did not typically have clearly defined borders and would roam around and see where the land was most conducive for their lifestyle. They also pledged their loyalty to a king who had to be a good warrior that could lead them to plunder, rape, and booty. These barbarians were not as much loyal to a nation-state and its values, so to speak, as they were to a strong figure that could lead them to victory in battle. This explains some of the strong barbaric figures like Attila the Hun. He could lead his tribe to victory and a lot of wealth as a result, and he was the scourge of God. These 'backwards peoples', as the Romans saw them, were able to eventually conquer Rome, a more advanced civilization, thus plunging the West into the Dark Ages and setting back once more the linear progress of civilization that we are so accustomed to thinking as part and parcel of the progression of mankind.

Though Rome was conquered by various barbarian tribes, it would be the Roman form of societal organization that would win out in the end on to our present day with regards to the modern nation state and how its citizens identify with it and pledge their loyalty to it and not the barbarian form of organization with its semi-nomadic way of life and lack of societal stabilty mixed with warring involving pillaging and plundering of other tribes and societies. These barbarian tribes would eventually settle and form their own cultures and civilizations which would evolve to our present day, with challenges and obstacles along the way both internally and externally, to the nation states we see in Europe which form of organization would also eventually spread the world over.

During the Dark Ages, the former lands of the Roman Empire were divided up in Western Europe among the various tribes, which would eventually but gradually, through the centuries, evolve into the modern European states of today. This is how we get the Latin states of Western Europe who belong to the Romance family of languages. It is a mixture of Latin and the local barbarian languages of that particular geographical region and is living proof of the breakup of the Roman Empire. It took centuries of feudalism and outside external threats like the Muslims and Vikings before these geographical entities would unite and forge themselves into modern nation-states with defined boundaries and common laws and a recognized monarch that ruled within said territory. These are the beginnings of the modern nation-states that we know of today, vying for their own self-interests no matter if it came at the expense of their neighbours.

Throughout the centuries, Europe has been a continent at war between neighbors trying to strengthen their position vis-a-vis their neighbors. One can name countless wars; The Hundred Years War, The Eighty Years War, The Thirty Years War, The War of the Spanish Succession, and many more. It was a continent that had seen much death and destruction on a large scale compared to other continents. However, since World War II, Europe saw an unprecedented era of peace through cooperation between European states, both economically and militarily, through the EU. Now the harmony was disrupted when the Russians invaded Ukraine. The last time this happened was in a fratricidal war in the former Yugoslavia in the 1990s. This unprecedented era of peace was still only a short period compared to the centuries of warfare that Europe had experienced. Because of this, it was still uncertain if this community based on cooperation economically and militarily would last.

The EU could regress back to the nation-state system that European states have been accustomed to if the EU cannot withstand the external challenges that it faces. This is because the EU is composed of many states with their own self-interests, which could be at odds with other member states within the EU. The nation-state system is easier to uphold since the individual states only have to worry about their own self-interests.

Chapter 11: Progression toward Superstates - The EU

The progress in the Western narrative is evident where the powers and rights of the modern nation-state were laid out in the system of Westphalian sovereignty. This system, as has been stated, is still largely in place today though one can see the beginnings of a system post-Westphalian, with superstates like the EU. The formation of this supranational organization was gradual from the nation-state system that Europe had known. Nation-states were not going to form a powerful organization like the EU overnight as states were reluctant to give up enormous powers to a central organization, so the transition was slow, and it first started with the European Coal and Steel Community. The ECSC eventually signed a treaty where their coal and steel industries that were formerly used to start wars in the past were put under common management so none could start wars against the others. Then came along the Treaty of Rome, which created the European Economic Community or Common Market that allowed free movement of goods, services, and people across borders. This shows a gradual step by step process in which states slowly but surely gave more and more power to a Central European authority so that they were not reluctant to give up their state rights all of a sudden. Thus, the formation of a supranational entity is gradual that first takes nation-states into confidence over time. And so, in the EU today, we see the movement of people and goods in a free-flowing manner which was unthinkable in the nation-state system of Europe in the past. It is this supranational system that Putin wants to break up and weaken in order for European nation-states to regress back to the Westphalian System, which would be a step back with nation-states vying for their individual state interests instead of their common interests. The EU has only been in place since the end of World War II, and with Brexit, there are still questions as to whether this system will be fully successful in the long run. The Western narrative would have one believe that this is the next natural step in the political arrangement of societies, but this is still in its infancy, and there are still questions if it will succeed, especially with external forces like Putin, and to a certain extent Donald Trump bent on having it weakened. Though the EU, in a way, tries to tame the selfish ambitions of state interests, state interests still boil to the surface, like when the UK went through with Brexit, and the Brexiteers argued that they do not want Brussels dictating rules and regulations in the UK which the UK is capable of legislating themselves. The UK has also had a history of not entangling itself in the affairs of the continent. It has historically played the role of a balancer of power whenever there was a state that became too powerful on the continent, like Napoleonic France or Nazi Germany.

During those conflicts, the UK remained defiant and continued the fight despite the fact that the continent had mostly already been occupied. Even during its stint in the EU, it still did not want to give up complete control of some of its sovereign functions like its own currency or not being part of the SCHENGEN zone. It also had different rules from those of the SCHENGEN zone. Even during the time that it was in the EU, the UK allowed Americans, for instance, to stay visa-free for up to six months, whereas Americans are only allowed three months in the SCHENGEN area. This establishes that national interests are still strong in states even if nation-states unite under the banner of international organizations like the EU to curb the adverse effects of national interests in favour of more international cooperation between EU states. There will always be those who argue how states are better positioned to legislate themselves as they know their own problems instead of a supranational organization doing it for them in Brussels. Thus a supranational organization like the EU might not actually be completely successful in the narrative of completely suppressing national interests in the hope of avoiding all future wars since no matter what happens, national interests will always boil to the surface when push comes to shove. In other words, the natural progression of the narrative is to go from states with selfish interests to a supranational entity like the EU to avoid future devastating wars, but it is not that easy since Europe has been accustomed to the nation-state system for hundreds of years so you have to wane them off slowly step by step before an entity like the EU can be organized with vast powers. It is like a drug. You cannot ween someone off the drug drastically. It has to be a step by step process. This is what we see with the ECSC and then the EEC. The transformation has to be gradual, and even then, there are relapses due to a desire to go back to the nation-state system, given its perks, like in the case of Brexit, since a state is accustomed to behaving for a long time as the ultimate authority. When it becomes part of the EU, it still has a tendency to go backwards in the narrative back to the nation-state system. Even in other European countries, there are right wing political groups that want to sever ties to EU institutions as they see the EU as a hindrance to national progress and interests. Marine le Pen, for instance, repeatedly argues that French leaders like Emmanuel Macron don't defend French interests but instead defend European values. In her 2022 debate, she argued that she wants a French foreign policy independent of Russia,

Europe, or the US.[37] This is, of course, what Putin wants as well as Trump. Thus the narrative is not perfect, as there are lapses and regressions. Again this takes us back to the conclusion that history has its ups and downs and that progression is not linear. Since supranational institutions like the EU are still new on the international scene, they are still a work in progress. It is easy for an outsider like Putin to chip away at its weak spots and identify where each individual state interest diverges in order to create fissures in the edifice that could bring the whole structure down. States are accustomed to the Westphalian nation-state system that they have been operating under for hundreds of years and could still have a hard time committing wholeheartedly to a supranational institution that has only been in existence for the last seventy-plus years. And the success of the EU is still not written in stone, which means if someone like Putin can weaken it, then this will be a step back in the narrative of societal progression, just like when the Dark Ages followed the Roman Empire. And signs of this weakening can be seen in the diverse responses among European nations to the Russian sanctions due to its invasion of Ukraine. But it can also be seen obviously with Brexit and also the various right-

---

[37] France 24. (2022, April 20). Le DÉBAT - Macron vs. Le Pen: Suivez en Direct le début de l'entre-deux-tours [Video]. Youtube. https://www.youtube.com/watch?v=PYr4IAjboAE

wing political parties in various European states who hold anti-EU platforms.

Chapter 12: The United Nations

Another example of post-World War II international cooperation apart from the EU is the United Nations. The UN is, of course, a product of the aftermath of World War II, and its predecessor, the League of Nations a product of the aftermath of World War I. Of course, international cooperation would be the result of a narrative of a continent that has been plagued by wars upon wars. Before these international bodies of cooperation, there was no such thing to prevent wars. There were only alliances in order for states to ally with other states, depending on what was best in the self-interests of nation-states. There was a time when it was generally believed that war was good every now and then to invigorate the nation and not let the people deteriorate into a state of decadence and complacency. Wars with states allying themselves with others based on their interests, therefore, happened again and again. For example, the Italian city-states of Northern Italy allied themselves with certain outside powers like France or the Holy Roman Empire or the Pope, depending on what best served their interests at that particular point in time or during the Thirty Years' War. During this time, various alliances were made across religious lines based on state interests to further objectives that were non-religious, like France trying to curb the power of Habsburgs, which is why it supported outside forces that were Protestant like Sweden despite France being a Catholic state. These systems of alliances only exacerbated wars as, eventually, there were multiple states vying for supremacy against multiple states. This is evidenced during the Napoleonic Wars, where numerous coalitions of various nations would combine forces to fight Napoleon. Another example would be the Crimean War, where the British allied themselves with the French, their longtime nemesis on the continent, to fight the Russians in order to prevent the Russians from acquiring the Crimea as the Russians were in desperate need of a warm water port. Now it was just revealed that Putin wants to annex Crimea in order to create a land bridge that connects it with the Russian mainland. Now Russia's reasons for invading the region are the industrial capacity of the Donbas and Donetsk which would be of benefit to Russia as it did previously to the Soviet Union. Yet another perfect example of these alliances closer to our time would be World War I. The assassination of Archduke Ferdinand was the spark that was needed for the European alliances to go to war. The situation in Europe was already tense at the time of the assassination, with each European nation having its finger on the trigger and about to pull. They just needed a spark to ignite the fuse, which was conveniently done by the assassination of the Archduke. These were alliances where each member was bound to the aid of the other if ever there was war. So one assassination caused a butterfly effect that plunged the continent into a war that caused the deaths of millions. The international community decided after the failure of the League of Nations, due in part to the US not being a member, which led to World War II, that the UN was going to be the ultimate forum for international cooperation which would end the centuries of war which culminated in the destruction and death of World War II.

But the important point that should be highlighted here is that even with the UN, wars still occur, though not major wars like the two world wars of the twentieth century. These wars have been smaller in scale, flaring up here and there the world over. The UN certainly did not stop the wars all over the globe fought during the Cold War, where the US or the Soviet Union made the world out to be their chessboard fighting wars all over the world, sometimes in person while other times proxy wars through allies that were backed either militarily through equipment or financially. There were also other conflicts that the UN was not able to prevent, such as the Suez Crisis of 1956 or the Six-Day War of 1967. In the latter, the services of the UN were extremely needed as an alliance of Arab countries wanted to annihilate Israel once and for all. Since February of 2022, there is a Russian invasion of Ukraine that has been bloody and atrocious which the UN has been impotent to stop. Similarly, the UN was also unable to prevent the Russian annexation of Crimea a number of years ago. These show that the UN certainly did not end all wars, which was its purpose similar to how it was widely believed that the machine gun would end all wars not that long ago in history or how nuclear weapons would end wars due to deterrence.

So the narrative always has its flaws as there are still conflicts, and the world still has not lived in peace. Thus, like any other narrative or international organization in the world, the UN's structure has some major flaws as well. Though the idea is that every state is equal, the five permanent members have a veto power which means they can block resolutions that go against their own self-interests. A perfect example of this is the Russian invasion of Ukraine where Russia can block resolutions passed by the General Assembly that goes against its desire to invade Ukraine. This goes against the UN objective that all states are equal because the power politics of the global order come into play with the five permanent members as they have veto power even if there is a resolution that is supported by a vast majority of states. So the combined weight of a majority of member states still cannot equal the power of one of the five permanent members when one member exercises the veto power against a resolution. This means that the narrative that the UN will end all conflicts and that all states will be equal to every other state is nothing more than a dream as the UN still operates in a realist world with powerful states exercising their self-interests over those less powerful.

Certainly, wars are part of the human condition, and no progress that mankind can make over time will take away the desire or the need for societies to go to war based on their interests. Even international law, which is the foundation of the UN, is still largely dependent on states to enforce law and order as there is no international police force that is purely stateless and enforces international law in a fair and just manner no matter how powerful the state is who is a party to a dispute. An example of this is how Russia has demanded that EU states pay for Russian natural gas in Rubles. There is no international police force of sorts that will stop Russia from changing the terms of the manner of payment. So the EU's only option is, if it does not want to comply because it will go against the sanctions that have been imposed on Russia, is to find its energy source from somewhere else like the US.

One sees the importance of nation-states and their interests when it comes to international laws. Of the various levels of international law, the highest level is treaties between states.[38] And if a treaty is violated, there is no police

[38] International law. (2022, June 21). In Wikipedia. https://en.wikipedia.org/wiki/International_law

force to enforce it except for international litigation. And when a decision comes down in favour of or against a state, it is up to the state who received an unfavourable ruling to comply or not. If a state does not comply, then pressure can be put to bear on that state by the international community. This pressure could be in the form of a threat of military intervention or other types of pressure like diplomatic and economic sanctions. The next level is customary international law which is derived from the consistent practice of states along with the belief that they are acting in accordance to opinio juris or a legal obligation. Here again, the law is dependent on the various states' actions which means that states, individually and not collectively, are still very important in the international system and international law. If there are state actors that deviate from customary norms, there is still no higher power that can make that state comply and act accordingly like law enforcement can arrest a citizen who has violated a law. Other states can put pressure on that state if need be, but we still see here the importance of state actors when it comes to international law. And when it comes to litigation, litigation in an international tribunal is considered the last resort. There is deference towards the various states on whether they can work it out on their own bilaterally. Only if these states cannot work things out on their own will an international tribunal step in to settle the dispute with the various states.

Therefore, no matter how the narrative is framed and sugar-coated about how the world is going into more and more cooperation through institutions like the EU or the UN, there will still be conflicts and national interests that show otherwise. States will always work to further their national interests that will work against the narrative of world peace and an end to wars that these institutions hope to end. The narrative of international law is also riddled with deference towards state actors and their willingness to comply with international law and norms. Even the rights to self-determination and secession in international law were originally crafted for the purpose of colonial states breaking away from their colonizers. The colonial and imperialist era lasted for several hundred years, starting with the era of exploration and ending in a cataclysmic manner with World War II, as some historians would say was the last of the imperialist wars.[39] The colonial and imperial powers, for several hundred years, were vying for supremacy through colonial acquisitions and fought each other for them, which resulted in some major wars over time. An example of the colonial and imperialist wars of past centuries was the Seven Years' War which engulfed not only the European continent but also other regions like North America, where the English

---

[39] Overy, R. (2021). Blood and ruins : the great imperial war, 1931-1945. Penguin Books.

and the French were vying for supremacy of the continent at the expense of the Indians and American colonists which the British eventually won taking Canada from France. It also extended to Asia, where the British were able to occupy Manila for several years and India, where the British fought the French for control over French territories.

In the twentieth century, of course, the two world wars were the major imperialist wars. Some would argue that powers like Italy, Japan, and Germany were late to the game of colonialism or imperialism since both Germany and Italy only became nation-states, in the modern sense of the term, during the latter half of the nineteenth century and Japan only industrialized at around the same time, so they had no choice but to stake their claim in the world by fighting the already established imperial powers for some slices of the pie. So at the end of World War II, it became clear that imperialism was an outdated way of diplomacy since it would only lead to destructive wars between powerful nations. So the major world powers decided that nation-states would be given their rights to self-determination like the Philippines in 1946 and India and Pakistan in a rather less than the amicable manner in 1947 (with violent migrations among people between the two countries when deciding in which country they would reside). The pivotal event which displayed that colonialism and imperialism were dead was the Suez War, when the British, French, and Israelis combined to fight Egypt when Gamal Abdel Nasser wanted to nationalize the Suez Canal. All three invading powers were chastised by both the US and the USSR. Eisenhower did not agree with the British and French outdated policy of imperialism that no longer held sway in a Cold War division of the world.[40]

Thus, it was in this environment, due to the events of the twentieth century, that self-determination was conceived. And beyond this, there is a preference in international law to maintain existing borders of states as they are. The argument goes that if any group based on race, ethnicity, religion, or culture can secede from an existing state, then there could be no end to groups who would want to secede, and there can be an infinite number of states which would undermine international stability and the rule of law. One only needs to look at the violent breakup of the former Yugoslavia during the 1990s to understand this. Yugoslavia was a multi-ethnic, multi-cultural state that was forced together during the Cold War and held together by the will of Marshal Tito. After the Cold War ended, these various groups wanted to control their own destinies, so a violent civil war ensued that

---

[40] Totten, M. (2017, February). We Are Still Living With Eisenhower's Biggest Mistake. The Tower. http://www.thetower.org/article/we-arestill-living-with-eisenhowers-biggest-mistake-suez-egypt-israel-ikes-gamble-michael-doran/

included ethnic cleansing. The case of the former Yugoslavia was very serious, and one could indeed have a very strong argument for secession due to the hatred that the groups within had against one another. If this happened all around the world, the various groups would want to secede due to the slightest infractions not amounting to oppression and having their own right to self-determination. As a result, there would be no end to wars and a complete breakdown of the civility and orderliness of the international system. So basically, there is no right for groups to secede in international law, but it can be considered a last resort and is only accepted if it is being so oppressed internally that it cannot practice its right to self-determination within the state. This can be argued with regards to Kosovo but not Quebec, where Quebec's claim to secede based on self-determination was denied.[41] Also, Russia invaded Ukraine because it was claiming to be fighting for the oppressed Russian speaking people of eastern Ukraine however flimsy the argument may be. In reality, it has interests in annexing that eastern portion of Ukraine as it wants a land bridge from Russia all the way through to Crimea, which blocks off Ukraine, and Russia also desires the industrial output of that region that the Soviet Union was able to take advantage of

[41] Reference Re Secession of Quebec. (2022, May 27). In Wikipedia. https://en.wikipedia.org/wiki/Reference_Re_Secession_of_Quebec

when it was still in existence.[42] If Russia was really sincere about the well-being of the Russian speaking minority in the Donbas and Donetsk region of eastern Ukraine, then it should first let the people of that region bring up this issue in the International Court of Justice in the Hague as prescribed by international law if there is no resort to a remedy under the local courts in Ukraine instead of resorting to an invasion that could hardly be supported under international law. This is another example that there can be no end to the creation of new states based on the slightest provocations. And an external state can use the oppression of a minority in another state as a pretext to forward its own interests by using the defence of the rights of the oppressed minority to further its own unstated interests in the guise of a humanitarian invasion or special operations as Russia calls its invasion of Ukraine. This shows the preference for the existing Westphalian nation-state system and how it is up to states to administer the laws with various existing groups within their borders. States also have to administer the laws themselves externally towards their behaviour with one another, whether by treaty or customary international law.

United Nations, with its unique international character and the powers vested in its founding Charter, can take

[42] Tracer, Transition in Coal Intensive Regions. (n.d.). Ukraine: Donetsk region (industrial characteristics). Tracer. https://www.scribbr.com/apa-examples/website/

action on a wide range of issues. It also offers a forum for its 193 Member States to express their views and defend their rights. However, despite all that UN is lauded for, the other side of the picture is that the progression of human development where there is more and more international cooperation is still a farce to a certain extent. This is because states are still behaving in their own capacity with regard to their own state interests in international organizations like the UN and under international law, not to mention organizations like the EU, where the UK exercised its right to exit from the organization due to its state interests. The UN was also not able to stop Russia's unilateral action of invading Ukraine, which was certainly not sanctioned by the organization and was condemned by a majority of the members of the organization. This unprovoked invasion was certainly something that an organization like the UN was meant to prevent. However, it could do nothing but simply voice its discontent. Another problem that goes with it is that Russia is a permanent member of the Security Council, which means it wields the veto power that it could use to block a resolution that goes against its interests.

Section 2 – Current Political Landscape

The world post 9/11 and especially the political landscape, in particular, has shifted from one of democratic gains and optimism to what can be best described as a political recession. While major changes were taking place all across the world, be it warfare, propaganda, revolution, or terrorism, perhaps the most notable change was the one that could be observed in the people in general. With political polarization from a left-right divide, the political landscape now moved toward politics based on identity. Moreover another major change was that of technological development, which not only raised stakes in governments but it also facilitated the rise of social fragmentation and political polarization. Similarly, the political landscape was further impacted by other less significant changes like the shift toward neoliberal economic policies and a lowered interest in democratic changes. Unlike in the past, the focus now shifted from faces to restructuring the legitimacy of the institutions in order to strengthen democracy.

When reviewing the political landscape in the light of the historical narratives, one cannot help but commend the thought put into the process of framing the constitution. It is interesting to note how much forethought was put into creating a system of checks and balances so that democratic governments shall neither be dynasts nor would they become

108

merely ideological clones that govern and administer the masses in choreographed synchronicity while disregarding the local constituents' needs and the freedom of expression that are the cornerstones of democracy.

Hence, with these barriers to a constitutional crisis and an illegitimate political approach, it becomes extremely difficult for governments to radically alter the direction of the country and its citizens. Furthermore, the last few decades have also been an era of information that has allowed people to be well informed and be more and more engaged in the administration or at least to have a say in policy decisions. Despite all those perks, it is still not rare that politicians often lapse into assuming that their approach or political viewpoints are the most important. They even tend to overlook the fact that people today have an almost amusing way of deciding what matters to them and what doesn't.

If the 2016 US election felt tense and explosive, the political situation that pursued only took a turn for the worse. While politics has gone through various different stages throughout history, to this day, it has continued to be an arena for marketing one's own political narrative. The divide that was created after the 2016 elections as well the distrust of news media is at an all-time high now. Unfortunately, the situation has been exploited to no end by many who consider politics nothing more than a game rather than a practical application of governance of the people, by the people, and for the people.

The need is for the politicians and people to realize that politics is the process of finding ideal governance while managing personal differences. It is only then we can begin to view politics as an intricate yet comprehensive process for finding unity and civilian supremacy. Until then, the question remains; is there hope for unity across political affiliations?

Chapter 1: The Trump Presidency

The events from Trump's initial campaign for the presidency up until the Capitol Insurrection have indeed been very chaotic and uncertain times in the entire history of the United States, especially at a time when a lot was going on around the world. This was a campaign like no other where his bombast caused controversy in American society among different segments of the population, depending on which religious or ethnic group were the subjects of his recurring insults. Strangely enough, this also happened to be his appeal to his supporters. They saw him as genuine as they believed he said what was on his mind instead of walking a delicate tightrope and worrying about political correctness all the time. This was also, at the same time, what enraged his critics and many others on the left. Perhaps not any other Republican candidate was hated as much as Trump for his hard-right policies and his lack of self-control against those who did not see things his way.

As will be discussed further in the book, various societies have their narratives on how they like to see themselves and how they want to portray themselves to the world for posterity. We will discuss the narratives of various countries, religious groups, époques in history, even Western civilization etc. All this and more will further elaborate the point that narratives are not what they are cracked up to be as there are always problems with them. For instance, the narrative of Western Civilization, where progress is the theme that goes back to the Dark Ages and then continues to present times, has been filled with setbacks and underlying sub-themes that shine a light on the ugly side beneath the narrative that people know or the one that a party or person wants to portray. As discussed in the previous section, no narrative is free of its sins. The fact that the Roman Empire was built on the backs of slavery and violence and how the Age of Faith was brutal towards heretics that is now turned a blind eye to today in the Cathedrals - the manifestations of the Age of Faith, and with the inter-city violence between the Italian city-states during the Renaissance which often does not get discussed in favour of the magnificent art and architecture that that time period in history produced, and with the appalling conditions in the factories during the technological leap forward that was the Industrial Revolution etc. only adds on to the evidence.

Similarly, the American cultural and historical narrative is no different. Americans like to think of themselves as exceptional, and they constantly portray themselves to the rest of the world as exceptional with its liberal democratic values and its portrayal of its history as progressing to a perfect union socially, especially with race relations. But in truth, there are still serious problems and deceptions with this analysis, especially now that all the societal and cultural problems have been brought to the surface during the four years of the Trump presidency.

Evidence of this can be seen in various facets of his presidency, especially in terms of how he behaves and acts. Though it was rather obvious that American society was not perfect with the police shootings of black men and the gaping deficiencies in the immigration system with illegal immigrants continuing to pour into the country and the lack of tracking of them, the Trump presidency has absolutely brought everything that was ugly in American society to the surface and gave these factions a voice and encouragement to continue believing in what they believed. The problems with the Trump administration and him bringing everything deficient in the American narrative to the surface will be dissected one by one in the following chapters.

Chapter 2: Comparisons of American Social Problems with the UK and France

The two different conglomerates of states on both ends of the world are similar in many ways and worlds apart in others. While the US has a federal and constitutional republic form of government, the UK has constitutional monarchy-parliament governance. But in both the regions, people have broadly similar views on certain social and political issues. So, when it comes to social problems, the UK and the US both face many similar challenges. A comparison of the two parts of the world can help us learn a lot from each other, but first, let's connect some dots.

The utter surprise, or rather shock, that I felt the day after Election Day in 2016, was only matched by that of the Capitol Insurrection on January 6, 2021, during the last days of the Trump presidency. Matthew McConaughey, in an online video, described it in the best way by referring to the US as a baby when it comes to being a country and that it is going through puberty.[43] This befitting analogy, however, totally contradicts how the US likes to portray itself not only to its people but to the rest of the world. The US likes to

---

[43] France, L. (2021, July 5). Matthew McConaughey declares America 'going through puberty' in Independence Day message. CNN. https://edition.cnn.com/2021/07/05/entertainment/matthew-mcconaughey-independence-day-trnd/index.html

propagate the idea of it being the pinnacle of a democratic society that has perfected the rules of this way of government, especially through its exportation of democracy to all corners of the globe. An argument could be made that modern democracy is still rather in its infancy that no society has yet perfected it even though a society like the US has been practising it for almost two hundred fifty years, and it is better at it than the other countries where it is exported especially the nation-states of the developing world. This period of time that modern democracy has been practised in various nation-states around the world is still a speck in time as compared to the entire span of human history. Therefore democracy is still evolving no matter if it is a nation like the US or others where democracy is still rather a novel concept. These facts show that the US is far from perfecting the ways of democracy and is still inching its way step by step through the problems of this way of societal and political organization. Basically, the US is still trying to work out this whole experiment in democracy, and I agree that the ugly side of our democracy has surfaced during the Trump administration. Just when everyone thought the US had its act together in how to run a democracy due to the centuries of peaceful transitions of power, here it proves that it still needs to grow and learn how the process works in all its facets. There is a tendency to think that the US has peaked as a democratic government, and all the governments that have only recently transitioned to democracies are the ones learning how it works and still have no idea how to go through it without any violence or regressions to autocratic rule. With the Arab Spring, for example, everyone thought that the Arab world was well on its way to democracy. But here we are years later, and that region of the world still has not figured things out, and what's worse, conditions are rather chaotic with wars in Syria and Yemen. Not to mention that autocratic rule is still pervasive in the Arab world. But the US, though not as serious, still has its problems with democracy as well. One only needs to step back and take a look at the big picture. And that is that the US is still relatively young as a nation compared to other nations that have had a long cultural history, even if not a long national history. Even when you overlook the fact that the US is a young democracy, you cannot ignore that it is also a young nation, plain and simple.

China, though not unified for most of its millennia of history, has had a long cultural and historical legacy and tradition. Similarly, Italy and Germany are other examples as they became nation-states in the latter half of the nineteenth century. Though not unified for much of their history until then, they have had a long cultural and historical heritage as the people were speaking the same language and practising the same religion, not to mention their art and architecture. These latter two are younger nations than the US in actuality. So when things are seen in this light, then the US really is still trying to work out the chinks in its armour. Democracy in the US may seem to be functioning well, but in reality, there are serious problems beneath the surface that are waiting to emerge if just given the right opportunity and motivation, which is exactly what happened during the Trump years. With the Capitol Insurrection, I could never have imagined images of a violent mob forcing their way into the halls of one of our branches of government being possible in this day and age in the most powerful country the world has ever known. Images of The Fall of Rome came crashing through my mind with the background of the neoclassical architecture of the Capitol reminiscent of that of Ancient Rome. Watching the mob all around the Capitol charging their way in through the lines of police protecting the structure made me think of Thomas Cole's painting 'Destruction' where Rome is seen in total and utter chaos as it was being ransacked and its inhabitants and women being killed and raped. The analogy to the fall of the Roman Empire is an apt analogy when it comes to the toxicity of American politics and violence in American society, from gun violence in the form of mass shootings to police brutality against African Americans. And the images of the Capitol Insurrection that we all saw on our screens were the physical manifestation of that toxicity. Rome, too, was facing many social problems as it was going through its downward spiral to its end, from the corruption and decadence of its elites to its increasing reliance on barbarians to defend its borders while shortchanging these very same barbarians when it came to social policies on how they should be treated. The sack of Rome under the Visigothic king Alaric was a vivid example of this. This was the first time Rome had been sacked in centuries. Americans alive today have only known peace and order on the American continent all their lives. No American was alive the last time the Capitol was invaded and burned, which was during the War of 1812. And no American was alive during the Civil War, which was the last time there was a war on American soil. Therefore images of the Insurrection could be likened to that of the Sack of Rome. Just like Rome was going through changes throughout the centuries until its fall, the US is also going through a lot of social changes. It does not mean the United States is going to crumble to dust. It just means that the US as a society needs to make it through these challenging times, and how it decides to tackle these problems will make it a greater or weaker nation than it was before. The barbarians in the Roman Empire were increasing in strength as the history of Rome progressed, but instead of incorporating them into the Empire, Rome decided to treat them as people that could be used and abused, from conscripting their children into the Roman Army to high taxes to forcing them to starve. Barbarian forces that were also incorporated wholesale into the Roman Army were used as fodder in battles as they were positioned on the front lines to take the brunt of enemy attacks and suffer higher casualties. The United States today does not have to deal with an influx of barbarians as much as it does with immigrants, particularly immigrants of a different race. The United States in the years after World War II was predominantly white, about 90%. Today it is now only 60% white. Immigration is changing the face of the country, and how it deals with its immigrants will result in the success or decline of American society. Just like the chaos during the final century or so of the Roman Empire was caused by many social changes in Roman society, the chaos in the politics of American society these past few years is due to the social changes that the US is currently undergoing. Immigrants and minorities are gaining more and more influence in society, as seen in the policies of the Democratic Party since the Johnson administration with the passage of the Civil Rights Act and into the early 1970s with the creation of the modern Democratic Party platform. These events have forged the Democrats of today with their liberal tendencies and their willingness to change, along with their unabashed cajoling of minorities into the party policies and political platform. The Obama administration was the personification of the rise of minorities on the political stage. The Trump administration can be seen as a backlash against the rising tide of minority/immigrant/ non-white power against that of the established white majority who has politically controlled American politics since its birth. Minorities have wielded less power in the past than they do today and were thus not seen as a threat to the predominant white majority. But now that minorities are making their voices heard through the policies in government, the white backlash in the form of the Trump administration is seen as strong to combat equally powerful minority policies and influence. The Trump years were like an earthquake that was the result of two equally large and powerful tectonic plates colliding, causing a massive trembling of the ground. The two tectonic plates are those of the old white establishment and of the new factions and groups gaining power in American society.

The four years of the Trump presidency can be analogized to the Bourbon Restoration in France after the French Revolution and the subsequent Napoleonic Empire that succeeded it. The French Revolution was a very radical change compared to the Ancien Regime, which preceded it. The Ancien Regime represented a rigid class structure where a small noble class along with the church and clergy held most of the power in society. Then the French Revolution boiled to the surface because the majority of the oppressed class of peasants wanted to change the social order and have more influence in policymaking. The changes were drastic, from social, to cultural and from scientific to religious. The mob during the French Revolution took their frustrations out on priests who were beaten and killed. It was during the chaos of the French Revolution when a new calendar was created where the names of the months gave an indication of what season it was to the creation of the Système International d'Unities or the Metric System, which made weights and measures logical based on increments of ten to the creation of the Cult of Reason where the Revolutionists even had a statute made of the Goddess of Reason and had it installed in Notre Dame Cathedral in Paris. The initial chaos of the revolution then gave way to the terror under Maximilian Robespierre, where executions were rampant of citizens suspected of being traitors or even of thinking or saying traitorous thoughts and statements. Subsequently, the Directory, composed of five citizens, came into power which was replaced by the Consulship composed of Napoleon and two other individuals who really did not matter as long as Napoleon was around. The end of the Napoleonic Wars resulted in the Bourbon Restoration as decided upon by the major European powers during the Concert of Vienna, which resulted in the redrawing of the map of Europe as its major outcome. The Royalists would now return to power at the expense of supporters of Napoleon and the Empire. This is borne out in literature like "The Count of Monte Cristo".

There was a lot of bad blood between those who supported the new order and those who wanted to go back to the old order, which could be read in the opening of "The Count of Monte Cristo". The Bourbon Restoration intended to turn back the clock of France to the time of the Ancien Regime as if the French Revolution and Napoleonic era never happened. The Bourbons learned nothing from the French Revolution and all the changes that France had undergone during the quarter-century. They acted like the absolute monarchs that they were in the past and were seen by the populace as out of date. The Bourbons had ignored that the French had experienced an entire generation of not having an absolute monarch. The Restoration in the big picture would not last long as Louis XVIII, Charles X, and Louis Philippe would be the last three kings of France (les trois derniers rois de France de l'ancien régime après la Restauration) before another Republic was declared. Charles the X and Louis Philippe left France for England in exile and adopted new royal names as pseudonyms.

After this, there were a lot of ups and downs, and many governments came and went, but France continued on its road to progress and the modern democracy it is today, with some bumps and bruises along the way as it went through several republics which included a Second Empire in between under the rule of Napoleon III and two World Wars which included Nazi occupation during the Second World War. It was after WWII that there were some major changes that happened in France and the ones that historians now call "Les Trente Glorieuses" (The Glorious Thirty). They included the liberation of women and the advancement of women's rights in society in particular. It is interesting to note that there was a time married women could not even have their own bank account in France without their husband's consent. This French narrative from the time of the French Revolution is another narrative that is not clear cut and dry with a steady linear progression as the French kept changing governments as they were trying to figure out which was the best form of government for them. For instance, Adolphe Thiers said in the 1870s that republicanism is "the form of government that divides France least".[44]

This is because France, at this point, had gone through almost a century of turmoil and revolution and changes of government as it kept changing governments and did not know what was best for them. Thus they had no sense of where their narrative was headed. It was not a clear and steady progression from the absolutism of the Bourbons to the democracy of France today. There were a lot of changes

[44] French Third Republic. (2022, July 23). In Wikipedia. https://en.wikipedia.org/wiki/French_Third_Republic

of government from monarchy to republicanism and back as they did not progress gradually to a more democratic government. It was back and forth from one type of government to another during nineteenth-century France. There were, in a nutshell, bumps, setbacks, and ups and downs. Thus the narrative breaks down and shows once again that there is not exactly a final state of progression that all governments will eventually attain, like some form of Holy Grail or paradise that the entire world will one day achieve. As an example of this, to this very day, there is a pretender to the throne waiting to claim the throne of France in case France decides to bring back the monarchy again, as bizarre as this sounds in this day and age.[45] This shows that democracy is not the end-all and be all of the societies because this small faction of the Bourbon dynasty is still actually contemplating a return to monarchy. These Bourbons believed that this government had problems, and one day somehow, France would yearn for the return of the monarchy to which the pretender to the throne would be ready to claim the throne.

Even today, French people love to protest against the policies of their governments. And one reason for a lot of terrorist activities among men of Muslim descent in France

---

[45] Louis Alphonse de Bourbon. (2022, July 30). In Wikipedia. https://en.wikipedia.org/wiki/Louis_Alphonse_de_Bourbon

is because of the lack of opportunities which is also demonstrated in the drug problem in France. Stalingrad, for example, is known as an area in Paris taken over by drug dealers and addicts (toxicomanes). It is so bad that it is a topic of discussion in the news, and the neighbourhood always has a formidable police presence. Stalingrad or "Stalincrack" is so bad that there have been citizen groups voicing their concerns about not being able to live normal lives in the neighbourhood.

Ethnic minorities like blacks and Arabs predominantly live in neighbourhoods located in the suburbs or banlieues which are just outside the city. It is worth mentioning here that this is the opposite of American urban areas where minorities have taken over the cities in the Post World War II period, causing "white plight" to the suburbs in the decades after the war.

These banlieues are breeding grounds for discontent and radicalization among its marginalized Muslim population, which is a societal problem in France due to the lower levels of affluence in these communities. These banlieues with their ethnic minorities, or 'quartier populaire' as the French refer to them, also have bad reputations in the eyes of many French citizens. Numerous times, terrorist attacks in France made the international news, like the Charlie Hebdo attack, the November 2015 terrorist attack that massacred many in

Paris, and the truck attack in Nice on Bastille Day. This shows that no matter how the narrative is framed that France is a developed democracy, it is just not so as there are a lot of underlying societal problems underneath with regards to discrimination based on religion or race, which is not how the French like to portray their narrative. There have even been incidents of police misbehaviour and even deaths of blacks in their custody whom they had arrested, like Adama Traoré, who even complained at one point to the officers that he could not breathe, drawing comparisons to George Floyd.

Watching the local news here in France, there are many numerous examples where one can draw a theme that the goals of French Republicanism and equality among all are still far from reality. One can see in the news police officers being killed by drug dealers or radicalized Muslims, police vans being set on fire by Molotov Cocktails by trouble-making youths or a teenager killing another teenager or a disgruntled employee killing his employer and another fellow employee and then fleeing and hiding in the woods as a fugitive, or a suspect being radicalized in prison then committing a terrorist act after serving his prison time. Some of these crimes have major underlying socio-economic and racial problems underneath. There are growing accusations in France about the police being racist and the 'Americanization' of relations between the citizens and police in France.[46] There was even an incident when the French police were attacked with fireworks. Such is the state of relations between the police and marginalized populations in France. And when it comes to headlines in international news, one can only see the major terrorist attacks in France (Charlie Hebdo, the Paris attacks of 2015, and the Nice truck attack on Bastille Day), while much more that are in the local news do not make the international news like a radicalized person who stabs or attacks law enforcement in France.

Combine these with the problems of disaffected youths in the banlieues who do not see many opportunities, who are getting in trouble with the law, and you get a volatile mix of radicalized youths who are tearing the social fabric in France and undercutting the values of republican cohesion. There was even a case of a schizophrenic who was radicalized in prison and ended up attacking the police when he was freed from prison. So not only is radicalization a problem, but if it is mixed with medical problems that an individual has, then it is a recipe for disaster. Plus, there are also all the socio-economic problems that I already mentioned, especially among youths and minorities. There was even a delivery

---

[46] Vigorie, C. (2016, November 2015). Vers une américanisation des rapports entre la police et la population. Agora.
https://www.agoravox.fr/tribune-libre/article/vers-une-americanisation-des-186537

man that was the recipient of racist taunts that made it to the news.

In another incident, a man was caught on video saying racist slurs. And there was a black couple who faced housing discrimination when trying to rent an apartment, and they recorded their conversation with the landlord. There are also racist incidents directed against black football players by fans. The theme here is that there are major segments of French society who have not been able to assimilate and are discriminated against, as there are elements among white French society who still see minorities in a negative light. This is in contrast to the sponge-like nature of American society, which has been successful in absorbing immigrants without major problems. One can see this in the lack of terror attacks in the US connected with radicalized Muslims. The 9/11 attacks were perpetrated by foreigners, not native-born Americans. Going back to France, with the examples I have just given, France still needs to make great strides in order to achieve "fraternité and egalité", as they like to believe are the foundations of their society. Society is still not colour blind as race still plays a determining factor in how fellow Frenchmen get treated.

On a side note, domestic violence or conjugal violence is also an ever-rising issue in France. There was a case where a man burned a house along with his former wife in it. And there was a former military man who was sentenced four times for domestic violence. He hid in the woods, and a manhunt was in full force to find him, using helicopters and police dogs. And there was an incident of a man throwing his spouse from the eighth floor of their residence. Domestic violence is an issue in France that needs to be addressed by virtue of the fact that there is a term coined for a husband killing his wife called "feminicide". I mention this as there are problems between the man-woman power relationships in France just like in any other society, which means there is still a problem that women may not be equal in relationships, once again undercutting French republican values of equality. And it also shatters the myth of the French people being so romantic and how Paris is the City of Love and all other stereotypical images people all over the world have of the French.

The UK is another state that likes to frame its race relations narrative as one of tolerance and racial harmony. This is far from the case, and there are many incidents of racial tension in reality that hammer cracks into the way they frame their society. We see this from the election of Sadiq Khan, who was touted as evidence that the UK is a society where people of all backgrounds can prosper and make something and somebody of themselves. The problems all surfaced during the mayoral campaign when there were a lot of racial undertones in the campaign for the mayorship as his opponents painted him as someone who had ties to extremism and terrorism, which is, of course, connected to his background as a Muslim of Pakistani ethnicity.[47]

And who could forget the bombshell interview between Prince Harry and Princess Meghan? They revealed that someone in the royal family expressed concern about the skin colour of their baby. The royal family, especially the monarch, is supposed to be the symbol of the kingdom representing every British citizen. One would think they would be accepting of all people as it would look bad on the monarchy for them to be racist in favour of one race over another. And the fact that the prince would leave his family to move to another country with his wife means that there is truth to the serious allegations, as the bar would be higher when it comes to proof for someone to go against one's own family. But that's exactly what happened. Similarly, the racist undertones of the tabloid press coverage against Meghan caused her distress and made her want to quit her royal duties as a member of the family through marriage. Even tabloid press coverage in the US is not as overtly racist as this, as the American public is still somewhat reined in by

---

[47] Booth, R. (2016, April 20). Tories step up attempts to link Sadiq Khan to extremists. The Guardian. https://www.theguardian.com/politics/2016/apr/20/tory-claims-sadiq-khan-alleged-links-extremists

the environment of political correctness (especially in the era before Trump) that curbs their outright racist tendencies. There are also incidents of racism among British football fans, like the British football fans who did not allow a black man to enter a train in the Paris metro and who were convicted for it in a criminal trial in Paris. And the UK, just like any democratic Western state, has laws protecting free speech. However, Black Lives Matter activists are apprehensive about their lives as there seem to be repercussions due to their activities. They have been at the receiving end of anger directed towards their activities and even threats of death and bodily harm on a regular basis which makes the threats routine for them. A government report hailed that the UK should be seen as a model for white majority countries when it comes to racial and ethnic disparities.[48] This is an example of how the British wanted to frame their narrative of race in their society. And the outrage that resulted from the report is the ugly reality underneath the narrative.[49] Despite the fact that the UK would like to see itself as a multi-cultural society where all

---

[48] Heffer, G. (2021, March 31). UK should be 'model for other white majority countries', finds government ordered race review. Sky news. https://news.sky.com/story/uk-should-be-model-for-other-white-majority-countries-finds-government-ordered-race-review-12261343

[49] Harriet, B. (2021, March 31). Race report which calls Britain 'a model for other white-majority countries' sparks outrage- here's why. indy100. https://www.indy100.com/news/race-commission-report-britain-sewell-b1824805

races and creeds live harmoniously with one another, similar to their American cousins, there are social tensions underneath hiding in plain sight with regards to racist incidents against blacks and people of Muslim background for instance. The British Empire has had armed forces of all races and backgrounds fighting among its ranks from the areas of the British Commonwealth.

These forces made substantial contributions to the Allied War effort, which was important in tipping the scales in the Allies' favour. Serving in the military is usually how marginalized groups gain respect from the majority population. In the US, for example, through the valiant heroism of African-Americans and other minorities during the war effort, these marginalized segments of the population who were perhaps not respected previously were seen in a different light by the government for whom they fought (even if not by their fellow citizens), and it was this change that was a substantial factor in the integration of the US military shortly after the war. The British, who probably looked down on the people they had colonized, should have gained more respect for them after contributing to the war effort. This should have been a sure way to break down racist belief system and improve race relations. However, this was not the case in the UK or in the US for that matter. Despite serving the country, which would usually make fellow

British citizens respect them and see them in a different light, there are still racial problems which show that they have not achieved full equality in British society despite all the service that people of all races have given to the state not to mention the labour they have contributed in the private sector to help fuel the British economy. The British have had experiences with people of all sorts of races and creeds as their empire at one point was the largest that the world had ever seen. As the saying goes, "The sun never set on the British Empire." It was only natural, at first, for the British to think that they were superior to all the people they had colonized as they were obviously more advanced technologically and at first glance, their civilization was more highly developed than those they subjugated. This can also be observed in the general attitude of people like the British slave traders, who did not see any human value in the people they were selling into slavery. And there are Englishmen like Rudyard Kipling who had the mentality of many of his countrymen who believed that white men had the burden even the duty to uplift these inferior and uncivilized people to a better state. And he was specifically imploring the US, who was not an imperialist power at that time and may have been hesitating on whether to colonize another nation-state, race, or, namely the Filipinos, to go ahead with colonization because, just like his countrymen who were supposedly civilized and uplifted all the people they had colonized, the US as a civilized nation had the duty to do the same. This was the typical mentality of the colonial and imperial powers for quite some time. But as history progressed, and as the colonizers spent more time learning about the cultures of the people they had controlled, their behaviour evolved beyond the initial first impressions. They realized, after spending time with them, that the subjugated people were also capable of all fields of culture and arts and the higher intellectual professions and pursuits just like any other capable human being and that they were not inferior in any way. The British should have moved on beyond the initial disdain that they probably first had in relation to these cultures towards more respect for people of various backgrounds, especially in this day and age with the archaic racist theories of the past being disproven. Everywhere in Europe and North America, and Australia, immigrants of different backgrounds, are excelling in the important professions that require a high education and that pay well. However much the British want to believe that they are indeed tolerant no matter what race or background someone is, the reality of the narrative is rather shallow contrary to what they had hoped. People today are still clinging to their irrational stereotypes and racist attitudes, no matter how ridiculous and outdated that way of thinking is. And racism is not relegated to any class. All are affected, from the royal family to average Joe, which shows that it is still a pervasive problem in society and must be taken in all seriousness. A huge contributing part to the problem is that people of all races and nationalities can be found in the major metropolitan areas in the UK. When walking the streets, all types of languages from different regions of the world can be heard. There are Brits who feel that they are losing their country to Muslims or whatever other minority they believe is taking over. And one cannot underestimate the sense that a person feels when they think they are losing their country to "foreigners". It can be a helpless feeling, however irrational the belief may be. Add to this the fact that Arabs, Indians, Pakistanis or whatever other ethnic groups there are have clung together in their communities. This makes it feel like one is walking the streets of Islamabad or New Delhi and not London. All this contributes to the sense of losing one's own country. I am sure there are many Londoners who believe that Sharia Law is being practised in some of these communities, even if the proof may be scant. There are always people who believe others behave differently than they do, and this cannot be changed no matter how much effort is put in to discourage such a worldview.

Though not as tumultuous, the societal changes in the US since the end of World War II were significant nonetheless. From the conservative household of the 1950s with a nuclear family that consisted of a working husband and a caretaker wife in a nice suburb in a society that was predominantly white to the tumult of the '60s onto the present day, the changes of the decades following the last Great War eradicated the "old society" so to speak of America, and these changes have boiled to the surface in recent years as embodied by Trump and his policies. The changes during the 60s, from the Kennedy assassination to the Vietnam War to Civil Rights to the rise of Women's Rights and Gay Rights, have been the most drastic of the post-war years. One need look no further than listen to Marvin Gaye's song "What's Going On" to understand the social changes that were transforming society during that extraordinary decade.

There were also major cultural changes that took place during the mid to late sixties, like the influence of the counter culture on the way people dress. Prior to this time, people were well dressed in public, even if they were just going to the supermarket or the mall or even out walking on the streets. Since the sixties, with the counter culture and hippies, people started dressing down, which is why we today are more casually dressed when we are out in public, unlike those who lived prior to the latter half of the sixties. Our tendencies to eat healthy organic food and our care for the environment also originated during that colourful and tumultuous decade. Though not as drastic a change since the decade of the 60s, it has been growing steadily, from Roe v.

Wade to the legalization of gay marriage in the past several years. The Democrats' cataclysmic defeat in the 1972 presidential election was due to the fact that the America they represented, whether true or not, was seen as too drastic a change from the America of the time. Richard Nixon was not exactly a charming and charismatic candidate but better him than drugs, sex, rock and roll, draft dodgers, or hippies for the most part (basically everything that was negative in society from the mid to late sixties up to that point) which the other side represented and was unfortunately embodied by the Democratic Party. White backlash is strong due to the fact that American society is seen as changing too drastically too fast. In another twenty-five to thirty years, it is estimated that whites will no longer be the majority, and the US will be a minority-majority country. This is just natural as humans are a migratory species.

From primitive times, we know that humans moved from one area to another based on where the animals were plentiful, and throughout history, humans have migrated from one area to another, like the barbarian migrations throughout the European continent and the migrations of whites to the New World and Australia and South America that were detrimental to the natives that were already there. One can even argue that even native Americans were not native to America, as archaeologists agree the first humans who entered America were from Asia by crossing the Bering Land Bridge. The point is people move and have been doing so throughout history. Trump's many followers, though far from all Trump supporters, want to stem the tide of change which they feel is overtaking their country, which is evidenced by the fanaticism of his followers during the years he was in office. I, personally, understand the anger against illegal immigration, and I believe in other ways to solve the illegal immigrant problem other than a wall, but one needs to understand that whether immigration is illegal or legal, they are just doing what is instinctual to humans - migrate to where conditions are better. I can understand the feeling that they are losing their country because of the immigrant numbers to the US, and a vast majority belong to other races, but people will move and migrate as humans will do. The situation in the US during the Trump years up until now is similar to the situation in France after Napoleon's abdication. Just like the Bourbon Restoration was a backlash to the drastic changes during the French Revolution and subsequent Napoleonic years, the Trump years were a backlash or 'whitelash' to the decades of changes going on in American society during the decades since the end of World War II. As Newton stated: "For every action, there is an equal and opposite reaction". Now Trump supporters (the equivalent of the Royalists in France during the Revolution and Napoleonic years) are making their voices heard, similar to the Bourbons and their Royalist supporters after regaining power during the aftermath of Napoleon's abdication. This is what happens when social forces and the changes going on in society are happening at a rapid rate. If change is too fast, the backlash from the old order will be just as forceful as can be seen by the Bourbon Restoration in France during the early part of the nineteenth century and the Trump presidency in the early twenty-first century.

The Nazis are a perfect example of how to handle drastic change. They realized that change could not be too forceful, and they knew people would not be too welcoming if the relative tolerance of the Weimar Republic would suddenly turn into an authoritarian state, skipping the intermittent stages in between. As a result, the Nazis had an agenda or narrative of their own, and they had to change the narrative of the Weimar Republic, which was that of tolerance, openness, and democracy. They knew that people would never accept a change of the narrative in a shocking and abrupt manner. And a change from democracy to authoritarianism is not only a mild step backwards; in fact, it is a complete swing to the opposite end of the spectrum. If you could say nothing else about the Nazis, they definitely had a good Human Resources Department. They had competent individuals who knew what they were doing and knew how to implement their policies. The initial boycott of

Jewish businesses to the horrors of the death camps did not happen overnight. It took time and stages where the Nazis implemented laws that slowly took away rights from Jews and certain German citizens as well. They slowly and gradually took over the media and slowly and repeatedly broadcast their anti-semitic propaganda so that the ordinary citizens were not even conscious of the fact that he or she was slowly getting indoctrinated into a radical ideology. This is why there was no revolution from within Germany to try and overthrow Nazi rule. Yes, there were people who tried to assassinate Hitler, like the July 20 plot. However, many were scared to even raise a voice against the Nazis even though they did not agree with what they were peddling. It was also a fact, however, that many Germans were indoctrinated and bought what the Nazis were selling. Needless to say, the Nazis had established themselves and had firmly implanted their narrative while in the process destroying a previous narrative of democratic progress, though be it imperfect in the form of the Weimar Republic.

This chapter has shown that history can be a chaotic tug of war between various factions in society. The tumultuous decade of the 60s demonstrates this social and political chaos perfectly with all the anti-establishment protests, race riots, burning cities, and Klan murders in the south in the years leading up to the Civil Rights Act. There is no linear progress towards societal and political cohesion and unity but only the various interests staking their claim in the social and political order. This is evident in nineteenth-century France, where we see a back and forth power struggle between the 'Ancien Regime' and its supporters and those supporting the Revolution and an end to the monarchy. France couldn't quite figure out what government it wanted, and so that century saw much social chaos in French society and political organization. The US during the present times with the culture wars is no different as minorities are increasing in numbers and are getting their voices heard in government and are increasing their leverage within government, most especially in the Democratic Party. The percentage of white Americans in the general American population has drastically decreased since the years after World War II, which will definitely cause a lot of political friction and social unrest in society, especially in connection with legislation and social policies. The Trump years represented a backlash or, as has been stated, 'whitelash' of the 'old order' of the values of 'white America' as there is an increasing perception among their numbers that they are losing their country. Thus the Trump years can be analogized to the Bourbon Restoration in the early nineteenth century in France when the Royalists took back to power after Napoleon's fall in an attempt to eradicate the gains made during the years of the French Revolution and Napoleon's reign. Trump, in his hatred of Obama, tried, in turn, to roll back the gains made by the left and minorities during Obama's two terms, with Trump's policies favouring the hard right-wing faction of the Republican party. Thus we see once again how there is a theme when it comes to history and politics that there is no historical progression to a societal utopia where there is no racial and social unrest and where everyone learns to live together in a democratic society where nobody is left out as the West, or probably more specifically the US, wants to think is the trajectory of their historical narrative. Examples of this are evident with all the policies and legislation from the '60s and '70s and on to the present day with regards to Lyndon Johnson's Great Society, civil rights, women's rights, gay rights, etc. There is only constant tugging and pulling from various factions and groups, which makes history and politics out to be more of a continuous plotline like a daytime soap opera or professional wrestling, where new storylines are created as well as new political and social alliances. There is also the ugly underside of society no matter how societies frame their narrative of racial and class harmony, like the racial problems in Western societies like the US, UK, and France despite being supposedly racially tolerant societies on paper.

The Nazis realized the social tensions and problems that would occur if change were to happen too fast. They wanted to go in a completely different direction from what Germans had known up to that point. So they had to implement their agenda slowly. All the death, destruction and suffering did not happen on day 1 when Hitler took power and became chancellor. As a matter of fact, Hitler wore a suit and tie on the day he was appointed chancellor by President Paul von Hindenburg and not his usual Nazi uniform with the Swastika armbands. He did this in order not to alarm the German nation and, more importantly, the people in government who pulled the strings and who mattered, like President von Hindenburg, who was not impressed at all by Hitler as he saw Hitler for who he was, that is; a cheap talking demagogue with the tendencies of a street thug.[50] Hitler started out wanting to show the German public that he was not a threat. He did this through a purge known to history as the Night of the Long Knives. Yes, the purge had the effect of consolidating Hitler's power by eliminating potential political rivals, but it was also meant to alleviate the worries that the German public had with the Nazis, as Hitler did not want to show his true colours just yet. This was demonstrated with the elimination of Ernst Rohm, head of the SA. The Nazis implemented their real agenda slowly by

[50] Clifford, A. (2022, January 25). Hindenburg and Hitler—How Germany's War-Hero President Set the Stage for a Nazi Takeover. Military History Now.
https://militaryhistorynow.com/2022/01/25/hindenburg-and-hitler-how-germanys-war-hero-president-set-the-stage-for-a-nazi-takeover/

passing laws one after another and not all at once, slowly tightening the noose. They started with a boycott of Jewish businesses way before they led Jews to the gates of Auschwitz and other camps that reverberate to this day as places of death and suffering. The Nazis knew what they were doing in order to avoid the unrest from within that would eventually happen if the change was immediately implemented. So they implemented their policies slowly and gradually in order not to alarm a public that did not share their fanaticism. And since they were implementing change gradually, the hope was Germans would be lulled into complacency.

This is in stark contrast to all the radical changes going on within American society during the mid to late sixties. The conservative American society with a white nuclear family living in the suburbs, which was the typical image of the 50s, was a thing of the past. America was rapidly morphing into a different society causing all the social and political problems we see starting in the 60's all the way to today with the culture wars, thus showing the problems with the orderly progression of historical narratives.

Chapter 3: The Narrative of Race Relations

One cannot ignore the pressing issue and narrative of US society which is the narrative of race relations. Today, the US has a thriving black middle class, which has grown in numbers over the years. But despite being such a large number, a majority of Americans believe that race relations in the United States are only getting worse. Obviously, these past few years have been rather tough on race relations, be it for the reason that black men are getting killed at the hands of police, anti-Asian hate connected to COVID or anti-immigrant anger and the lack of humanity with regard to undocumented immigrants being placed in cages. Even African American pundits are of the opinion that today's police officers are the equivalent of yesterday's slave bounty hunters. But this is not the narrative that the US wants to relate to or even imply in its historical narrative from the past to the present.

The US, from the very start, when it became a nation, had high ideals for its Republic. Its founding documents like the Declaration of Independence and the Constitution talked a big game. It ideally gave the same rights to everybody and made racial discrimination unlawful in work, social, and public places. It reiterated that everybody is equal under the law, which was radical for its time as this was not the case in the old world with its rigid class structure and differential treatment under the law if one belonged to the nobility as opposed to if someone belonged to the peasantry. The US, with its history, even its laws, both legislative and judicial, wants to portray its history in a different light by teaching students of its narrative that it is a society that is becoming more accepting and tolerant of other races, religions, sexual orientations etc. However, this is a failure of the narrative as it is. It is as if different races and groups only got their civil rights as time went on when the truth is, as has been said, the US founding documents had high ideals from the very start, which were not actually followed in practice at the founding of the nation. Thus one can say there is the narrative on paper which was not fulfilled by the actual narrative, which came up way short. This can be seen in court rulings, especially the Supreme Court, and with Congress with regard to legislation. Blacks up until the Civil War were slaves and were not even considered humans under the law as they were literally considered chattel. The southern slave states fought for slaves to be counted for purposes of representation, and the 3/5 rule was established where slaves were counted 3/5 in representation which gave those states more political power than they otherwise would have had had the slaves not been counted. Slaves were treated harshly in the south with their plantation-based economy based on field labour of their important crops like sugar, tobacco, and cotton. There was the Dred Scott case which was a judicial affirmation of slavery. The Supreme Court, in that case, ruled that slaves were not citizens and could not have the rights of citizens no matter what, even if a slave was brought by his master to a free state. With the south's defeat in the Civil War, the slaves were freed, and the Civil War Amendments were passed, which goes along with the progression of the narrative of more rights for more marginalized groups of people as time and America progressed.[51] These amendments gave more rights to marginalized former slaves that they did not possess previously. Thus the narrative progressed with more rights being given, which was an improvement in their status. Consequently, there were also blacks elected to Congress in the aftermath of the Civil War during the Reconstruction era. Despite improvement in the narrative of race relations, blacks were still not completely equal as they lacked education and were relegated to menial jobs despite being free as the best jobs were still held by white citizens due to the advantage they had with regard to being more educated than blacks from the Antebellum era and the endemic racism and prejudice was still present in society despite legislation from above. This separation among the races was affirmed in the court ruling of Plessy v. Ferguson. Racial segregation

---

[51] Dred Scott v. Sandford, 60 U.S. 393 (1856)

was made constitutional by this ruling.[52] Thus, even in society at large, blacks had to endure an inferior status. They were expected to step aside from a sidewalk if whites were walking by or give up their seat if a white person had nowhere to sit. African Americans also had to suffer lynchings if they were suspected of committing a crime, no matter how slight the suspicion or the evidence was. These lynchings usually went unpunished by the authorities, and lynchings were not relegated to the south. For instance, there were three black men lynched in Minnesota in 1920 when they were suspected and accused of raping a white woman.[53] This demeaning servitude in which blacks were forced to live eventually changed post World War II partly due to the way blacks conducted themselves in service of their country, which resulted in the integration of blacks in the military not long after the war.

There were also individuals who would stand up to the system, like Rosa Parks, in the mid-'50s, who refused to give up her seat to a white passenger. Also, in the mid-'50s, the Supreme Court decision of Brown v. Board of Education was passed, which brought down racial segregation in public schools.[54] In civil society, there were protests and sit-ins at

---

[52] Plessy v. Ferguson, 163 U.S. 537 (1896)
[53] Duluth Lynchings. (2022, June 30). In Wikipedia. https://en.wikipedia.org/wiki/Duluth_lynchings
[54] Brown v. Board of Education, 347 U.S. 483 (1954)

lunch counters in the '60s, and the Civil Rights legislation was passed after massive resistance by white segregationists. All these events were another step in the improvement of the narrative for a marginalized racial minority after unequal treatment for a century after the Civil War. So now, on the level of the law, blacks have indeed made great strides through a combination of legislation and case law which shows progress in the historical narrative of creating a fairer and more equal society. No longer are there the whites-only water fountains or restaurants. So while there has been some progress in racial relations, it is also true that racism has transformed to become more subtle that does not make the newspaper headlines. No longer are there overt signs of racism like there were in the days of slavery. The visible manifestations of racism cannot be seen by the public. This current form is otherwise known as systemic racism. This can be manifested in the lower-income gaining capacity and lower educational levels of blacks due to the racism of the past. Blacks also still get stiffer penalties in the legal system compared to their white counterparts and will more likely be given the death penalty compared to a white person who committed a similar type of murder. And, of course, there is the police brutality of the present day. Thus the narrative has gone far from the days of slavery, but it still has a long way to go to achieve true equality.

Needless to say, one can separate the narrative of race into two layers. One is on the level of the law, where indeed tremendous gains have been made, and another on the level of social structure, where the racism is now systemic and does not make national headlines like the Jim Crow laws of the past, where the racism was blatant and could be seen with one's two eyes. This racism in civil society has really been brought to the surface these past several years with Trump's dog whistles directed at racist elements in society. The American presidents in recent history have always been above racism and have tried to improve or heal the racial divides in society. Trump, however, poured salt into the wounds of this festering social problem. White supremacist/nationalist groups like the Proud Boys were encouraged by Trump's statement during the debate with Biden, which increased their membership in the aftermath of that debate. During the Capitol Insurrection, many Capitol police officers suffered racial abuse at the hands of the insurrectionists.

Thus all of this shows how the American race relations narrative is not the end-all and be-all of all narratives since there are problems beneath the surface, and there are bumps and setbacks where the narrative actually gets pulled back and the progress made gets nullified. And if this is the case, what more when the Western narrative is imposed on other nation-states. All kinds of problems will surface that will be unseen since the other nation-states will have their own cultural and societal issues to deal with, similar to how the US has racial issues. There are also ethnic tensions in other countries and whole groups of people within societies with different cultures from the culture of the majority. It will be harder to impose Western-style Jeffersonian democracy and equality in these other nation-states, especially if the US, the model of democracy and equality itself, has racial problems despite the narrative of a democratic society where all are welcomed and treated equally. What if these other societies that do not have the economic, social and political development like the US go on to follow the US model? Their problems will be different and even more destructive to this social experiment.

When it comes to the narrative of the West and the US, more specifically, beauty is only skin deep because there are societal problems underneath the narrative that is portrayed for the world to see. The US likes to think that its system is there for the world to emulate because it is the highest form of social progress and equality. But the truth is that with someone like Trump at the helm with his overt racist overtones and dividing Americans into groups, it only shows that the American narrative has problems, and its progress is not all that it is cracked up to be. Be not mistaken; there has been much progress made on many levels in American society, both legislative and within civil society. But there are still serious problems and a long way to go to be a truly perfect union.

Chapter 4: Disrupting the Narrative of the Presidency

Donald Trump himself is a disruptor of the narrative of American progress. He has not acted accordingly in numerous ways in both how the American people expect him to act and how the world expects an American president to act. As has been already discussed, there is a clear progression in American cultural and societal norms, laws and demographics that have shown an acceptance of blacks and other minority groups as well as other religions and sexual orientations due to case law and societal changes. Actually, from the very start, the American Constitution, as well as the Declaration of Independence, talked a big game with its lofty language about all men being created equal. But the reality was far from the ideals which the forefathers set out for themselves. But even then, there has been a narrative of the improvement of rights among various groups within American society as American history progressed. Barack Obama's election to the Presidency can be seen as the ultimate symbol that race relations have come a long way. But as can be seen by just watching the news as I have been doing across the pond, there are a lot of racist factions in American society boiling under the surface that have no outlet due to the fact that it is not the normal expected behaviour in today's America. The end of Jim Crow, the

Klan marches in Washington DC and lynchings etc., were all thought to be a thing of the past. But the Trump presidency has brought all the social problems of the past boiling back to the surface due to his rhetoric. He started it right from the moment when he announced he was going to run for the Presidency by saying that something had to be done with illegal immigrants because many of them were criminals and rapists, even though some of them were good people paraphrasing what he said. It was just blatantly stereotypical, racist, and tactless. This is not in accordance with the narrative of how a president should act.

Presidents of the past were not this blatantly tactless and racist. Richard Nixon's bigotry only came out in the Nixon tapes, which were not supposed to be meant for public consumption, as Nixon knew what was expected of a president and how he was to act. A president had to be representative of every citizen and cannot be seen as seeing one group as inferior to another. It just is not presidential. Many vulgar things were said on the Nixon tapes, but Nixon never thought in his wildest dreams that the public would ever listen to the tapes. Donald Trump was Nixon and more in public, just like how Nixon was on the tapes. He out-Nixoned Nixon with his public speeches compared to how Nixon was in the privacy of his conversations with Haldeman or whoever he happened to be talking to in private on those tapes. Another example of this behaviour is George Wallace during his run for the Presidency. There was a different George Wallace when he was governor of Alabama and a different George Wallace when he ran for the Presidency. George Wallace, the governor, said, "Segregation now, segregation tomorrow, segregation forever." However, when he ran for president, though the American people knew who he was as governor of Alabama, he couched his language in terms of support for law enforcement and rights and stated not a word about segregation or used his race bating language that he used as governor of Alabama.

Wallace knew that there was a narrative of how a president or how someone who runs for president is supposed to behave. But it did not hide the fact of who he was as a governor with his racist politics and policies. Everyone knew he stood in front of the University of Alabama's front door to try and block an African American student from attending. Despite this, he still had a successful showing as a presidential candidate, winning some southern states, which means to show that there were still very conservative and racist elements in society that were willing to support a candidate with a racist, segregationist past. This also meant that the US had still a long way to go to be a colour blind society which America ideally likes to portray itself to be though the reality is much different. Thus, be it Wallace or Nixon, every American president knew that there were certain expectations of a president and some standard way of conduct that the highest position of the country demanded. On the contrary, Trump did not care for any of that and disregarded it altogether. As proof, Trump bragged on Twitter about rescinding an Obama era rule that was intended to combat housing discrimination.[55] He did it to try to gain a larger share of the vote of suburban women, which he was losing according to polls in the weeks leading up to the 2020 election, but it was still in the spirit of who he was.[56] He was still showing himself to be against minorities and that he lacked compassion for the marginalized community, and in doing so, he was, in a way, endorsing the discrimination against minorities in society. As always, this was true to who he was all along; pro-white and racist when the going gets tough, and he had to make decisions that would divide the electorate. And if one thinks this is just an act by a politician to gain votes, one needs to consider that Trump has faced litigation going back to the 1970s for

---

[55] Kurtzleben, D. (2020, July 23). President Trump To Repeal Obama-Era Fair Housing Rule Aimed To Combat Racial Bias. npr. https://www.npr.org/2020/07/23/894794169/president-trump-to-repeal-obama-era-fair-housing-rule-aimed-to-combat-racial-bia?t=1659458444898

[56] Flaherty, A. (2020, July 23). Trump officially dismantles Obama fair housing rule he's never enforced. abc NEWS. https://abcnews.go.com/Politics/trump-officially-dismantle-obama-fair-housing-rule-enforced/story?id=71942284

housing discrimination.[57] This shows that this behaviour is in keeping with his character that time and progress in the country had no effect on.

---

[57] NPR STAFF. (2016, September 29). Decades-Old Housing Discrimination Case Plagues Donald Trump. npr.
https://www.npr.org/2016/09/29/495955920/donald-trump-plagued-by-decades-old-housing-discrimination-case

Chapter 5: Trump Paraphernalia

If you wanted to see version 2.0 of Hitler and his rallies, then you needn't look further than the Trump rallies.

Their rallies included people who wore gear to stand out as their supporters, cheering every word they uttered during their speeches. The difference was Hitler was more serious as he always made Germans proud of their nationality in his speeches. Trump tried to get people excited about what he was saying, but with less eloquence and more buffoonish antics than someone like Hitler, who wanted to lift people to high levels of emotions, making them feel them. And if one were to see all candidates do this, Trump overdid it because he held rallies throughout his four-year presidency even though they were unnecessary without the upcoming election. His four years consisted of these rallies in various cities, and they happened at regular intervals at taxpayer expense, even while he was the president.

Wearing unique attire was another way that Trump disrupted the narrative of how a president should behave. Across America, people wore their red 'Make America Great Again' shirts and hats. Usually, these rallies were only done during the campaign when running for president, but that wasn't the case with Trump. Many saw this as a waste of time and a way for him to satisfy his ego. But though this was not the narrative of how an American president behaves, this is how dictators behaved with their mass rallies while showing themselves off to the nation and the world at large that they were well-loved by their people.

Trump took a page out of a dictator's playbook. The Nazis did it best, however. They knew how to present themselves in the best light and use their widespread support among the German people to their advantage, though not even close to 50% of Germans voted for them in their best election.[58] From their mass rallies in arenas where everyone did the Nazi salute, swastikas flying everywhere, to Hitler driving by and everyone in the crowd giving him the Nazi salute, to youth parades - image for them was everything.

Through their propaganda and rallies, the Nazis showed that all Germans supported them though this was most likely not the case. Those voices who opposed them were kept silent due to the terror the Nazis could wreak upon them, which made them tremble with fear—even the thought of raising a voice against the regime caused chills up and down the spine.

Trump was similar in how he wanted to portray how popular he was and what he could do to the people against him. I wanted to believe that he knew there was much anger towards him in society. So how did he get around this, one

[58] March 1933 German federal election. (2022, July 22). In Wikipedia. https://en.wikipedia.org/wiki/March_1933_German_federal_election

may wonder. It was by constantly holding rallies with people wearing MAGA attire. During the demonstrations for his campaign, he'd tell the cameraman to pan the camera around because he wanted to show how many people attended his rallies. It showed that he was more popular and that those against him were merely marginal voices.

Even though Trump showed he had everyone's support by taking Hitler's leadership qualities as his inspiration, he failed to do two things: he could not organize and sponsor youth organizations in his name with kids in MAGA attire similar to the Hitler youth. He also did not come up with meaningful gestures they could use to recognize one another, such as the Nazi salute. Trump did not have a personalized greeting for his supporters, so in this way, he did not copy the Nazis entirely. But despite these shortcomings, there were similarities between Trump, his people, and the Nazis or dictators in general. Yes, there were the issues of being a narcissist and that he constantly needed the affirmation of his admiring audience, but there was no doubt that he was copying the style of a dictator.

The difference was that he was still operating in a constitutional democracy where he could not silence his critics and detractors, so the voices against his administration could still make themselves heard through demonstrations and social media. But make no mistakes, it was unheard of until Trump held rallies throughout his presidential term. It was a waste of taxpayer money and time he could've used doing his job.

Chapter 6: Donald Trump and His Lies

If Donald Trump said "good morning" to me, I'd make sure to bring a raincoat or an umbrella when I went out the front door. Whenever Trump's lips moved, oh well, you can imagine the rest. The point was that Trump lied a lot. It was not even up for an argument as it became a known fact. We, as humans, do not appreciate when people lie to us, and it was something we taught our children at an early age. We respected and honored truthful people who kept their word because that spoke a lot about who they were.

We usually trust people in authority due to the position they hold. We trust lawyers, doctors, and other professionals to give us correct advice, and we believe their advice without question due to the authority they hold by virtue of their position, so we don't think for a second that they are being untruthful. When we are approached by salesmen, strangers on social media, or people with quick rich schemes that are too good to be true, then we naturally have our guard up as to the veracity of their statements. I guess one can say this is human nature. We make a lot of calculations based on people's circumstances, and we hold professionals in higher regard than someone on the streets whose background we don't know. We, as humans, like to make judgments on people. We judge people who are better dressed differently from those who aren't. And our prejudices usually come out on the streets where the other people we come into contact with are a blank slate due to the fact that we don't know anything about them. But once we interact with people in a school setting or office setting, then our prejudices go away, as there is now context surrounding the people with whom we are interacting. This is the same with how we gauge whether someone is to be believed. We have high regard for professionals and people in authority and believe them to be telling the truth by virtue of their position, especially when they are talking about things in their area of expertise. And the President of the United States is the most powerful man in the country, if not the world, so naturally, Americans will believe what he says and hang on to his every word. This is why many Americans still believed what Trump said, no matter how outlandish they were by virtue of the fact that he was the President.

Combine that with the fact that he's supposedly a successful billionaire businessman. However, this is debatable as he has filed for bankruptcy numerous times. But nevertheless, by virtue of the fact that he was President, many believed every word he said. This is because the aura of the position holds a lot of weight in people's minds. If someone on a street corner said to drink Hydroxychloroquine as a cure for COVID, we would be hard-pressed to believe such a statement coming from such a person. But because Trump said it, then it is much more believable by virtue of the surrounding circumstances. This is why he has betrayed the public trust when he outright lies to the American people.

In the olden days, people would have a gentleman's agreement based on their word and a handshake, and that was good enough for the two parties to trust each other to go through with their end of the bargain. Some books on law labeled lying as an element of an offense like fraud or libel. The basic foundations of these offenses were untruthful statements or declarations, and we certainly are not allowed to lie in a court of law. But Trump was not afraid to disrespect the idea that the truth should be told to the public. Still, it is unforgivable for a country's president to lie to its people because their livelihood and respect for their country depended on how he treated the people who belonged to that country.

We cannot imagine our friends and family lying to us, let alone a president lying to the entire country and its people. I am not saying that previous presidents never lied in the past. It is just that Trump took it to a whole new level. And if the president was not telling the truth, there was no reason to expect each other to tell the truth either. Trump has set a poor example for our children, even adults, as he has made lying seem rather applaudable.

I recall the only other person in recent history who blatantly continued to lie was "Baghdad Bob" or Mohamed Saïd al-Sahhaf. He was the spokesperson of the Iraqi government during the 2003 Iraq War. Despite the Iraqis being in a desperate situation against Coalition forces, he kept painting a rosy picture of how things were going great for Iraq and that the Coalition forces were nowhere around. But soon, the truth came to light when Iraq's defeat was imminent.

Who would have thought that there would be an American administration that would lie to that extent?

Well, the world found Saïd al-Sahhaf's match in Donald Trump. People who kept track of Trump's lies counted them in thousands.[59] Even his press secretaries pretended to believe his every word and, when asked to validate the facts, acted incredulously and continued to outright lie as per the administration policy. He was so sure that he would sell his lies that he uttered his "alternate facts" with a straight face. Compare this with the previous presidents who, instead of acting like the Trump government, avoided answering the questions, rambled on about a completely different topic, or, at worst, tweaked the truth a little. But that was it because

[59] Kessler, G., Rizzo, S., Kelly, M., (2021, January 24). Trump's false or misleading claims total 30,573 over 4 years. The Washington Post. https://www.washingtonpost.com/politics/2021/01/24/trumps-false-or-misleading-claims-total-30573-over-four-years/

they avoided sounding incoherent and incompetent in front of the public.

In a State of the Union address, many remember Gerald Ford famously saying, "The State of the Union is not good." And some presidents talked in a mildly lecturing tone, trying to relay important information to the American people that they needed to know, just like how an adult would speak to an adult. In Franklin Roosevelt and Jimmy Carter's fireside chats, they conversed like adults speaking to adults explaining to the public the nation's problems instead of treating the American public like children.

Trump, however, did not think of remotely talking to the American people in this manner and treated them with disdain at best. Trump would flat out lie if he thought it was best for him. It all started on Inauguration Day when he continuously claimed that his inauguration was the most attended event in history. When the video footage of the crowd emerged, it showed that was not the case.

Trump's string of lies didn't end even during one of the deadliest pandemics in the history of the world. He played it down and said that there was nothing to worry about even though Americans were dying at an alarming rate every day. He went so far as to claim that COVID-19 was a "hoax." Trump also lied significantly when talking about how to combat COVID-19. He said that Hydroxychloroquine would be an excellent way to fight the deadly virus.

Widespread speculation took place regarding why he played down the pandemic. It was not to affect and disrupt his upcoming election campaign since he knew he had failed to keep the country safe from it. Someone spoke during the Democratic National Convention who said her father believed every one of Trump's lies, which cost him his life. It only shows how serious it can be when a president lies because sometimes, the people find no other option but to believe the words of their leaders.

And so, the leaders should be mindful of the things they say and the promises they make, as it is a president's moral duty to relay the truth because of the position he holds. But his lying was worse as it cost people their lives, from not wearing masks to believing Hydroxychloroquine works. He even claimed to have a health care plan that he never unveiled. He also had other lies like saying Biden would do away with pre-existing conditions or how he won Michigan's Man of the Year, which Trump should have known did not exist. Trump claimed to have graduated at the top of his class at the University of Pennsylvania. It was yet another lie he conjured up to suit the title of the 'President of the United States.'

And of course, who could forget the "Big Lie" that he won the election even though the facts contradicted the statement. No president had acted like this before and claimed to have won an election he had lost. It is all part of the narrative that presidents accept how the game is played, and when one fails, it is best to acknowledge the results and concede for the country's sake and present an orderly and peaceful transition.

When the previous presidents took to the office and media confronted them, they wanted to look like someone the American people looked up to, even when they told lies. But they did in ways that did not come off as unprofessional and inadequate by either avoiding to answer or giving a more structured answer so the media frenzy would die down. During the Trump administration, the media involvement reached its peak where they kept track of all the lies he had told.

This statistic has not been tracked with any previous president. It only shows how much Trump ruptured the role of a president and made a mockery out of the office because no other president laid a foundation for such statistics to be tracked.

One can compare Trump's untruthful statements to other presidents to see how serious they really are. When Bill Clinton denied having sexual relations with Monica

Lewinsky one could argue it was his private affair and had nothing to do with the national interest. When the Bush administration claimed that Iraq had weapons of mass destruction which justified the invasion of that country, it could be argued that the US government couldn't take a chance even if it turned out Iraq didn't have nuclear weapons because the stakes were too high. Or if the real reason to invade Iraq was its oil, then it is a lie but it still has the objective of serving the national interest since the US is a huge consumer of fossil fuels. Trump's lies however only served himself and were detrimental to the national interests. This is how Trump's lies were worse than other presidents which make it all the more detrimental to the national interest.

Chapter 7: The Media Climate Today Enables Trump's Lying

The media played a huge role in enabling lying.

The media has changed from what it used to be like before. People of every persuasion can now find a media outlet that affirms their beliefs and worldview. The media and the people who watch it are like the chicken and the egg problem. We can argue on and on as to which came first, but it is surely a never-ending cycle that repeats itself.

I want to shed light on: are media outlets that expound on a certain viewpoint created due to the enormous numbers of people who espouse said viewpoint, or are these media outlets built with a certain view in mind. Then the viewers who tune in will then buy into their perspective?

Whatever the case may be, technological progression in terms of communicating through the internet and social media has come at a cause of social fracturing by giving a voice and platform to demagogues like Trump and those of his ilk. Thus the narrative of technological progression with the internet and social media, satellite TV, etc., has aided and abetted social regression similar to how the printing press aided the advancement of the Reformation especially Lutheranism.

The said situation was a godsend for marketing purposes because they could target their audiences. Brands could now sell to the right demographic through cookies on the internet, enabling companies to target their audience based on their websites. They could also do this by running the relevant ads in connection with the subject matter of the websites or TV channels (for instance, running video game ads on the video game channel or women's products on the Lifetime channel).

So, politicians also took advantage of these marketing techniques to gauge their audience if they chose the right media outlet. I saw and experienced this firsthand. I was googling what foods were good for the keto diet, and eventually, I viewed a commercial on the keto diet on YouTube. The setup of the modern media was also a way for demagogues to get to the audience of their choice, whom they believed best conformed to their views based on the TV channels or websites visited.

In the past, only a handful of media outlets had to cater to the entire viewing audience. The outlets then had to cater to all tastes and persuasions and at the same time not offend factions or any group of people whatsoever. Due to the absence of the internet or even multiple cable channels, these few media outlets monopolized the dissemination of information. Thus these 'gatekeepers,' media outlets that controlled the diffusion of knowledge, could easily call out a lie, and there would not be any enabling of it.[60] If these media outlets acted in a very partisan manner, they could lose huge segments of the consuming public, and thus the ratings war with their competition.

Now that there is a media outlet for anyone with a particular political persuasion and worldview, someone like Trump can lie intolerably. He could find a media outlet that would enable it. And now, with different media outlets serving the entire spectrum of political persuasion, both on TV and on the internet, there is a possibility for such media outlets where one could lie. The media outlet would take the lie for the truth, and so will its viewing audience as long as that media outlet shared the politics and worldview of the person lying. So when Trump lied appallingly about many things, the wider viewing audience had to keep in mind that he was not directing his information to them but to his 'own' audience, who shared his worldview and hung on to every word he said.

Now due to the numerous media and communication channels, one need only find the right channel to get his point of view across to the right audience willing to listen to every word that person said, no matter how outrageous it may sound to the wider public. In this way, the media enabled

---

[60] Gatekeeping (communication). (2022, April 4). In Wikipedia. https://en.wikipedia.org/wiki/Gatekeeping_(communication)

Trump's disruption of the narrative of presidents telling the truth to the American people. It was why the people speculated that Trump only reached out to his base. One reason his supporters loved him so much was not only that his politics conformed to theirs' but also influenced them.

He was spontaneous and said what was on his mind without any care for political correctness that had consumed all forms of communication, political or otherwise, in American society. The media is so diffused now that he could find an outlet like Fox that would validate his wild claims and alternate truths to a certain extent. They called him out sometimes, which got him mad at Fox, but for the most part, they enabled his actions, especially with people like Sean Hannity or Tucker Carlson. Previous presidents always tried to talk to all factions of the American population decently and maturely, no matter their political persuasion, so they were not as controversial.

Trump always sounded immature and did not care for those who did not support him. Before the media's diffusion, Trump's tactics would not have worked in the past.

In conclusion, Trump's lying was another way he disrupted the narrative of how presidents behaved through his skillful manipulation of all types of media and his celebrity status before he was president. The fact that he was a celebrity gave him weight and credibility among his supporters, which more than made up for his wild antics and lack of political experience.

The Media Climate Today Enables Trump's Lying: I, for one, did not buy into his celebrity status as I did not watch "The Apprentice," which is why many of his supporters thought he was a good businessman. I did not care for such bells and whistles and cared more about the reality behind the myth-like how he declared bankruptcy, how Trump University was sued and had to pay a settlement, how he wasn't really a self-made man but inherited millions from his father. I definitely was not Trump's target audience in the current media climate where there are various channels of communication to reach various audiences who hold different viewpoints.

An example of what I am talking about of how the media today is so diffused is in the realm of TV programming. Back in the days, when you gave the name of popular TV shows like Seinfeld or Cheers, practically everyone knew what you were talking about unless they were living under a rock. However, today there are so many cable channels that are equally as good if not better than the major networks that the major networks no longer have a stranglehold on the viewing audience. If one were to give the name of some TV programs today, there are people out there who may not have even heard or said programs, or even if they have, they probably haven't seen a second of it. This is because there are so many channels to choose from that it doesn't mean everyone is watching the same shows on TV. Throw in the internet with sites like Netflix, Amazon Prime Video, Vudu, and Hulu, along with numerous others, and one really has a lot of choices to be entertained. This is all to the advantage of marketing and advertising because all one has to do is choose the right sites and channels to advertise one's products. The same goes for politicians. A Republican like Trump needs only concentrate his efforts on marketing himself to right-wing media like Fox and talk radio which tends to be very conservative.

Chapter 8: Trump's Coddling Of Dictators

Trump was also a disruptor in that he openly liked dictators, like his kissing up to Putin or his bromance with Kim Jong-un, or that he did not think that Duterte was a bad guy. Openly coddling dictators have not been how American presidents, the "leaders of the free world," typically behaved. Past presidents have normally been diplomatic with dictators and nothing more; they did not openly admire them or give them complements.

Past American administrations did not openly show their admiration for them even though they supported them economically and militarily behind the scenes. Even if Trump did not mean it and was only joking for the sake of argument, it still sends a wrong message domestically and internationally. The way he engages with Putin and how he refuses to say anything bad about him is the most glaring example, which was the punchline and butt of many jokes in the media, social media, and political cartoons. It made it seem like he was Putin's stooge. Yes, American presidents had to deal with dictators in the past, but it was in a diplomatic manner. They did not openly admire these dictators (at least not in public). In many instances, especially during the Cold War, it was in the best interests of the US to support right-wing dictators who were bulwarks against Communist movements or insurgencies. These dictators were seen as the less evil alternative as their removal from power would utter in chaos and a power vacuum that would be dangerous for their neighbors and the US. But for the most part, they kept this from the public as it would not have been a good image for the world's leading democracy. Reagan was an exemplar of this with his administration's support of the Contra rebels in Nicaragua and El Salvador's brutal right wing regime which was fighting Communist rebels among others.

The US government has always portrayed the narrative to its people that it is all about freedom and supporting democracies in other parts of the world. Because the US is the world's most powerful democracy, it would follow that it also supports only freedom and democracy the world over. At least, this is what it portrays on the surface and what it wants its people to think. The reality, however, is far from this idealistic narrative. In no way is a US president going to openly admit their support for a dictatorial ruler to the American public. US government support of despotic regimes has happened everywhere in the world, like American support for Saddam Hussein in the 1980s in the Iran-Iraq war or American support for Pakistan during their conflict with India despite India being the world's largest democracy and was ironically supported by the Soviet Union and even Americans not raising a hand when Marcos declared Martial Law in the Philippines in 1972. Martial law still happened despite the Philippines being groomed as a democracy in Asia along American lines during the American colonization of the Philippines in the first half of the twentieth century. But because Marcos allayed fears of possible Communist plots, he declared Martial Law. The US simply allowed it since it was also thought to be in America's best interest that communism be stopped anywhere it flared.

No way would Martial Law be declared in an Asian democracy in a region where democracies at that time just didn't exist without American consent. But the most blatant American support of right-wing dictators happened in America's own "backyard," namely Central America." The US supported numerous right-wing dictators in these countries as Communist movements were strong in these countries where wealth was based on land. The wealth gap was enormous between the few rich landholders and the huge population of people connected to the land through their labor who lacked any wealth whatsoever.

There are many many examples. One would be Fulgencio Batista in Cuba before the Communist takeover of Cuba by Castro. Cuba had an open economy that catered to the wealthy and exploited the poor as per a typical Hispanicized country in the Central America/Caribbean region. It was a paradise for wealthy Cubans, complete with casinos. It was the mafia that made Cuba a center for entertainment, a Caribbean Las Vegas. There was an extravagant meeting of mafia bosses from around the US immediately after World War II, which resulted in Cuba becoming an entertainment destination and playground for the rich.[61] This meeting had a parallel in The Godfather during the rooftop scene where the mob was present for Hyman Roth's birthday. No better scene in motion picture could better depict the decadence of the American big brother exploiting a Caribbean country that needed massive amounts of investments into its economy by its giant neighbor to the north. This was an American-backed government that ran a society where there were a wealthy few who exploited the majority of the masses who were poverty-stricken. Meyer Lansky would occasionally travel to Cuba and give Batista a briefcase full of money so he could proceed with his activities in the country.[62]

American interests were in line with that of Batista, who opened up his economy to the US which could then take advantage of a country like Cuba economically and

[61] Havana Conference. (2022, July 12). In Wikipedia. https://en.wikipedia.org/wiki/Havana_Conference
[62] The MafiaRUs 1. (2012, October 15). MEYER LANSKY [Video]. Youtube. https://www.youtube.com/watch?v=Q9zutu_qqAk

politically up until the Communist takeover of Cuba by Castro.

Another good example would be Carlos Castillo Armas of Guatemala. Right before Armas' ascension to power, Guatemala underwent land reform programs to redistribute land to make land ownership somewhat more equitable vis a vis the big landowning families and companies and the majority of the peasant population. United Fruit Company, a large landowner and an important American company disdained these reforms and made its desires clear to the US government. At this time, the Cold War atmosphere made the US government view these reforms through the lens of the East-West conflict and thus conclude that these reforms were Communist in nature. The US government had to find factions in the country that would support its ends, and they found the right officer in the military in the person of Armas. The CIA supported Armas' invasion primarily through propaganda. The current president at the time, Arbenz, did not have the support of his military who supported Armas and was therefore forced to resign.

There were negotiations among various factions until Armas eventually gained power. It was primarily because of the CIA that Armas became president and therefore was seen as a dictator that promoted American interests. Another example was Ngo Dinh Diem, the president of South

Vietnam, who initially had the US government's support but was seen as increasingly hard to control due to his discriminatory policies against Buddhists. The US then wanted to see him gone. That ultimately led to the assassination of him and his brother with the intriguing and conniving of Henry Cabot Lodge Jr.[63]

The ouster of Salvador Allende, a Marxist who was elected President of Chile, is another example of American interference in other nations' affairs in support of a brutal right-wing dictatorship. Due to Allende's policies of wanting to nationalize major industries, redistributing land, and government control of health care and the educational system, he earned the ire of the US, who wanted him gone. The US found their man in the military, Augusto Pinochet, who, with support from the US, removed Allende from power via a coup d'etat. As Allende was making his final speech in La Moneda, the Presidential Palace, gunfire could be heard in the background as he was being closed in. He committed suicide rather than being captured. Again US support of a right-wing dictatorship overthrew a democratically elected government.

Though contrary to its principles of supporting democracies, the US also supported right-wing

---

[63] Henry Cabot Lodge Jr. (2022, June 19). In Wikipedia. https://en.wikipedia.org/wiki/Henry_Cabot_Lodge_Jr.

dictatorships, especially during the Cold War when opposing groups or factions were seen as Communist. The mere hint that a particular guerrilla group or opposing faction was perceived to have ties with the Soviet Union was enough for the American government to support its elimination, even if those that the US government supported had less than savory credentials. Even if these governments or opposing factions to governments were not completely Communist/Marxist on the Soviet model, the appearance of Communist policies was enough to persuade the US in the form of the CIA to have these governments removed from power. There are numerous other operations where the CIA tried its hand at subversive operations, like the botched attempt to overthrow the Albanian Communist government in the early years of the post-war era.

But due to Soviet espionage and help from Kim Philby, a British mole, the government knew about the operation beforehand.[64] The 1953 Iranian Coup d'Etat also installed the Shah with backing from the CIA, who paid people to start riots on the streets.[65] The democratically elected government of Mosaddegh was overthrown because he wanted to

[64] Fatjona, M., Fatjona, M., (2017, February 24). Albanian Anti-Communists' Families Remember 'Martyrs' Deaths'. BALKAN TRANSITIONAL JUSTICE. https://balkaninsight.com/2017/02/24/albania-honours-families-of-anti-communist-martyrs-02-23-2017/
[65] 1953 Iranian coup d'état. (2022, July 27). In Wikipedia. https://en.wikipedia.org/wiki/1953_Iranian_coup_d%27état

nationalize Iranian oil to the detriment of the West, as a British corporation had a stake in Iran's oil. The Shah was installed and ruled Iran for twenty-six years until the Iranian Revolution in 1979.

The big difference between all this and Trump was that all this happened without making announcements about it to the American public. The US was not open and proud of its relationships with these governments, and even the media was hush about it. Trump, on the other hand, openly flouts his admiration for brutal tyrants to the embarrassment of non-Trump supporting Americans and to the horror of many around the world who sees the US as the world's leading democracy (though there are also many who see the US as the imperialist power that it is). What's worse is Putin and Kim Jong-un are not allies of the US, but geostrategic rivals whose interests are not aligned with American interests. No American president should get inappropriately friendly with leaders who are adversaries of the US. In this way, he has been a disruptor of the narrative in that he has not done something that his predecessors have done, which is to flout admiration for tyrants. In the past, unless you were really into world events and politics, you would have to do a lot of research, without the internet, to find out what and who the US is supporting internationally as it was not told by the media nor by the American government for fear of the public backlash and embarrassment that it was supporting non-democratic governments.

The US always held itself up to the world as a society with lofty ideals and that it was willing to spread those ideas to the four corners of the earth to the best of its ability, whether through force or persuasion. But secretly, it supported many dictatorships that did not align with the narrative that America held up for itself as long as these governments were willing to fall in line with the economic interests of the US. I myself learned about who the US government was supporting in college when I took classes on Latin America. But normally, it is not taught to students at the lower levels. And it is certainly not covered in great depth by any media outlet or in an American history class.

Chapter 9: American Isolationism

The US had come a long way from its isolationist past before it became the superpower it is today. However, Donald Trump's isolationist policies harken back to a time when the US was more isolationist. He has demonstrated his isolationist beliefs by berating NATO members to increase their share of expenditure.

Again, this was against the grain of the narrative, especially since the US has been increasingly involved in world affairs since World War II. It is a major factor in the US becoming the world's foremost superpower. The US has come a long way since it gained independence in the late eighteenth century. It was nowhere near the power (much less superpower) that it is today. The US could not even gain independence on its own against a power like Great Britain. It needed the aid of France, who provided essential naval support. Even in the first century or so after independence, it had to play second fiddle to the great powers in Europe. And it was also more concerned with its domestic affairs like the expansion of the frontier, slavery, slavery in the newly incorporated states, policies towards the Indians, etc.

US interests hardly extended beyond its borders except trying to keep the British at bay, which they did in the War of 1812, or extending its territories through the Louisiana Purchase and the Mexican War. After the Civil War,

American industrial production and output went into overdrive with projects like the transcontinental railroad. The US was now closing the power gap between itself and its European rivals. During the late Nineteenth Century, about thirty-three years after the end of the Civil War, the US got its chance to play ball with the other imperial powers by getting involved in the Spanish American War and subsequent Philippine-American War. This was a chance for the US to engage itself in a common patriotic cause and heal the divisions and animosities that were wrought from the Civil War, which persisted afterward with Reconstruction. Now the US wanted to be an Imperialist power and would get involved in affairs beyond its borders which shows a progression in the narrative in that more power equals more involvement and influence in international affairs. Its victory against Spain and subsequently the Philippines now made it an imperial power with territories like the other European powers. The US was now higher up the pecking order than it was previously. But despite its higher stature in international affairs with overseas territories, it still was initially isolationist from the end of the nineteenth century up until the start of the First World War. It entered on the side of the UK and France later in the War, helping them win the war against the Central Powers.

The US then retreated back into its shell by not joining the League of Nations in the aftermath of the War despite Wilson's lofty ideals at the Versailles conference. It was again isolationist at the moment World War II started but was forced into the War early with the bombing of Pearl Harbor. It came out the big winner in World War II as it became the world's superpower as the other powers involved suffered heavy losses and a loss of their previous prestige due to the devastation wrought on them. The Soviet Union, the other big winner since it gained Eastern Europe, still suffered heavy losses, having had over 20 million of its people killed. The other victorious nations were even less fortunate as they were just war-weary and exhausted. Their cities were decimated.

They suffered heavy military and civilian casualties, and they lost much of their industrial and agricultural output. China, for instance, is estimated to have had 15 to 20 million casualties compared to the Soviet Union, which was estimated to have more than 20 million casualties. And both these aforementioned countries were on the victorious side. With this newfound American preeminence on the world stage that it has really yet to relinquish, the US became more involved in world affairs, with its influence reaching all corners of the globe. And the American military is also the most deployed military overseas, with bases and military personnel present all over the world. Since World War II ended, the US has been involved in many events that demonstrated its willingness to engage. For example, there is the standoff in Berlin during the Berlin crisis before the building of the Berlin Wall, the Cuban Missile Crisis, the Vietnam War, and many others where the US has supported factions overthrowing established governments, as has been previously mentioned.

Former CIA director William Colby spent time in Italy after World War II during the 1950s. He made sure that the Communist party which was backed by the Soviet Union was defeated in elections so Italy would remain firmly in the Western orbit politically, culturally, and economically when Italy was tenuously holding on to its connection to the West as it was still unsure if communism would win out. Then Colby was assigned to Vietnam to continue his anti-Communist undercover work there.[66] With examples of Cold War warriors like Colby and many unnamed others, the US has basically played a preeminent role on the world stage that it has been reluctant to relinquish until Trump came to power with his isolationist policies of not starting any more wars during his administration and forcing NATO countries to increase their share of spending. This is a step back from

---

[66] Colby, C. (Director). (2011). The Man Nobody Knew: In Search of My Father, CIA Spymaster William Colby [Film]. Act 4 Entertainment

the narrative of the increase of power and influence of the US in world affairs. Suppose the US steps back from its preeminent role and becomes more isolationist.

In that case, that power vacuum will be open for another power to fill in the void left vacant by the US, like Russia or China perhaps. The US cannot afford to be isolationist. The result will be a loss of its power vis a vis other nations and a loss of its prestige as the world's leading democracy. Thus Trump is moving the US backwards when it comes to its narrative of industrial growth and American preeminence on the world stage. The US cannot afford to step back now, as the world is now multi-polar, and the Cold War paradigm no longer applies where there were two superpowers and every country in the world lined up behind one or the other.

This is similar to Samuel P. Huntington's theory in the Clash of Civilizations. He basically theorizes that future wars will be fought between cultures and civilizations. This is the world that he claims we have lived in since the end of the Cold War. The Cold War suppressed the various civilizations for the most part under the banner of the East-West conflict. Now that the Cold War is over, there is now a multi-polar world that he groups under various cultures or civilizations and that future wars will be fought along these lines.[67] Whatever the case may be, the point is that the Cold War is over, and various powers are now emerging from the ashes of the Cold War's demise. Suppose the US becomes isolationist as Trump wanted and continues down this path under future administrations. In that case, that power vacuum will be filled in by the other powers in their respective regions to the detriment of American power.

And what's more, the US would be less prepared if there were a future major war or another world conflict. The American isolationist stance will hurt it because it will have to build up its military, which will take time to engage in said conflict. This is what happened in World War II. The US, at the start, had nowhere near the military capacity of the other powers and so had to build its military capabilities and train its soldiers before it could engage in the fighting.

According to Sir Alan Brooke, it takes approximately two years to properly train a soldier. This is why D-Day happened when it did in 1944 and not earlier. That is when US military capability was sufficient to fight that War. In the early years of World War II, there were serious discussions between the US and the British on where they should begin operations. The US wanted to strike at the heart of the European continent right away, while the British wanted to

[67] Huntington, Samuel p. (1998). The Clash of Civilizations And The Remaking of the World Order. Simon & Schuster.

work around it first, like, say, North Africa, before going into Europe in order to get much-needed training and weaken the Nazi military capability in the periphery before the eventual landings in Europe which would be much more difficult. An argument for not striking at Europe first was the unpreparedness of Allied forces, as the Germans were just way ahead of the game when it came to being on a war footing. If D-Day or Overlord happened earlier in the war, say in 1942, a strong case could be made that it would have spelled disaster for allied forces. Americans were ill-prepared at the beginning of World War II, which is why the British had more of a say in the early years of the War than the Americans when it came to operations and such, as they typically got their way. All the US could do was threaten to shift resources to the Pacific instead of keeping them in the European theatre.

As the war continued and the US could manufacture more planes, tanks, weapons, and train more soldiers, they were increasingly gaining leverage over operations vis a vis their British allies and could thus decide on where and when the landings in Europe would take place as well as the choice of supreme commander. This is a major reason why Dwight Eisenhower was chosen as a supreme commander rather than

Sir Alan Brooke, who was also a strong candidate for the post.[68]

The US today is much more prepared for a war than it ever was at the start of World War II. If Trump's isolationism were to be followed, then it would go back to these days when a war would catch the US off guard, and the US would need to bide its time before going on the offensive. On top of this, American allies who are more prepared will have leverage when it comes to command and control of military operations to the detriment of American interests. Thus Trump and his narrative of stepping back from the world stage and going isolationist is bad due to the fact that there will be unnecessary problems in future conflicts due to the US scaling down its military and leaving a power vacuum. It will not be prepared for a future war from the get-go and will be in a position like it was in World War II, where it had to build up its forces before it could engage in the conflict.

The Taliban's swift defeat of Afghan forces shortly after the US pulled out is a perfect physical manifestation of the results of American isolationism throughout the world. Images of the chaos in Kabul when American forces pulled out brought back to the collective memory the American pullout from Saigon in 1975 with people in both countries

---

[68] Roberts, A. (2009). Masters and Commanders; The Military Geniuses Who Led The West To Victory In WWII. Penguin Books

trying to hitch a ride with American forces in order to leave the country. The world has become a multi-polar world, and no longer is power monopolized between the two superpowers, as was the case during the Cold War when every other country just fell in line. The US needs to keep its guard up and face the challenges in this complex world with various power dynamics at play throughout the world. This is not the time to step back and shirk international responsibilities. If the US were to continue down the road of pursuing Trump's policies (and I don't think it will), it would only be to the detriment of American power and prestige on the world stage.

China is already flexing its muscles with its neighbors, especially in the region around the South China Sea. Suppose the US goes down the path of isolationism. Who's to stop the Chinese juggernaut from being more emboldened and taking up more islands and territorial waters from its surrounding neighbors. Russia will also be more emboldened in Crimea and Syria, where its interests lie and where they already have a presence. As a matter of fact, Russia has already invaded Ukraine and taken over the eastern part of the country. Allies like Japan and Germany will start to wonder and suspect America is wavering towards their allies. North Korea will be even more determined to become a nuclear power with no obstacle in their way in the form of the US presence in South Korea. Despots will be encouraged to be even more brutal to their people. There is no conscience or force in the US to look over their shoulder and criticize their every action.

If the US is more isolationist, it will have to scale down its military bases worldwide. This will be to the detriment of the US in future conflicts as these bases can be used as jumping-off points toward the areas of conflict. This can be seen in the war against Afghanistan in the early 2000s. The US needed to smooch Pervez Musharraf in order for the US to use Pakistani facilities to fight the war in Afghanistan. Musharraf, in agreement, had to toe the line between various factions in Pakistani society who were either mistrustful of the US or welcomed the American presence as beneficial to Pakistan. Clark Air Base and Subic Naval Base in the Philippines, as well as bases in Japan and Korea, were also beneficial to the US during the Vietnam War as the US could use those bases as staging areas for pouring troops and equipment into Vietnam. They can make use of those bases as resupply depots as well as where the injured can get medical care.

The US did not need to cajole a government in the vicinity of Vietnam in order to use their facilities. Overall if the US becomes more isolationist, the world will become a more unstable place with various powers jockeying for position in the pecking order by force if necessary. With the US as an engaged world power, other powers which would otherwise be aggressive without the US presence will now think twice about their violent tendencies in the face of an engaged Superpower. American military presence overseas is a manifestation of American power. When those bases disappear, so does American power in the eyes of those in the regions where those bases are located.

China is already aggressive as it is right now, with the US as an engaged superpower in the region. One can only imagine China's bold agenda with the isolationist US. And just like in the Cold War, an American presence in Europe is just as much needed today as it was then. The threat to Europe is now very high with the Russian invasion of Ukraine. Putin has shown his menacing nature with the Ukraine invasion to demonstrate his threat to the European continent. He also supports Brexit and nationalists like Marine Le Pen. Putin would be ever brasher if Trump continued his policies of scaling down in Europe. He has already invaded Ukraine based on the fact that he thought that the US would be less engaged in the world. Like today, an American presence in Western Europe during the Cold War benefitted Western Europe from Soviet domination. During the Berlin Wall Crisis, when tensions rose between the two superpowers, the US could easily deploy tanks for a standoff at the border between East and West Berlin. And now with increased American troop numbers in Eastern Europe under the Biden administration, the US and its NATO allies are ready for any eventuality in case the Russian invasion of Ukraine flares up into a larger regional war.

Now the US and the West can easily go on the offensive. With the East liberated from Communist rule, it has now increased its engagement and presence in Eastern Europe. There is now an American military presence in Poland. Who would have thought this during the Cold War, as Poland was firmly behind the Iron Curtain within the Soviet sphere of influence? The Iron Curtain is now further East. Russia does not have the buffer that the Soviet Union had in Eastern Europe. If the US were to scale down and be isolationist, it could put Putin on the offensive and further his designs beyond Crimea and Ukraine. It would be a disaster for the US to follow the path of isolationism as per Trump's agenda. For example, China is flexing its international muscles vis a vis its neighbors and further out through a military presence in Djibouti. Chinese citizens are also traveling the world over, which is a symbol of Chinese economic power. It wasn't that long ago when Asian tourists were almost exclusively Japanese. They have since been taken over by the Chinese. Chinese citizens are also buying businesses all over the world, like vineyards in the south of France.

And it goes without saying, North Korea continues to test missiles from time to time. This is not a time for the US to recoil and go back into its shell. The power vacuum will only be readily filled up by any of these powers in their respective areas of interest. The US will lose any influence and/or goodwill it has earned in regions where it will scale down its presence militarily. NATO members are now determined to increase their military spending so as not to be too dependent on the US due to Trump's assertions that they increase their share of military spending according to the guidelines of NATO. These pronouncements by Trump put the fear of God in them. Once these states go further down the line of becoming less and less dependent on the US, the more they will assert their interests which may not exactly be similar to American interests despite being allies. Even traditional allies like the Philippines under Duterte have pulled away from the 'American orbit' and have increased economic ties and diplomatic overtures to China. With an isolationist America, the Philippines may continue down this line.

The US will lose influence in this vital Asia Pacific region where it has held sway for so long since the twentieth century. Duterte is not like former Filipino presidents who were firmly pro-American in outlook and politics. The

197

Philippines has traditionally been a firm and constant US ally ever since the Philippines became independent in 1946. Manuel Roxas, the first Philippine president of the Republic after independence, signed the military bases agreement. The Philippines has been a close ally since, through the 50s, with American help against Communists in the Philippine countryside and all the aid given to the Philippines through the years. And the Philippines is always a must-stop for a US president visiting the Asia Pacific region. China is now making inroads and making dents on this traditional alliance between two close allies. Following Trump's policies of leaving other countries alone, the result will be detrimental in the long run to American interests as China will continue to improve its relations with the Philippines to the detriment of the US as long as China does not try to take advantage of the Philippines by exerting its leverage in its dealings with the Philippines

Trump is a disruptor this way as a traditional and consistent ally is slowly being sucked into the 'Chinese orbit' even though China is less than respectful with the Philippines, as demonstrated by their encroachments into Philippine waters. Trump was a disruptor in a positive way, though, when it came to US-Philippine relations. It was under the Trump administration that the Balangiga Bells were returned to the Philippines after more than a century in

US hands. During the Philippine-American War, a regiment of American troops was ambushed and massacred by townspeople wielding machetes.[69] This angered the Americans even more because Aguinaldo formally surrendered a few months previously, which was seen as the legitimate end of hostilities as Aguinaldo had the authority to surrender as he was the leader of Philippine forces as president.[70]

This embarrassment from the massacre needed to be avenged, and American troops executed men and children ten years old or over who could bear arms in order to turn the region into a "howling wilderness" as ordered by an American commander. And American troops also took these Balangiga Bells as 'souvenirs' and had kept them through the years despite calls to return the bells.[71] Duterte increased the volume on the return of the bells. Previous Philippine presidents may have asked for the bells' return, but nothing had been done. And Trump, who believes in isolationism and believes in states determining their own destinies, was more than willing to return the bells. However Duterte

---

[69] Battle of Balangiga. (2022, July 31). In Wikipedia. https://en.wikipedia.org/wiki/Battle_of_Balangiga
[70] Umali, J. (2021, April 27). Did Emilio Aguinaldo's Surrender Mark The End of the Philippine-American War?. Esquire. https://www.esquiremag.ph/long-reads/features/philippine-american-war-emilio-aguinaldo-a2212-20210427-lfrm
[71] Balangiga Bells. (2022, August 2). In Wikipedia. https://en.wikipedia.org/wiki/Balangiga_bells

played it off to the Philippine people that it was his determination that got the bells back to the Philippines. In this way, Trump positively was a disruptor because it finally healed wounds between the two nations that were more than a century old.

Overall, America's greatness on the world stage did not come about through isolationism. Through its military presence throughout the world, it has made America the superpower that it is both economically and militarily, and Trump's isolationist policies, if continued, will be a step back in the narrative and leave America a less influential player in the world stage.

Not only that but the international community, as well as American allies the world over and, more specifically, Europe, will lose any and all adulation and respect they will have for the US. They will chart their own course independent of the US, and the US will also lose its influence with its allies. These are all the negative results that could happen if the US were isolationist during the Russian invasion of Ukraine at this point in history. The US has a lot of responsibilities on the world stage, and an isolationist position could have a butterfly effect that could lead to a less stable world with other more aggressive and unstable actors filling in the power vacuum in the wake of American isolationism. The Marshall Plan in the post-World War II era was also a time when the US needed to be engaged in the world as Europe needed to rebuild from the ashes of World War II. And the US did indeed step up much-needed economic aid to various European countries in the form of the Marshall Plan. That led to European gratitude toward the US, which continues to this day. If the US did not step up with aid at that time when Europe needed it, then the Soviet Union could have swept in and exerted its influence over Western Europe as well, but thankfully that did not happen. Back to the present day, even though the US is engaged now in world affairs under Joe Biden, a future administration could follow Trump's isolationist policies, which will not bode well for the world and American interests as the US has a lot of interests and responsibilities the world over and a more unstable and unpredictable world order could be the result of an isolationist US.

Thankfully the Biden administration has committed itself to being engaged in the world. Everyone knew this right away when he started out his presidency by saying, "America is back." And just in time, too, as the Russian invasion of Ukraine happened during his administration. Ukraine was invaded by its bigger, well-armed neighbor, Russia. They have much more weapons and ammunition than Ukraine. According to news reports, some have estimated that Russian weaponry may outnumber Ukraine weaponry 10 to 1.[72] And Volodymyr Zelensky keeps pleading for arms from the international community. This is not the time for American isolationism because if the US decided to be isolationist at a time like this, then Russia would smell blood and move in for the kill. They may make their move to further their interests beyond Ukraine and try to dominate that entire region of the world to the detriment of American respect and power. It is good that Biden has decided to send billions upon billions of dollars' worth of weaponry. If not, it will spell doom for Ukraine.

[72] Seligman, L., Miller, C., Forgey, Q., (2022, June 16). Outgunned. Outmanned. Outnumbered. Outplanned?. POLITICO. https://www.politico.com/newsletters/national-security-daily/2022/06/16/outgunned-outmanned-outnumbered-outplanned-00040024

Chapter 10: Trump and the Emoluments Clause

The forefathers knew how officeholders could use their office to benefit themselves over the public interest. They were very well aware that people misuse and abuse their power in politics. Once one is elected president or elected in any position of power, that person becomes a public servant, and it is his duty to serve the national interest and not his own. The president or any elected official or public servant cannot use the office to enrich or benefit himself or herself as that would be a breach of the public trust. One way they decided to curb this problem was through the Emoluments Clause.

The Emoluments Clause, through its text, basically prohibits the president from benefitting from his office both with foreign actors and domestically as well. Many questions are raised about whether Trump or the people around him violated the Emoluments Clause and actually gained personal benefits using the office of the presidency. One of the ways Trump may have violated the Emoluments Clause is through his use of Trump properties during his time in office. His security, among others, would have to use the properties, which meant the government was paying Trump.

Trump also played an endless amount of golf; he played way more than his predecessor despite complaining about

203

how Obama was always on the golf course instead of doing his job. Not only did he play golf a lot more than Obama, which meant more taxpayer-funded vacation time for him, but he was also playing on his own golf courses, which meant that once again, he was benefitting from the office and using the presidency for personal gain. No other president has been caught in this conundrum because they did not have the wealth in real estate that Trump has, and this is the very situation that the forefathers envisioned, which they tried to prevent with the Emoluments Clause. These are some of the controversies which showed that Trump was definitely benefitting from the office.

A big factor in making this happen was the fact that Trump still continued to own and profit from his organization.[73] This was a potential setup for widespread corruption. The US had not faced this situation before as no other president had the wealth and real estate assets that Trump has in order to be able to benefit this way. But it is this very situation for which the Emoluments Clause was crafted. Trump and his advisers should have played it smart and avoided controversy by playing perhaps on military or government golf courses to avoid any hints of impropriety.

---

[73] Alexander, D. (2021, July 19). Trump's Business Hauled In $2.4 Billion During Four Years He Served As President. Forbes. https://www.forbes.com/sites/danalexander/2021/07/19/trumps-business-hauled-in-24-billion-during-four-years-he-served-as-president/?sh=3120f19d10c0

And also, perhaps in the future, every single cent of tax expenditure should be accounted for and reported to the public. How every single cent of tax dollars is spent should be shown transparently to the public, especially at the level of the executive branch, the highest office. This will make it less controversial and political as everybody will see where the public coffers are being spent and judge whether the taxpayer money is being spent properly. There will be no more debate as to how much is being spent and whether it is 'fake news' or whatever other reason those who don't believe the news accounts can conjure up.

Trump also has interests in countries all over the world. While he was in office, his policies and attitudes towards these countries should be scrutinized to see if he directly or indirectly benefited. Some of these countries where Trump has foreign business interests are China and Russia, which is all the more worrisome as they are geopolitical adversaries of the US. There is also the issue of Ivanka Trump and her trademark requests which were fast-tracked in China.[74] The approval of her trademarks was faster after her father was elected president. Trump also had trademarks granted to

[74] Beer, T. (2020, September 22). Ivanka's Trademark Requests Were Fast-Tracked In China After Trump Was Elected. Forbes. https://www.forbes.com/sites/tommybeer/2020/09/22/ivankas-trademark-requests-were-fast-tracked-in-china-after-trump-was-elected/?sh=c06f3da1d60f

himself as well.[75] The question of speed raises issues if the Chinese wanted or were expecting something in return. Even if the Chinese gained nothing of value, it still raises impropriety issues in the country's highest office. There were also many individuals from foreign governments who stayed at Trump's properties.[76]

This, of course, could set up a situation where Trump, in exchange, could advocate favorable policies towards those countries, whether it is in the national interest or not, simply because these individuals patronized his properties. This could potentially be dangerous as one is blinded to the national interest since the office holder (Trump in this case) is thankful that these foreign guests paid to stay in his properties. So now he is blinded to this fact, and it will not matter if his policies will benefit the nations of said individuals to the detriment of American interests. No other president has brought this much controversy to the office in connection to the fact that his financial dealings could affect his behavior which is why this is another disruption of

---

[75] China provisionally grants Trump 38 trademarks - including for escort service. (2017, March 8). The Guardian. https://www.theguardian.com/us-news/2017/mar/08/china-approves-trump-trademarks-businesses

[76] Davis, W. (2020, October 23). 150 foreign government officials have paid visits to Trump properties. CREW. https://www.citizensforethics.org/reports-investigations/crew-investigations/150-foreign-government-officials-have-paid-visits-to-trump-properties/

presidential behavior on a rather major scale compared to those of his predecessors in the highest office.

Though there is corruption in American politics, corruption is typically associated with other nation-states that are less developed, where poverty is prevalent in society and politics. These are countries where one takes advantage of making money through various illicit sources by virtue of the office held, which otherwise would not be available to common citizens who have to live in poverty or misery due to lack of status or power in society, so these individuals in positions of power can use their leverage due to their status to make money. In other countries, for example, at each stage of the process that one has to go through in the government bureaucracy in order to get what he or she wants, it is typical to pay a bribe in order to get approved or make things go faster. This is how a lot of people in those governments make money. In the Philippines, for instance, the ten percenter has entered the common lexicon. These people are go-betweens that individuals have to go through in order to get what they want. It is common for politicians in other countries to be involved in corruption scandals. Corruption, though ever-present, is not something that we typically encounter in politics in America today as much as in other countries. In times past, however, during the nineteenth and early twentieth century, make no mistakes about it, there was a lot of corruption in American politics and elections, especially in the big cities with "machine politics" like Tammany Hall in New York. And more recently, there are the Daleys and the machine in Chicago. These political machines would take advantage of the immigrants who would enter the country by getting them to vote for them by providing them in return with employment, services, etc.[77] These needy families may get Thanksgiving turkey compliments of the local party machine during Thanksgiving. This was why the same party kept winning election after election due to their stranglehold on the voting public. They knew their constituency and made sure their constituency was dependent on them for their needs. This was largely done away with via the civil service system, which was instituted in order to do away with the rampant corruption in government.[78]

Though there is still corruption today in American politics, it is nowhere near the levels of times past, like the days of machine politics of a century or so ago. More recently, some politicians were notorious for their corruption, like former Governor Edwin Edwards of Louisiana. These were exceptions to the norm, though.

---

[77] Political machine. (2022, August 2). In Wikipedia. https://en.wikipedia.org/wiki/Political_machine
[78] Spoils system. (2022, July 28). In Wikipedia. https://en.wikipedia.org/wiki/Spoils_system

Trump, however, changed all that as he took it to another level. Trump's blatant corruption is another way he disrupted the narrative of how presidents behave, with his outright corruption, like having Stormy Daniels paid $130,000 to shut up, or how his inner circle has all been indicted and/or convicted because of doing things connected to him or for him, whether under his instructions or not. They were convicted for things connected to the Russia probe. Whether there was something to the Russia probe is up for debate, but there was a lot of lying and covering up involved which is where the corruption is. He has also outright practiced nepotism appointing members of his own family in his inner circle purely on loyalty since they are family. However, many more individuals could be qualified for the position. The corruption was blatant and obvious to everyone, with the exception of his supporters, who believed he could do no wrong.

The other prominent incident of nepotism was John F. Kennedy appointing his brother Robert as Attorney General. But if one were to compare Trump's nepotism with Robert Kennedy's case, it was just one family member, and he was at least qualified for the position of Attorney General as he was a lawyer with experience. In Trump's case, his daughter and son-in-law were not specifically qualified for the positions they were holding but for the fact that they were members of his family. Yes, they have their own financial interests, but it cannot be argued that they were appointed but for their relation to the president. It is as if his supporters gave him a pass because he is a celebrity and so are members of his family, and he is just being himself. The problem is that he is held to a different standard compared to others. If it is considered corrupt and nepotistic for others, it should be for him. His being held to a different standard is a major factor in disrupting the presidential narrative. He ran his campaign and his presidency like a TV show that needed to get high ratings. No other president has acted this way. It was all about how much attention he could get from his non-presidential, crass, and uncouth manner.

He also 'projected' his faults to his opponent Joe Biden and how he was supposedly corrupt by 'getting' his son Hunter Biden a job with the Ukrainian company Burisma. Whether or not there was any impropriety, it did not look good for Joe Biden and his son Hunter, and it did have the appearance of corruption. The problem is Trump is not clean of corruption with his nepotism, payments to Stormy Daniels, and associates obstructing the Russian investigation. Trump was so corrupt that many of his associates got indicted for actions relating to his interests. There were also photos of him and Ivanka promoting GOYA products after GOYA'S CEO complimented him. If this is not considered corruption, I do not know what is. No other president has advertised a product on his desk during his presidency with the office's clear manifestations in the photo.

This uses the prestige of the position and office as leverage to promote the product. The danger here is that Trump did all of this because of the CEO's compliment. This demonstrates that if it is that easy to manipulate Trump (by simply flattering him), what more with foreign leaders who are adversaries of the US who would like to influence him by making him behave to promote their interests instead of American interests? Trump has also pardoned his entourage, who have been convicted of crimes. This is an abuse of the pardon power. The pardon power has been used sparingly and only for those who deserved it and were truly repentant and have shown that they have changed. For Trump, it was obvious that he was getting his friends out of prison because they were loyal by not ratting him out or whatever other reason. Who knows? But by doing what he did, he is making people think that is what is going on, and it stinks to no end. No other president, first of all, has had so many around him get convicted. And his pardoning them just made it worse.

Not even Nixon used the pardon power in the way that Trump used it to show the depths that Trump would sink to serve his interests and his most ardent loyalists. Of course, just to put things in perspective, Bill Clinton pardoned his half-brother Roger Clinton for a conviction for cocaine possession and drug trafficking.

Even playing devil's advocate and assuming the intent was corrupt, it was still just one pardon. Of course, there was the infamous pardon of Richard Nixon by Gerald Ford. Even if one could argue that Nixon made a deal with Ford that he would resign so Ford could be president in exchange for being pardoned, Ford's reasoning is just as plausible. Watergate was taking up a lot of the nation's time, and it was just time to move on to other important things, and a pardon was the best way to do it. There was also the pardon of Andrew Johnson of all soldiers who fought in the Confederate Army.[79] Again here, it can be argued that soldiers are less culpable than the leaders of the Confederacy, and it is best to just pardon them so they can go back to live their regular lives, whereas it was the leaders of the Confederacy who had the decision making power to secede, go to war and continue fighting the war. So this can be argued, which makes the pardon reasonable and explainable.

There are others, too, like George Washington pardoning two men who participated in the Whiskey Rebellion and

[79] Pardons for ex-Confederates. (2022, July 8). In Wikipedia. https://en.wikipedia.org/wiki/Pardons_for_ex-Confederates

Andrew Jackson's pardoning of George Wilson, who committed a violent crime.[80] Still, these are just isolated incidents as these presidents just have one controversial pardon and not many like Trump. Trump is still worse compared to these examples, as he did it multiple times to people in his inner circle who were convicted. And it can be assumed if more of his loyalists were convicted, he would pardon all of them as well, no matter how many they were. It was as if they were all a one-crime family with Trump as a mafia boss. There is just no plausible argument that could be made on why Trump should pardon these individuals. There is no public good that is served as these crimes were committed for the president's benefit and probably at his command. But even if the president did not order them to do what they did, which got them convicted, it still reeks as they were committed for Trump's benefit. Trump has thus demeaned the presidency by his less than honest reputation and behavior while in office, thus disrupting the narrative that presidents were not corrupt individuals or, if they were, their corruption did not stoop down to the depths where Trump dragged it.

---

[80] Whiskey Rebellion. (n.d). George Washington's Mount Vernon. https://www.mountvernon.org/library/digitalhistory/digital-encyclopedia/article/whiskey-rebellion/. United States v. Wilson. (2021, November 26). In Wikipedia. https://en.wikipedia.org/wiki/United_States_v._Wilson

Trump has also disrupted the narrative in that he seems to have put himself on top of national interests. This can be seen with him refusing to criticize or just say anything bad about Putin when it is not in America's best interest to get 'chummy' with Putin, a geo-strategic adversary of the US. This simply emboldens Putin and makes him think he can do whatever he wants without worrying that the US, under Trump, will stand up to him. An example of this is in Ukraine, specifically with the civil war going on there with Russian-backed separatists. Russia has interests in Ukraine as it is their neighbor and a former Soviet Republic. Concomitant with this is their need to control Crimea in order to control the coast along the Azov sea and cut off Ukraine's access to the sea.

This was so important to the Russians that they fought the Crimean War over this during the nineteenth century. They lost to the combined forces of the English and French. For the US not to do anything in Ukraine and giving Ukraine a hard time by saying that they need to investigate the activities of Hunter Biden in exchange for weapons is playing right into Russian hands. Because the weaker the American alliance is with the Ukrainian government, the better it is for Russian separatists fighting them. It is also in Putin's interest to have the Western Alliance weakened, which Trump is doing with his more isolationist policies and wanting other NATO members to increase their share of NATO spending. The US needs to be there for its allies no matter what.

Giving conditions and sending out signals that the US may not be there for its allies is not good for these allies because they will think that the US cannot be depended on in future conflicts. The fall of Kabul to the Taliban is a perfect example of making American allies wonder if the US will be there for them through thick or thin. This is playing into Putin's hands because it is in his best interests that the western alliance is weakened as he still views the West as well as their interests and foreign policies through the Cold War paradigm as anti-Russian. The US needs to support its new allies in the East since the fall of the Berlin Wall and communism has opened up an opportunity for the US to extend its influence in the region.

The US could now extend its interests to the countries of Eastern Europe and befriend them to take advantage of trade with them and extend the reach of American power to these previously closed-off lands due to them being behind the Iron Curtain. There are already US forces in Poland and even a few in Romania. To ignore Ukraine and be reluctant to give them aid if that was Trump's intent would be giving up a golden opportunity and opening up a vacuum where the Russians can easily take advantage. Putin needs to be aggressive in countries like Ukraine. During the Cold War, the Soviet Union had Eastern Europe as a buffer to protect it from the West. Now with the fall of communism, that buffer is gone, and Putin feels he has to fight off the West at the Russian borders as American power has now reached the formerly closed-off Eastern Europe. It is also in America's best interest to have safe and secure elections and make sure that no agents of other countries are spreading 'fake news' regarding their own elections on the internet and social media sites.

The fact that American intelligence agencies say that there is truth to this is worth investigating. And Trump's efforts to curtail these findings and play them down are not in America's interests because it emboldens those who are behind the election interference. It is not in America's best interest to have its own president believe Vladimir Putin over America's own intelligence services. It emboldens Putin that if he can get away with this, he can do more. The same goes with despots like Kim Jong-un. When Trump shows that he admires him, it not only emboldens Kim Jong-un it also gives him a sense of legitimacy. US presidents have always shown themselves to be strong towards leaders who are adversaries or potential adversaries of the US.

When a US president shows he likes them, then he shows his hand, and the other side has the advantage and can play and/or control the US president in the way they like, almost like a puppet. Putin has done this by telling Trump he had nothing to do with election interference, and Trump believed him and said so in a press conference. Trump also withdrew US troops from Syria and left the Kurds defenseless by saying that the Kurds did not help in the Second World War. Forget the fact that the Kurds did not have the manpower, resources, and capability to fight a war on the level of the great powers; this is just not how the US operates. Trump sees everything as transactional or contractual.

Basically, a party must get something in return for something that is given. Realpolitik does not always work this way, and the US government does not work this way. The US has always supported governments overseas, whether they be dictators or not, by giving them weapons, aid, and help when they need it when a natural disaster occurs. All this goodwill comes with tangible and intangible benefits for the US in the long run. Even though these countries do not pay back what the US has given in aid, the US gets benefits by having policies and maybe laws passed in these countries that help the US, or these nation-states will pursue interests consistent with American interests.

These countries may allow US troops, for instance, to operate in their territory or allow bases and facilities to be used by US forces which could help the US in a future conflict. This may also benefit the US businesses by allowing them to operate in these countries without many obstacles as they normally would have, had there not been any assistance. If one travels to other countries around the world, one can easily see American power manifested in its soft power/non-violent power. The US military displays US strength all over the world. But this is hard power as it has the appearance of violence attached to it. US soft power is its non-violent exports worldwide in the form of businesses, culture, etc. This can be anything from electronics, food, music, movies, clothes, etc. Even language can be included here. People all over the world try to imitate American expressions (bro, dude, what the hell, etc.)

American brand products are ever-present in countries all over the world. And this promotes American goodwill in other countries because when people all around the world eat McDonald's or use Apple products or have things delivered via UPS etc., they know these are all American companies. Thus these businesses are all ambassadors of American goodwill. Make no mistake; the American military does a lot of good as well when it gives aid to disaster-stricken areas around the globe. It gives food and relief to populations in need that are on the brink of collapse in the aftermath of a disaster. But they still wear the symbols of violence in their uniforms and equipment and are thus not a perfect substitute for American soft power in the form of businesses and brands that people all over the world have come to admire.

This is why the US was a staunch opponent of communism. It was not because their governments were oppressive and anti-democratic. It was primarily because those markets would be closed to American trade and commerce. If those governments eventually became democracies, then that would be a bonus, but it was not the priority. Let there be no doubt that the primary purpose for being a staunch bulwark against communism was that the US wanted those markets open besides the domino theory connected to communism. This is why the US got involved in Central America. Companies like the United Fruit Company have a lot of clout with the government and are a big part of the American economy for better or worse. This is why when UFC called 911, the US government made sure that they would do everything in their power to overthrow the government that was redistributing land to the detriment of UFC.

In one of the more recent debates for presidential elections, one of the democratic candidates, Mike Gravel, said something that stood out. He said that Vietnam would still have turned out the way it is today with American businesses operating in the country even if the Vietnam War had not been fought. He was asked about a comment he made about American soldiers in Vietnam dying in vain. And Gravel replied that American soldiers died in vain because if one were to go to Vietnam, that person could easily buy a Baskin-Robbins ice cream cone. And Gravel added that the US has the most favored nation trade with that country.[81] This goes to the point of what I was arguing that the US' primary objective in fighting communism was to open markets for trade and commerce. There is nothing wrong with this, as American economic power depends largely upon American corporations being able to do business and maneuver abroad. American government officials are usually not that blunt about it and couch their reasons within the framework of support for liberal-democratic governments. If trade and commerce did not motivate the American administrations but rather exported democracy abroad, then why the backing of anti-democratic, right-wing governments?

This shows that spreading democracy is not America's number one objective when spreading its influence abroad but rather economics. Thus the primary mover of American foreign policy boils down to money which means trade and American access to foreign markets. Mike Gravel was just honest about it. I, for instance, did not agree with the Iraq

---

[81] jpeters. (2007, July 27). Dying in Vain in Vietnam and Iraq. Mike Gravel. https://mikegravel.com/dying-in-vain-in-vietnam-and-iraq/

War in 2003 as I thought the reasons for it were an excuse for something else, namely the oil. Though I did not agree with the politics of George W. Bush, I still believed he was doing what was in the national interest. The US is a major consumer of fossil fuels, and if we ignore the Middle East and allow it to be under the orbit of other world powers, then the US president would not be doing his job. This is why George W. Bush was working in the national interests even though many on the left, as well as I, did not agree with the decision to go to war with Iraq. Even Lyndon Johnson was doing what was in the national interest by being a bulwark against communism during the Vietnam War. The Cold War demanded that a US president stand up to Communist threats around the world. If not, then the US would come off as weak, and the USSR and Communist movements around the world would smell blood and move in for the kill.

As the old saying goes, hindsight is twenty-twenty. We may think today that the Vietnam War could and should have been avoided as a waste of time or whatever reason certain factions of society today can think of, but this was not the way the West saw the world back then. If one Communist uprising or movement were not prevented, then this would embolden them to rise up all over the world against non-Communist governments. So Lyndon Johnson was definitely doing what was in the best interests of the US during the Vietnam War regardless of whether it was right to fight the war or not. The same goes for the Korean War as well. It was definitely in the best interests of the US to prevent North Korea from controlling the entire Korean Peninsula. Trump, on the other hand, does not meet the very low standard of doing what is in the national interest but instead does what is in his own interest. There is no reason to think being friends with Putin serves American interests. Putin will think that the US is weak, and it will embolden him in places like Ukraine and Syria, which gives him a vital foothold in the Middle East, an important region where he can thus get his hands eventually on oil. And there is no reason to take away assistance from the Kurds, who is a steadfast ally of the US in the fight against ISIS or Daesh as the British and French call them, in order to deny them their claim that they are representative of true Islamic thought, as it is a more derogatory term that does not make them a real government as well as representatives of authentic Islam.

This is all the more so dangerous as Turkey and Syria want to see the Kurds weakened. There is a reason why the US does not abandon allies, no matter how tyrannical, and the Kurds are definitely not in that category. The US has many leaders all over the world on its "payroll," so to speak, and they make it easier for the US to conduct its interests within their borders. Once the US abandons one ally, all these leaders the world over will also think that the US can abandon them in the blink of an eye if the US has no more need for them, like how a villain gets rid of his friend or his henchmen in an action movie. Just imagine if the US did not aid the South Vietnamese government during the Vietnam War.

Communism would have just rolled over the south like a bulldozer in a speedier way early on in the conflict. Yes, the Communists did eventually win, but it took them until 1975 to finally march into Saigon. With no US intervention, there is a strong likelihood the south would have been overrun during the 1960s. The same could be said about the Korean War. If the US did not intervene, then we would be looking at a Communist Korean Peninsula today, which already did happen in the initial stages of the war before the American landings at Inchon.

But today, because of American intervention, at least there is a South Korea that exists that is progressive and democratic who is allied strongly to the US and knows that the US can be relied upon through thick and thin. No other president constantly thought of himself first and what was best for him and his family on top of the nation, and so this is another way he is a disruptor of the narrative of how presidents act and behave.

Chapter 11: American Soft Power Is Important

The greatness of America is created by its economic power manifested by American businesses and American ingenuity. All the soft power that America can muster that one sees worldwide with American companies and American brand products are America's best ambassadors. But all this is dependent on American hard power in the form of its military, which is why the US must remain engaged in the world instead of being isolationist. Trump's isolationist stance puts American soft power in jeopardy and not just American hard power.

The liberation of Europe after World War II created a stable, peaceful continent that fostered American goodwill through the Marshall Plan. And eventually, once prosperity returned, the continent was fertile ground for American businesses to prosper since these were developed countries with a high standard of living and high amounts of disposable income. This was why it was in America's best interests to liberate the continent during the Second World War. It benefits the US today as the EU is one of America's important trading partners.

Another sign, albeit a negative one, of American soft power throughout the world is the growing trends of obesity the world over. In many countries, obesity is gradually increasing. A major factor is the exportation of the American lifestyle the world over.

This includes American fast food, processed foods, sugary drinks, and salted snacks. These products of the American lifestyle can be found worldwide and contribute to health problems among all the world's citizens. Unhealthy and fatty foods, which are also temptingly delicious, are so cheap that ever-larger numbers of consumers can afford them. Being overweight is becoming more and more of a health epidemic in more and more parts of the world. Brands like Coke and McDonald's are marketing to school children in schools in developing countries through activities and the like where it is clear that they are sponsoring these events. Even these global brands like McDonald's have different menu items in different countries with specific items sold in particular countries that are popular in those countries. Even KFC, for instance, makes their chicken spicy in India to cater to the Indian palette. And according to a documentary, all the fast-food giants, in general, put higher amounts of salt in their food in India compared to others like France, for example, where there are stricter health regulations.[82] Thus there is an incentive for these fast-food corporations to invest and take advantage of the lack of health regulations in

---

[82] ENDEVR. (2021, March 14). Global Junk Food: How the Fast FoodIndustry is Making Poor Countries Fat | ENDEVR Documentary [Video]. Youtube. https://www.youtube.com/watch?v=uEJwbGBrXfk

developing countries where they can get the population addicted through the higher amounts of salt and fat that they can put in the food. The exportation of unhealthy American industrialized food is very evident in Mexico, America's southern neighbor. Obesity has been a recent health issue in the country starting around forty years ago. This is partly due to trade with the US and the introduction of processed food into the Mexican food market.[83]

Previously much of Mexican food consumption was fresh, and the health problems that Mexico had were undernutrition and malnutrition, whereas obesity was a problem relegated to the rich.[84] Since the 1980's Mexican nutrition consumption has transformed from fresh foods to factory-made processed food due to the increase in the market share of food products of multinational food corporations. This is the double-edged sword of the exportation of the American diet. Though there are still segments of the population in developing countries that suffer from malnutrition due to poverty, there are also rising rates of obesity never seen before. These multinational brands are also creating video game apps children play who

[83] Osea, G., Rieger, M., Rotunno, L., (2018, February 2). Weight gains from trade in foods: Evidence from Mexico. VOXEU. https://voxeu.org/article/weight-gains-trade-foods-evidence-mexico

[84] Barquera, S., Rivera, J. (2020, August 18). Obesity in Mexico: rapid epidemiological transition and food industry interference in health policies. Elsevier Public Health Emergency Collection. https://www.ncbi.nlm.nih.gov/pmc/articles/PMC7434327/

do not realize these brands are subconsciously marketing to them. Subconsciously, if children or anyone else see these symbols of the brands repeatedly, they will crave those foods and want to buy them.[85] Though not a positive outcome of American soft power, it still shows the economic might of American soft power, albeit to the detriment of the health of foreign citizens. Examples of this unhealthy lifestyle can be seen with the phenomenon of the video game streamer, where video gamers play games for hours on end while streaming them live for an audience to watch online. These streamers make money through donations or ads played on their channel. The streamers are facilitated by platforms such as Twitch and Facebook. Both are American platforms that make money off their streamers and facilitate the streamers in earning an income since the streamers are using their services as a conduit between them and their viewers.

Streamers from all over the world can avail of the services of these two sites, which facilitates the streamers' sedentary lifestyles or professions since they are sitting in front of a computer screen playing games for hours upon hours. Again all this is American soft power at work. However, it does have negative side effects like an unhealthy diet or a sedentary lifestyle from the exportation of

[85] ENDEVR. (2021, March 14). Global Junk Food: How the Fast FoodIndustry is Making Poor Countries Fat | ENDEVR Documentary [Video]. Youtube. https://www.youtube.com/watch?v=uEJwbGBrXfk

American food products to sitting down in front of a computer and playing games for hours upon hours while making a living from it.

This entire ecosystem where a sort of symbiotic relationship exists of American soft power working hand in hand with American hard power will be ruptured if America goes down the path of Trump's isolationist policies. If Americans travel all over the world, they will come to appreciate the 'tentacles' of American economic power all over, with American businesses ever-present, whether it be clothes, food, music, movies, internet platforms, etc. Americans need to realize that when a foreigner says they like an American singer, movie, electronic device, or clothes, that is beneficial to America economically. And it also promotes goodwill as that is one less person who will want to join in a war or commit a terrorist act against America. It is not just American hard power where the US can display its power all over the world. The US also gives aid to governments all over the world. This aid helps those countries and garners American goodwill in those countries. The aid also has "strings attached" to them, which means there are also tangible benefits besides just goodwill that the US receives from these countries to which aid is given. Obviously, this influence comes at a benefit for American businesses, which are ever-present the world over. Every item that the US sends to other nations that has US AID written on it helps promote American goodwill and influence in other parts of the world. If the American government was simply doing it out of the goodness of its heart, then why the need to label the items?

The reason for the labels is to further American interests all over the world. Many in other countries do not like the American aid because of all the strings attached to the aid. But this is exactly how the US furthers its interests. This entire symbiotic relationship of American government influence, whether in the form of aid or its military presence, and the influence of American businesses all over the world work together and will certainly get disrupted with an isolationist America. That is a disruption of the narrative of American power which is what will happen if Trump's policies are implemented to the fullest extent possible.

Chapter 12: Trump's Tactless Manner of Speaking

Trump is also a disruptor in that he does not care about the social upheavals that his language causes. Presidents have always been careful about what language they use. Presidents have traditionally risen above the hate and petty politics in the government around them. They have always shown themselves to be unifiers of all Americans by inspiring them with their words and speeches.

Lincoln, for instance, said, "A house divided against itself cannot stand." And John F. Kennedy said, "Ask not what your country can do for you. Ask what you can do for your country." Trump is not one of those presidents. He always says things that his base wants to hear. He probably thinks that he will only pursue the policies of those who vote for him, which means they are also the audience he targets in his speeches. This was evident in his inaugural speech when he reached out to nobody but his base of supporters after a bitter election.[86] Trump directed his speech to those who have lost their jobs and all the forgotten Americans whose jobs went overseas due to cheap labor abroad. He did not reach out and allay the fears of the left who were

---

[86] Full text: 2017 Donald Trump inauguration speech transcript. (2017, January 20). POLITICO. https://www.politico.com/story/2017/01/full-text-donald-trump-inauguration-speech-transcript-233907

frightened by his campaign rhetoric and were angered by his victory. The problem is he is supposed to be the president of all Americans and should speak in tones that uplift Americans together as a people. For one, he is oblivious that his constant calling COVID the China Virus is the cause of much anti-Asian hate in the country. Previous presidents would never have called COVID the China Virus as it made them sound crude and bigoted, but it also made them sound immature and uneducated. Something like naming a virus the China Virus would also fall under the category of being politically incorrect.

Trump also does not care about the consequences of his lies. He does not care that when he tells the 'Big Lie' about winning the election, it leads to consequences like the 'Capitol Insurrection' because his supporters hang on to every word he says. No other president caused anything like this. Imagine a president causing an insurrection toward another branch of government. No American could have imagined it. Presidents were always careful to always be acting in the country's interests and not cause chaos domestically.

They always took their oath seriously to "preserve, protect, and defend the Constitution of the United States." This is all the more appalling as Americans have long ago accepted the principles of fair play in government.

Americans have always accepted the outcome of an election. And if a party loses an election, there is always another presidential election in four years. Because no matter who wins, Americans still abide by the principles of reaching out across party lines to get things done. But I guess this is a sign of the times of how toxic American politics has become in recent times, especially during the Trump presidency.

Since Trump wholeheartedly supported one side over another, it seems like Trump supporters think they will now be punished if and when Trump leaves office as the new administration will not pass legislation following their wishes. Regardless of these realities in the current American political environment, Trump's bold declarations also disrupt the smooth transition of government which is the unwritten rule that presidents abide by. Trump is undermining the credibility and the ability of Joe Biden to govern as long as he continues his antics because people who did not see the election as legitimate will not see Biden as a legitimate president. This is not good for the country as the subsequent government is weakened, which could embolden foreign governments against the US and will work against Biden's policies and agenda domestically.

Chapter 13: Trump's Antics and Behavior

Trump's overall antics and demeanor are also a disruptor to the office of the presidency. His non-presidential behavior cheapens the office and makes him a laughing stock domestically but just as important internationally. People worldwide view the US in high regard as an economic and military superpower. And the president is seen as the representative of the American people.

When Trump acts the way he does, he diminishes the office and the country and its people. The US president is the head of state which means he is the symbol of the nation. In this way, he is like a monarch in a country which has a constitutional monarchy. Queen Elizabeth was the symbolic embodiment of the British people, and she was well loved by her people as evidenced by all the people who have nothing but nice things to say about her as well as all the people lining up to see the Queen's coffin while lying in state in Westminster Hall. Compare this to Donald Trump who brought out emotions of loathing and detestation among huge segments of the American population. This is not how a symbol of the nation should be viewed. And it is embarrassing to see how one symbol of that nation (Donald Trump) is viewed by his people compared to another symbol of the nation (Queen Elizabeth II) and how she was viewed by her people.

Whatever goodwill the US has earned previously will be tarnished as they now see that someone like Trump can get elected as the leader of the US by the people. Before Trump's election, people all over the world probably never would have imagined someone like him leading the free world. Citizens of other countries realize that other nations can have unstable, dictatorial leaders who are unhinged but not the US. The US has always had good presidents who have acted and behaved according to the high standards of the office. But Trump has now erased all people's expectations of an American president. The US will no longer be held in high regard like it did before due to Trump.

He insulted John McCain's getting captured and said that he liked those who did not get caught. He made fun of someone's disability. When someone died, he insinuated that the person was in hell. He also claimed a judge would not be fair in his ruling due to his Hispanic background. And he also had negative nicknames for his opponents. Once again, this shows that the lofty expectations of people both home and abroad can be erased with the election of one man. Who would have thought that someone like Trump would be US president? There are dictators all over the world who have acted outrageously and erratically, but we do not have high expectations for the leaders of those countries.

In other words, those leaders are not held to a high standard, so the bar is rather low as to how people all over the world expect them to behave. Mommar Gaddafi, for instance, was rather buffoonish in his behavior in front of the camera, but there were no high expectations for the head of state of Libya. This is not the case for the American president. Therefore there are very high standards for the American president, and when one behaves as Trump has, then those high standards are lowered. Thus the narrative of presidential behavior was destroyed by Trump's election. He made the presidency like a TV show which kept people watching his every action due to its outrageousness. US presidents have always been rather boring with their proper behavior when in front of the public. His disruption of this narrative has now lowered the expectations that one has of the presidency.

Chapter 14: Trump and Social Media

Trump also regularly used Twitter to say what was on his mind or even future administration policy decisions or plans. Just as a general concept, social media has changed the way people communicate with others, and it has given people a way to craft their image for the world to see.

Kim Kardashian is an example of this. Her fame and wealth are a product of reaching her audience through social media. Any one of us can, through social media, craft the image that we want to portray for our social media friends or the world to see. This can be our hobbies or lifestyle, whatever image our hearts desire for all the world to see. Trump has done exactly this in his run for the presidency. He can be considered the first social media president.

Previous administrations used the news media to make speeches or hold press conferences. But now, due to the easy accessibility of the public through Twitter, Trump used it to announce upcoming events and policy decisions. He said whatever was on his mind, however spontaneous and irrelevant it was. He disregarded diplomatic norms and was blunt, and lacked political correctness. Due to the instantaneousness of Twitter, Trump, just like many others, said what was on his mind without thinking of how to say it intelligently and eloquently. That is something individuals typically do when writing a formal letter, holding a press conference, or making a speech in front of a TV audience, but not Trump. These are the various ways presidents normally communicate to the American people.

Thus with Twitter, his every thought was exposed for all to read. This made him the butt of many jokes among his detractors. The comments were filled with Twitter followers mocking him with memes and political cartoons. Through Twitter, Trump has tarnished the aura of the presidency by bringing it down to a mediocre level similar to that of a jester who makes a fool of himself for people's amusement. No other previous president debased himself or the presidency in such a manner. Presidents have always intelligently and carefully crafted speeches, statements, and responses in order to minimize controversies and not give fodder to political opponents.

However, Trump seems to crave controversy and diffuse fodder in spades to opponents, things that previous presidents were extremely careful about. Obama, for instance, was very careful during his campaign and his presidency not to have any missteps. His eloquent speeches were a testimony that he was careful with every word that he relayed to the American people. The only other thing that came close to Trump's erratic statements were the Nixon tapes, where one could listen to the raw and uncensored Nixon. But the difference was that Nixon kept recordings of his conversation to have a record of them. He did not imagine that the tapes would be available for everybody to hear in his wildest dreams. He fought tooth and nail when the Supreme Court ordered him to release the tapes.

Trump would also mimic people with disabilities like a comic or a buffoon. Imagine any other president besides Trump doing that. It was unimaginable before Trump. But he is a disruptor in this way. His supporters allowed him to be like this since he was evaluated with a different standard than other presidents or presidential candidates. It was so bad that he was eventually banned from Twitter after the Capitol Insurrection for fear of what other things he may be capable of leading his followers to do. This was how dangerous and outrageous he was on Twitter. The image that he created for himself was digested in a certain way by his supporters and in a different way by his detractors, but it does not change the fact that this was a new way of reaching out to the voting public for good or bad.

Chapter 15: The Electoral College and the Party Conventions

One cannot ignore the history and narrative of the Electoral College and also that of the respective party conventions. The Electoral College was meant to be above the passions of the masses.

It started as the body that voted its conscience irrespective of how its constituents voted. The way the Electoral College operates now is a long way from what the forefathers intended. Now it is simply a rubber stamp of the states' popular votes. And Trump is a perfect example of why the forefathers created such an august body as the Electoral College. The forefathers did not want a demagogue elected who simply played to the people's basest instincts instead of the issues. The evolution of the Electoral College created demagogues like Trump, which shows the sagacity of the forefathers with the original intent of the Electoral College. Thus the narrative of making the Electoral College more responsive to the people had the consequence of allowing a demagogue like Trump to be elected president.

The narrative of the party conventions is also similar to that of the Electoral College. It started as something where the party leaders chose the best nominee regardless of how the party constituents voted. This clash of the party faithful and party leaders came to a head at the Chicago Democratic

Convention of 1968. There were protests outside the convention to protest the activities of the party elite within the Convention. Hubert Humphrey won the nomination but was far from who Democratic Party members wanted. At the start of the 68' campaign, Eugene McCarthy gained an early advantage in the field of Democratic candidates. As the campaign progressed, Robert Kennedy jumped ahead of McCarthy in the poles.

But when RFK was assassinated, the candidate most likely to win the nomination was gone. And during the convention in Chicago, instead of McCarthy winning the nomination outright due to his early lead, the sitting Vice President Humphrey won the nomination. There was chaos during the convention. Humphrey was handicapped in the race for the presidency against the Republican candidate Nixon. The 1968 Democratic National Convention was a major factor in why the party conventions evolved into what it is today, which is a rubber stamp of the popular vote of registered party members.

Though the narrative is that of more power to the party voters with the system in place now compared to previous times, the downside is a rabble-rouser was nominated by one of the parties who eventually was elected president. Avoiding an incendiary candidate was the original purpose of the party conventions. The party bosses voted for who they thought was the best candidate regardless of who party members voted for. They believed that cooler heads would prevail when the party bosses deliberated in the smoke-filled rooms where they would choose a nominee. The evolution of the narrative of the Electoral College from a deliberative and contemplative body to simply following popular whims ended up with the election of an inflamer, an instigator, and a fomenter.

Many learned and wise men in all ages of humanity believed that the masses were not always the best deciders of who should be their leaders because they were excitable and exploitable. The masses could be swayed by someone who dug into their fears and passions instead of the issues and will thus make them vote against the community's best interests. This is why many learned men like the forefathers wanted a buffer or filter in between the candidate and the masses who would not be swayed by cheap rhetoric but would vote for the best candidate for the nation based on qualifications and past performance instead of what they told the people in their speeches and in their rhetoric to garner support.

The breakdown over time, especially after what happened in 1968, of this filter or buffer between the people and the bosses who voted for the candidate, resulted in the election of someone like Donald Trump. For example, during the early years of the republic, only propertied white men could vote. The theory behind this was that they had sufficient interests in society to vote responsibly for the right people who would maintain law and order instead of someone who advocated radical policies to overthrow the status quo. This was a good thing for society in order to have a sense of continuity and predictability without any radical changes depending on who was in power based on who the masses supported.

The belief behind this was that propertied white men were responsible and rational enough not to be swayed by one radical inciter who wanted to topple the existing status quo, which the masses at large would be more likely to be swayed by. Thus the result of allowing every citizen in society, regardless of income, education, etc., to vote would be opening up the masses to vote for a demagogue that appeals to people's fears and emotions due to the fact that many people are voting who do not follow the issues sufficiently enough but are swayed by emotion which are the perfect target audience by someone like a Trump. People are susceptible to simple and direct phrases and soundbites as they are easy to follow and understand. The masses will readily believe in simple solutions to complex problems, which is why over and over, demagogues can hold audiences captive with their policies. This downside is to open up the franchise to every citizen without any qualification except age.

The narrative is always that we have come a long way from the country's early years. We have stepped into a country where everybody can now vote regardless of race, religion, sex, etc. In the beginning, only a small minority could vote, which were propertied white men. The bad side of this is that the masses are malleable and can easily be made to follow the tune of an inflamer dressed as a pied piper. James Madison gave an apt quote pertinent to democracies everywhere: "Knowledge will forever govern ignorance, and a people who mean to be their own governors must arm themselves with the power which knowledge gives." I think we can all agree that democracy will only be as successful in proportion to how knowledgeable its citizens are about the issues. This is why there are only a few successful democracies in the world.

Democracy is not easy. There are rules that everyone in society must abide by for a democracy to work to its best potential. And so we see one of the causes of the problem on why someone like Trump got elected in the world's most powerful democracy. The American educational system has some deficiencies and is running behind compared to other industrialized democracies.

Americans are testing poorly internationally in math and science. And suppose they are testing poorly on these subjects. In that case, it can be inferred that they are also not being taught sufficiently in the other subjects as well, like civics and government, which educate students on how government runs and where the political parties stand. And if they are not educated on government, then they cannot make educated decisions on how to vote because they did not learn the basics of the party system and their political platforms.

A problem is the enormous disparities in the country's public educational system. Funding for public education comes from property taxes, so the taxes in affluent neighborhoods can pay for better schools, teachers, and school equipment, translating to highly educated students.[87] And there are many impoverished urban areas in America where public education is definitely a joke or inadequate at best. How many Americans know who their representatives or senators are? Even worse, how many Americans know what the three branches of government are? The political parties, however imperfectly, do the work of organizing the candidates into opposing camps based on where they stand on major issues. But sometimes, you get a candidate like

[87] How State & Local Dollars Fund Public Schools. (n.d). Allovue. https://blog.allovue.com/alloversity/how-state-local-dollars-fund-public-schools

Trump whose force and personality can eat up the party itself and can cause the party system to go haywire and explode on its face. So if people were not adequately educated in civics class, then you get a candidate like Trump, who people always see on TV. Such an individual will be a clear choice of who to vote for. Another issue is when Americans are out of school and have joined the workforce, Americans just do not have the time to keep up with politics as work takes up their time. And when they are relaxing, they would rather watch sports or a good show on TV. Who wants to watch CSPAN?

And because of all of this, you get a less than adequately informed electorate who does not know the issues and will be swayed by someone who peddles hate and fear instead of another candidate who actually talks about issues. Another reason for voter apathy is the fact that the US has been a prosperous nation for quite some time now, and democratic government and its transition of power have been the norm ever since the founding of the republic. There have been no times in American history when the republic was somehow overthrown and replaced by a dictatorship, nor has the US been conquered by an outside power.

Thus Americans have a complacency that even if they do not vote, whoever the president is will not change their lives one bit. So why go to the polls? They will still have their freedoms and will still continue with their everyday lives. There just is no sense of urgency to get out and vote. In other less affluent countries than America, eligible voters really vote, and there are high turnout rates in elections. These countries may have just recently experienced democracy which means their people appreciate the values that democracy brings. They still feel that urgency that they need to vote for the right government or the right person in order for their country to be on the right course, which means they really care and are highly informed about the issues and the candidates and talk about politics regularly. Basically, the citizens in these countries are still excited about democracy, and enthusiasm for its values is still very high.

However, in the US, due to electoral complacency and the stability of the government for almost two and a half centuries, it is easier and more entertaining to watch someone being bombastic and outrageous instead of someone who actually talks about and cares about the issues. In a way, Trump brought back that voter interest in the election because he was controversial. You either loved him or loathed him, which really drove people to the polls in 2020. But otherwise, if he were not on the ballot, then it would be a typical election with high levels of voter apathy.

Another major factor that lends itself to deficiencies in the American democracy is the low levels of voting compared to other democracies. If people do not vote, they cannot have their voices heard, and worse, the candidates will know not to target their campaign to those voters. This is why candidates have a tendency not to talk about issues important to young Americans due to their low levels of voter turnout. Trump targeted those who were angry and felt their voices were not being heard to get them to the polls to vote their anger and fears even though they may not have known the issues in depth.

Perhaps the US can take a page out of other democracies that penalize people for not voting, ranging from a fine to imprisonment to infringement of civil rights. Then if everybody had to vote, they would force themselves to know the issues, and candidates would then need to campaign for them and the issues important to them. If not, then a demagogue will get more coverage in the media through his antics which in turn helps the candidacy of this person, which does not serve the best interests of anybody. The forefathers and their generation were aware of this, and we forget the lessons they warned us about.

Chapter 16: Soundbites and Simple Solutions to Complex Problems

Like a typical rabble-rouser, Trump has tried to give simple solutions to complex problems. He kept advocating for building a wall that Mexico would pay for to keep out illegal immigrants. No president before had ever advocated building a wall on the Mexican border as a major campaign issue in his run for president.

First of all, there is much irony in the US building a wall to keep people out. The US has always been an open and welcoming society, as embodied by the Statue of Liberty with its message about welcoming the poor, huddled masses, homeless, etc. And who can forget Reagan standing in front of the Berlin Wall, imploring Gorbachev to tear it down? Building a border wall to keep people out even though targeted at illegal immigration is completely contrary to America's image to the world as an open and welcoming society.

What is more ironic is that Gorbachev himself admitted that walls are ineffective when asked while speaking at the University of Texas-Pan American. He even said that the US does not have infinite money to spend, so why should it be spent on something as silly as an ineffective border wall?[88] What is just as ironic or even more so is Berlin Mayor Michael Müller saying that his city, which was the symbol of Europe's separation and freedom of Europe, cannot just sit on the sidelines.[89] At the same time, the country, which was the primary force to tear down the Berlin Wall, wants to build its own wall. All this aside, a border wall ignores the fact that many overstay their visas which completely makes a border wall irrelevant. The problem with a border wall is it plays into people's stereotypes that people who cross the border illegally are people from Latin America who are poor and looking for fieldwork at less than minimum wages that Americans refuse to do. It completely overlooks Europeans or Australians who have entered the US legally but have overstayed their visas and refused to leave.

These individuals are just as illegal as those who have crossed the border illegally. Therefore the wall is a stereotypical solution to a problem with stereotypical overtones. And even with a border wall, illegal immigrants will find a way to get in if they are determined. They have traveled a long way to escape their poverty-stricken lives,

---

[88] Gorbachev: World Should Embrace Globalization. (2007, October 9). THE GORBACHEV FOUNDATION. https://www.gorby.ru/en/presscenter/publication/show_25702/
[89] Berlin mayor tells Trump: 'Don't' build this wall!' (n.d). DW. https://learngerman.dw.com/en/berlin-mayor-michael-müller-tells-donald-trump-dont-build-this-wall/a-37311389

and a border wall will not stop them from entering. How will a wall stop immigrants hidden inside trucks? How will a wall stop immigrants who enter from the northern border with Canada or illegally as stowaways in ships? And the border wall also ignores the life in border cities and the massive international trade between and among border cities. Many Mexicans who live in Mexico may cross the border to the US for work and then return home to their residences in Mexico. Many Mexicans also cross the border to shop and return home. This amounts to massive amounts of money crossing the border back and forth, issues that a border wall completely ignores. Americans in other parts of the country are completely ignorant or oblivious to these issues, which they take for granted once someone says that a border wall is a solution. A demagogue takes advantage of the fact that he knows his audience is not educated on all the details and complexities of the particular issue and offers simple solutions that the intended audience takes at face value.

Scapegoating is a typical tactic used by inflamers. Trump implies that Illegal immigrants are taking away jobs. The issue is much more complex than that. Multi-national corporations are moving their activities overseas with lower overhead in the form of cheap labor. Corporations are all about maximizing profits, and lower labor costs overseas are a way of doing that. They are also moving their operations overseas, where those jobs are appreciated and highly desirable compared to how Americans see those jobs. For example, call center agents are prestigious and highly coveted jobs in India and the Philippines. However, these are much less prestigious jobs in the US, not to mention the higher rate of pay for American workers compared to what these corporations have to pay call center agents in other countries.

All of this is compounded by the fact that it is not considered a job with as much dignity as it has attached to it in other countries where employment opportunities are scarce and working any type of office job has its social benefits. With the new information economy, traditional businesses are losing to new ways of doing business and making money online. People are now making money through the internet that would have been unimaginable not that long ago. A demagogue would like to blame these job losses to the new internet economy on illegal immigrants since it is an easier solution to something inherently complex. The fact of the matter is that workers need to adapt to the times and transform themselves to make themselves relevant in the new economy of the future.

But if a politician were to say this, it would be extremely unpopular and sound the death knell to their run for office. The fact of the matter is that workers need to be open to change and be open to training or educating themselves for new skills relevant to the current economy. This is a major reason for the success of inflamers with divisive rhetoric. They feed the audience fodder that they can easily digest. Trump has disrupted the narrative because no one could have imagined a demagogue becoming president in the world's largest democracy that would have advocated the building of a wall to keep people out in contradiction to its image of welcoming immigrants embodied by the nation's symbol, the Statue of Liberty. Demagogues, as many believe, come to power in other countries but not in the US, the world's bastion of freedom. American presidents are supposed to be able to walk a tight rope and unite all the various ethnic and religious groups into one cohesive vision of what it is to be American and not divide Americans along racial lines. Obama was very good at uniting Americans with his high ideals and lofty rhetoric.

The immigration crisis has very racial undertones connected to it. Trump uses the language of illegal immigration as a dog whistle to 'nativists' that the illegal immigrants are not white and are therefore not wanted and cannot be Americans. Throughout his presidency, this has been borne out from his reluctance to speak out against right-wing white nationalist aggression or crimes to his statement during the presidential debate to "Stand back and stand by."[90] Let us face it. Trump was simply trying to plug holes in a dam that would eventually burst. Immigration is inevitable that no one man can stop, even with his divisive rhetoric and race-bating. These immigrants will inevitably come from other regions other than Europe.

Europe is a highly industrialized and developed continent with a high standard of living which means there is no need for Europeans to immigrate to the US, unlike in the past, when there was a lot of social, political, and economic upheaval in Europe which meant massive European immigration to the US.

Immigration will continue to the US as many people all over the world are looking for a better life somewhere else, and they see the US as their best bet where they can live in peace and to their full potential. And on the other side of the ledger, the US needs educated and professional labor. It can get that from immigrants to keep its competitive edge economically. The process is done through the H-1B visa program, which allows the temporary employment of foreign workers in occupations that require specialized knowledge and a bachelor's degree or the equivalent in work experience. As long as qualified workers are needed in particular industries, it will not matter what race these

---

[90] INSIDER. https://www.businessinsider.com/proud-boy-membership-tripled-trump-stand-back-and-stand-by-2022-6?r=US&IR=T

immigrants are as long as they qualify for the jobs. This makes economic sense as opposed to racist policies that do not make economic sense.

In one of the cases in front of the court, the reasoning came down to a "negative impact on interstate commerce."[91] Basically, the court was saying the US could not make money under Jim Crow. Due to all of the wealth and allure that the US has in the eyes of other countries, it will be difficult to stop the tide of illegal immigrants even if a border wall is erected. And legal immigration will continue just the same because it brings a lot of benefits to the American economy.

An argument can be made legally that Mexico violates its treaty obligations under the Treaty of Guadalupe Hidalgo by simply allowing illegal immigrants to cross the border into the US. In the Treaty, both the US and Mexico are obligated to respect the boundary between their two countries, and by simply allowing illegal immigrants across the border, it can be said that Mexico is disrespecting the boundary between itself and the US and making Mexico pay for a border wall is thus legal in order for Mexico to be in accordance with its treaty obligations as paying for the wall

---

[91] Katzenbach v. McClung, 379 U.S. 294 (1964)

will ensure that Mexico is respecting the boundary between itself and the US.[92]

The problem is that Trump is not eloquent enough to explain this to the American people. If this were brought up, then there would be a possibility that people who were against a border wall paid for by Mexico might change their stance in favor of it. People are also more inductive to simple soundbites and solutions, and this sort of legalese is complex and does not lend itself to campaign slogans when a candidate needs to convince citizens to his side. However, there are still other ways to deal with the illegal immigrant situation instead of a medieval solution like a border wall. It is just that a border wall is a simple solution that voters can buy into and understand. In the past, societies in the Western world have discriminated against other races like in Nazi Germany with its policies on genetics due to its beliefs that the idea of the blond hair blue-eyed person was the ideal human and also probably because he or she was intellectually superior due to the fact that they themselves could see how far advanced Europeans (especially those of the Germanic persuasion) of their time were compared with other races all over the world.

---

[92] Treaty of Guadalupe Hidalgo (1848). (n.d). NATIONAL ARCHIVES. https://www.archives.gov/milestone-documents/treaty-of-guadalupe-hidalgo

This was a reason the Europeans needed to colonize the rest of the world. They believed they had a mission to spread their culture to the other peoples of the world to uplift them. And this was seen by the Europeans as the only way the power relationships in the world worked, so when this was reversed, it caused a lot of consternation among Europeans, like the case of the occupation of Germany after World War I by the allied forces. Not all occupation soldiers were white. The French used colonial soldiers from Africa etc. as occupation troops. Even before the Nazis came to power with their racist ideologies, Germans feared the colonial troops of other races who were assigned to Germany under the French in the aftermath of World War I.

This was seen as going against the natural order where Europeans were supposed to subjugate these "backward people," but these backward people were now lording it over defeated Germans. There was talk of how they were sexually raping white women or how their genetics could defile the German gene pool.[93] Even German president Fredrich Ebert spoke of this menacing threat to Germany as an affront to European Civilization.[94] The children of these mixed marriages between occupation soldiers of other races and

[93] Black Horror on the Rhine. (2022, July 5). In Wikipedia. https://en.wikipedia.org/wiki/Black_Horror_on_the_Rhine
[94] Spickard, P. (2012). Race and Nation: Ethnic Systems in the Modern World. Routledge

German women were eventually forced to go through sterilization by the Nazis when they came to power, so these offspring could no longer produce their own offspring, which could dilute the purity of the German race.[95]

In the US, there was a quota system in times past for immigrants of 'less desirable' races like Italians, Poles, Greeks, and Jews, among others. Asians were excluded altogether, at one point, through the Asian Exclusion Act as they were considered completely undesirable and unassimilable. Obviously, those of Northern European or Nordic stock were those who were seen as the ideal immigrants, a similar view held by the Nazis as they were most lenient to the Scandinavian countries that they occupied. This can be seen when Trump complained about all the immigration from "shitty" countries and desired more immigrants to come from "Norway," which caused a commotion among political opponents domestically, and there was an international outcry as well. This is in parallel with the traditional view of racists that Northern Europeans/Scandinavians are the race that is on top of the totem pole with all other races playing second, third, or fourth fiddle, depending on what racial group they are.[96]

---

[95] Forcibly sterilized for being Afro-German 'children of shame'. (n.d). DW.
https://www.dw.com/en/forcibly-sterilized-for-being-afro-german-children-of-shame/a-56175531
[96] Nordicism. (2022, August 4). In Wikipedia.

Even other divisions of whites, like the Latins, Slavs, etc. are considered inferior to the Northern European stock of people.

Not only was this in the immigration policy of the country, but this also reflected the attitude as well of American nativists (those of traditional English ancestry) in society. Well, known are the signs from back then like "Irish need not apply." To top it off, these immigrants from Eastern and Southern Europe typically lived in the slum neighborhoods of urban areas like New York, where politicians took advantage of them in spades.

The border wall plays into these racist stereotypes that the only way these non-whites should be treated is like animals which means a wall needs to be built so they can be caged out and not enter. Along with this is the fact that the border wall will keep non-whites out, which means there are definitely racist undertones to building a border wall. No previous president, in recent history, has used an issue with obvious racist connotations like Trump has. No other president has made the erection of a border wall with Mexico a major platform in his campaign for the presidency. Trump has certainly tarnished America's image on the world stage by trying to symbolically close itself off from its neighbor.

---

https://en.wikipedia.org/wiki/Nordicism

Chapter 17: Racism and Racist Attitudes Debunked

Today, views of racial superiority, which Trump espouses (explicitly and/or implicitly), are less viable as the West no longer has the technological edge that it had in ages past vis a vis other peoples and regions of the world.

Asia, for instance, has closed the gap with Europe in terms of industrial and economic outputs, especially concerning Japan, China, and South Korea, whose output is much more than its other Asian neighbors. Japan has outpaced the industrial and economic output of its European counterparts. We see this in industrial output like cars, electronics, and video games, where Japan has almost cornered the market in video game consoles. A good amount of technology and tech gadgets comes out of the Far East. And Asian students tend to outperform other racial groups in international testing, especially in science and math. For instance, even in schools in the US, students of Asian background tend to outperform their peers. Even Nixon, in the tapes, said that Asians were the smartest, followed by whites.[97]

---

[97] Ian mcafee. (2016, March 31). Nixon talking about IQ tests and other things [Video]. Youtube.
https://www.youtube.com/watch?v=PwXOEFK6Swo

This is a view held by a lot of people. Therefore, Europeans cannot act as they have in the past with their ideas of intellectual and cultural superiority because the gap they once held has vanished. This is another disruption of a narrative, the narrative of European superiority. I am sure Europeans of past times thought that their intellectual, industrial, and cultural edge, in contrast to the rest of the world, would remain that way forever. European powers could foresee only a little the massive industrialization of a country like Japan in the second half of the nineteenth century. Japan transformed itself from a feudal to an industrial society in a matter of a generation. The Japanese victory against the Russians in the Russo-Japanese war was the first time an Asian power defeated Europeans since the time of Genghis Khan and the Mongols.[98] One could draw a straight line from the Japanese industrialization during the Meiji Era to the Battle of Port Arthur to the attack on Pearl Harbor. Each step along the way proved Japanese ascendancy as a formidable power. None of the European powers or the US could argue that they underestimated Japanese might at the beginning of World War II when the

---

[98] Baby, G. (2021, November 26). How this conflict in a northern Chinese port changed the world. FINANCIAL REVIEW. https://www.afr.com/world/asia/how-this-conflict-in-a-northern-chinese-port-changed-the-world-20211123-p59b8t

Japanese gave the Russians the business less than forty years previously.

Another cause for the race of Asian parity with the industrialized powers of the West is the massive economic and industrial output that China is currently undergoing in our present day. China has come a long way since its image of being a 'backward society in the years after World War II. Especially as seen through the lens of the Cultural Revolution, which purged any remnant of capitalistic elements left in Chinese society and reimposed vigorously Maoist thought, they have come a long way from where they were just forty or so years ago since the rapid modernization they have undertaken since the 1980s under Deng Xiaoping to become the power economy they are today. Thus Trump's dog whistles to racists and his own racist rhetoric with his stereotyping of other races are debunked and fall flat on its face due to the strides that other races have made on the world stage to earn parity with their white counterparts. Racism is no longer viable as other cultures and races have proven themselves to be capable of what whites are capable of doing.

Racial theories have also widely been discredited since times past when they were all the rave. Gone are the days when Nazi scientists were made to go to Tibet to measure the skulls of the locals in order to support their racial theories or when conquistadors destroyed any relic or artifact related to the native cultures they encountered for fear that they were the work of the devil and had no intrinsic cultural value whatsoever to contribute to humanity or the understanding of the world in which we live.

Social scientists and anthropologists have come to accept other theories to explain why some societies or regions developed at various rates compared to others to make it seem like the people of those regions are superior to those in other parts of the world. In the book Guns, Germs, and Steel by Jared Diamond, he argues that Europeans are not genetically superior to other races but rather that other factors come into play which is why European civilization developed exponentially more than other civilizations. Factors that determined European hegemony are environmental differences, geography, and resistance to endemic diseases.

I believe geography favored Europe due to the ease of travel from one European region to another when it came to advancement. Ease of travel facilitates trade, and more importantly, it also facilitates an exchange of ideas and technological breakthroughs. In other world regions, there are imposing geographical barriers that prohibit ease of travel, etc., like the Sahara or Gobi desert in Africa and Asia. This also prohibits development as the exchange of ideas is made more difficult by these geographical barriers. Europe does not have these imposing geographical barriers that prohibit travel from one region of the continent to the other, so the exchange of ideas is easier on the European continent. Though Jared Diamond also adds that the natural barriers on the European continent allowed for competing European nation states which drove them to innovate as opposed to the Empires like China who stagnated due to lack of competition among its neighbors.

Europeans have also developed resistance to endemic diseases, which helped them when encountering the natives of other continents. Due to the lack of immunity of the natives that the Europeans encountered, these indigenous peoples died in unimaginable numbers.[99] Therefore, they were easy pickings for the less numerous Europeans who wanted to dominate them. This phenomenon was instrumental in the Americas, where natives died in unfathomable numbers. Suppose Europeans were genetically more intelligent than other races, then why were the Arabs superior in every way against them during the Dark Ages.

The Arabs were more advanced in every field than the Europeans, from culture to the arts, medicine, and science.

---

[99] Diamond, Jared M. (2005). Guns, Germs, and Steel: the Fates of Human Societies. New York :Norton

The Arabs were already using surgical techniques when Europe was still bleeding sick people to expel evil spirits or bore a hole through the skull, both of which would inevitably lead to death.[100] In the movie "The Agony and the Ecstasy," there is a scene where Michelangelo collapses due to work fatigue from painting the Sistine Chapel. He is nursed back to help by the Contessina de Medici, the daughter of Lorenzo the Magnificent. While Michelangelo was lying sick in bed, the Pope's physicians were sent to bleed him of the evil humors. They were promptly dismissed by the Contessina and were told that in Florence, they no longer bleed patients but instead use the Moorish methods.[101] Here we see how it took time for the advanced methods of the Arabs to reach the West.

Renaissance Florence was open to the ideas of the Arab world, and it took time for these advanced methods to be diffused throughout Europe. Historically, only after interaction with the East through the crusades did the West close the gap with the Arab world. The Enlightenment and Renaissance, which followed afterward, made the West gradually overtake the Arab world, and they have never

---

[100] Tasci, Ufuk, N. (2020, May 5). How a 10th-century Muslim surgeon revolutionized surgical procedures. TRT WORLD. https://www.trtworld.com/magazine/how-a-10th-century-muslim-surgeon-revolutionised-surgical-procedures-36039
[101] Reed, C. (Director). (1965). The Agony and the Ecstasy [Film]. 20th Century Studios.

looked back since. The Arabs took control of all of the Near East, including North Africa. It was where most, if not all, of the knowledge of the ancient world was stored, for example, in the library of Alexandria. Once again, it was reasons other than genetics. The various stages of European development show that they are not inherently genetically more intelligent than other races but rather were favored by geography and other such factors. All this points to the destruction of the narrative of racial superiority by believing that certain races are more intelligent than others. Trump's advocacy of the narrative of bigotry is thus outdated and out of touch with reality.

All these modern theories of race make Trump look foolish. His actions are relics of times past, especially with the examples I have just given. With its notions of white superiority, they are a disruption of the narrative as no president has implicitly supported white supremacy in his policies, rhetoric, or actions, or lack thereof, like not condemning right-wing acts by staying silent. This is much more so shocking as these are the actions of a US president of the twenty-first century. It is more understandable if these were the actions of someone in a bygone era like the nineteenth century when notions of racial superiority were more acceptable and tolerated as part of the natural order of the world but definitely not the actions of a president in the times that we live in now. It will not matter anyway, as these are the actions of a man trying to stop the inevitable.

More and more immigrants of other races will come pouring in who are in need by US businesses and US society in general due to their professions connected with intelligence like medicine, engineering, and computer skills. Heck, there are numerous black doctors and lawyers despite blacks having a stereotype of being intellectually inferior. I myself have not seen so many black doctors and lawyers as I do when I watch CNN. And many of the African immigrants that enter the country are professionals and highly educated. Even Nigerians in their home country tend to be educated and intelligent, but due to a lack of employment opportunities in their home country, they turn to crime like internet scams. Though not legal, these are still white-collar crimes that involve the intellect where cunning and trickery are involved in order to get money from the intended victim.

And neither has a president explicitly based a major part of his platform on a border wall that will be paid for by Mexico. Until this point advocating a border wall with Mexico that would be paid for by Mexico was unthinkable as a major policy platform by a presidential nominee from one of the two major parties. Something like this would typically be thought of as something that would be advocated by one of the fringe parties but not one of the two major parties. The Know-Nothing Party was the closest parallel to "Trumpism." They were nativist and anti-immigration in outlook though they were progressive in social policies. They were so nativist and anti-Catholic that they stole a piece of stone donated by the Pope meant for the Washington Monument, which was then still being built.[102]

The stone was broken up into pieces, and the rest thrown into the Potomac, where pieces of the stone would surface a long time after.[103] This event is a major reason why the stone of the Washington Monument has different colors. But this was in the nineteenth century, and they were not a major party that had as huge a following as Trump in the Republican Party. If one were to believe in the progress of the American narrative, then one would think that the racism of that time would have ebbed away by the first few decades of the twenty-first century. If one were to follow the narrative of American history, then it has become more and more inclusive as time has progressed through case law and legislation, so how can a major party candidate for president be advocating such policies even though hidden in the

---

[102] Washington Monument, A History. Chapter III: THE INTERIM PERIOD, 1856-1876. (n.d). NPS. https://www.bibliography.com/apa/how-to-cite-a-website-with-no-author-in-apa/
[103] Veroske, A. (2013, July 16). They Mystery of the Pope's Stone. WETA. https://boundarystones.weta.org/2013/07/16/mystery-popes-stone

language of laying the hammer down against illegal immigration and supporting legal immigration.

Even a viable third-party candidate like George Wallace, who was a staunch segregationist as governor of Alabama before he ran for president twice, had some practical policies in his platform that were not as outrageous as Trump's policies. Wallace advocated things like support for law enforcement as an answer to the riots breaking out in cities all over the US in the late 60s. A major reason for this was the fact that there is a major far-right presence in the Republican Party that there has not been in times past. In times past, for example, during the Reagan years, the Republicans were not too far to the right and could lay claim to the center, which attests to Reagan's success in both the 1980 and 1984 elections. He did not adhere to the program of right-wing religious fundamentalists and was actually open to immigration and did run on limiting immigration numbers.[104]

Obviously, some practical solutions to the problem of illegal immigration instead of an impractical one or a "medieval one" as some of the detractors of the border wall say is better enforcement of the current laws, keeping better

---

[104] Mettler, K. (2018, December 22). Analysis: Here's what Reagan actually said about border security. President Trump inaccurately described the former president's view. The Washington Post. https://www.mercurynews.com/2018/12/21/analysis-heres-what-reagan-actually-said-about-border-security/

track of those who overstay their visas, better detection of illegal immigrants crossing the border as well as those hiding in vehicles, hiding as stowaways in ships, and keeping track of illegal immigrant traffickers known to authorities who traffic illegal immigrants across the border.

The problem with these solutions is that they are not politician friendly because people do not see the positive results from these policies. A wall, on the other hand, can be seen and touched. And a barrier is a simple concept that people are blocked from going through, which is why it is so popular with so many though if one were to dig deeper into the pros and cons, there are many flaws with that particular solution. In other words, a demagogue just gives the people what they want to hear to make them happy.

Other presidents refrained from demagoguery but not Trump. This is how he broke the narrative of how presidents behave. In any event, his demagoguery has no basis in reality, as notions of racial superiority have been and can easily be debunked through interaction with other races and peoples.

Chapter 18: Trump and Hypocrisy

Hypocrisy is the worst thing in government. Suppose a politician was revealed to be a hypocrite; that usually was the death knell for his or her career. This does not seem to be the case for Donald Trump, as his supporters were oblivious to his hypocrisy even though it was so blatant.

He texted that Xi Jinping should engage with protesters and that he also should talk to Xi Jinping, and also that the Michigan governor Gretchen Whitmer engage in dialogue with white protesters in her state who were protesting lockdown measures. But then, when it came to black protesters, he texted that the powers that be come down on them hard. Trump also tweeted about Obama's incompetence during the Ebola virus crisis. Need I say more?

He refused to do anything about COVID, even saying it was a hoax. And his tweets criticizing Obama about playing golf did not age well also, as he played golf way more than he did, and his detractors criticized him. Congruent with this, he has complained about taxpayers paying for Obama's vacations, whereas he has cost the taxpayers a fortune with his trips to Mar-a-Lago.

He complains about the media being "fake news," yet he constantly lies with his alternative facts. He criticized Hillary Clinton's unsecured emails while talking about national security issues with Japanese Prime Minister Shinzo Abe at Mar-a-Lago. He complained about the Electoral College when Mitt Romney lost but did not have a problem with it when he won. He has complained about anonymous sources but admitted in court that he had used the alias John Miller. He promoted himself and ran his campaign on law and order when his foundation, the Trump Foundation, was shut down for fraud, and Trump University was sued and had to close down. He is also silent on law and order being imposed on his supporters who cause trouble like right-wing instigated violence.

He has also accused Hunter Biden of nepotism and corruption in connection with his father, Joe Biden when Trump himself has placed his family members in cabinet positions with no prior government experience. During the debate, Trump had also attacked Joe Biden for being at the bottom of his class or near the bottom when Trump himself did not have a stellar academic record. He has also had a photo of a Bible in front of a church. Obviously, to show himself to be a good Christian man and in favor of Church values.

Trump as a man of the Bible, well, we can go all day! No other president has been so hypocritical in his actions and pronouncements for all the world to see. There were presidents previously who were hypocrites, but one could argue that they were products of their time. One obvious example was Thomas Jefferson, who was behind the phrase "All men are created equal." Yet he was a slave owner and even had a slave as a mistress and fathered children with her. These descendants have been proven to be descendants of Jefferson through DNA and attend Jefferson family reunions.[105] James Monroe thought slavery to be evil yet owned many slaves.

It can be argued that these two presidents need to be placed in their historical context in that they were products of their times. They had aspirations of an ideal society, yet they could not escape the shackles of the reality of the society and times in which they lived. Andrew Jackson said that he wanted to treat Native Americans with justice, yet he prompted Congress to pass legislation that forced Native Americans to move west of the Mississippi River. Again this hypocrisy can be explained as being a product of the times. White settlers were populating the continent in ever-increasing numbers, and Native Americans were seen as inferior and unassimilable and had to be moved in order to make way for progress.

---

[105] Spencer, H. (2018, June 21). Sally Hemings Descendants Visit New Exhibit: 'We Knew Our Story Was Real'. VPM. https://vpm.org/news/articles/3074/sally-hemings-descendants-visit-new-exhibit-we-knew-our-story-was-real

There is no historical context for Trump's hypocrisy other than the fact that he says things that suits him from one minute to the next, and if he changes his position, he will do it if that is what is best for him. Add this to the fact that he knows his base does not care or will make excuses for him. Thus Trump's hypocrisy is much worse than those who have come before him. He has also done it on numerous occasions on various subjects. This shows that he does not care if he contradicts himself from one moment to the next. One also cannot argue that Trump's being hypocritical should be placed in historical context and that he is a product of his time. He simply lies to suit his ends.

One could say that 'alternative facts' are a way of how things work these days, but it really does not give a good excuse for how one shifts position from one to another. At least with slavery, it could be said that Jefferson and Monroe's aspirational language was drowned out by many in society, they included, who thought blacks were not equal to whites.

Chapter 19: Trump Continues To Have a Stranglehold on the Party

Though he lost to Biden, Donald Trump is still eligible for another term under the Constitution. The only president who has served two non-consecutive terms was Grover Cleveland, the twenty-second and twenty-fourth president. And because of this, Trump still has a hold on the party among members of his party, which means the Republican Party will still be clinging to' Trumpism' in the near future.

For the most part, Trump forged his own brand or platform quite distinct from the mainstream Republican Party platform, which made him attractive to many voters along with his alleged 'authenticity.' This is how he ran for the presidency, and this is how he was when he was president. His was truly a 'cult of personality. It is typically in other countries where the individual candidate's personalities and qualities are the deciding factors that voters vote on and not so much the party. This is not the case in the US. The US has a strong two-party system where the two major parties have dominated American politics for the vast majority of American history. Trump has broken through the stranglehold of the two major parties by making himself bigger than the Republican Party by virtue of his brand and cult of personality. His supporters were voting for him because of who he was and not so much because he was running as a Republican. Normally the two party system dominates American politics instead of a cult of personality as politicians fall in line with one or the other party depending on what their values are. But Trump came in like a storm and his supporters were voting for him instead of what he stood for which shifted from day to day as he changed his mind and policies whenever he felt like it. What he stood for was not exactly in line with the standard Republican platform.

There was a stint in the first half of the nineteenth century when for a time, there was just one dominant party which included the "Era of Good Feelings," but for the most part, the American political system is based on two major parties due to the winner take all system. In other countries, where there is a proportional representation based on how much a party got on the ballot, the party wins seats in proportion to the percent of votes it got. In the US, where the loser gets nothing, the two-party system is the best way to win elections since it whittles down the choices that voters have into just two, which simplifies things for the voting public. In large part because of this, the parties are bigger than the candidates. I mean that politicians for either party have to tow the party line, or their voices will be drowned out by those who do. This is why candidates are either to the right or left of the center during the primaries. But then they move to the center during the general election. Thus people vote for either one party or another because their views align with the parties.

Trump has been so much bigger than the Republican Party that he does not have to conform to the party platform. This is why his hold on the party is so strong because Republican voters see other Republican candidates as 'politics as usual.' This is a big reason why Trump's followers still believe in him and why Trump still has a hold on the party even after defeat. And even though Trump lost the election, his supporters have still made their voices heard in local elections for representatives who support Trump and his policies. Evidence of this is seen in the elections of individuals like Marjorie Taylor Green, Madison Cawthorn, and Lauren Boebert, who are wholehearted Trump supporters and support his politics as well. First of all, when the votes were about to be certified, various Republicans contested the results of certain states right before the Capitol riots, after which some of them had a change of attitude.

But Trump's hold on the party could be seen there with the contestation of election results and his hold on his supporters by getting them to march on Congress. Trump's hold on the party can also be seen in the fact that Representative Kevin McCarthy visited Mar-a-Lago shortly after Trump left office to make sure that the Republican faithful knew he was still 100% on board with Trump and his policies.[106] And in Arizona, there was another recount of the ballots several months into Biden's presidency.

Through the force of his brand and personality, Trump has broken through the dominance of the hold the parties have on the individual candidates. He is his own party, and at the very least, he has definitely changed the face of the Republican Party in the short term, if not the long term. Typically, once a party's candidate lost an election, the party looked to the next election and moved past the previous one that was lost. The party tries to figure out where they went wrong and try to attract an important constituency that they lost last time for the next election. This is not the case with Trump's loss. Despite losing by seven million votes, the GOP is doubling down and staying steadfast with' Trumpism."

Republicans all over the country are also tightening election laws to try and disenfranchise voters. American voter turnout is bad enough as it is compared to other countries, and here are legislatures all over the country trying to disenfranchise segments of the American population. On the opposite end of the spectrum, there are numerous

---

[106] Cohen, S. (2021, January 29). GOP House leader McCarthy meets with Trump at Mar-a-Lago to discuss 2022 strategy. DENVER abc. https://www.thedenverchannel.com/news/national-politics/rep-house-leader-mccarthy-meets-with-trump-at-mar-a-lago-to-discuss-2022-strategy

countries that penalize its citizens for not voting in elections. Our representatives should encourage people to vote so citizens will inform themselves on the issues instead of following Trump's destructive policies and suppressing the vote of those who are likely to vote for the opposing candidate's party.

A less than informed Electorate is why we have candidates like Trump and others of his ilk who say stupid things and get away with it. Some people will vote for Trump because they are conservative and will not vote for a candidate of the opposing party no matter what. Still, there are a lot of people who also do not vote, and I can bet you that many of them do not vote because a lot of candidates are grandstanding and avoid the real issues. This shows the imperfections of democracy and how Trump exacerbates them. This especially demonstrates that Trump has a stranglehold on the GOP, and the GOP cannot look past him.

Another reason for Trump's control over the party after his presidency is career politicians who want to win re-election. Career politicians are something the forefathers frowned upon. Career politicians were ever-present in England, and the forefathers did not want the American government to be filled with them. The forefathers wanted citizens to have regular professions and probably run for a government position in public service and then return to their regular lives. George Washington set the tone for this practice after he stepped down voluntarily after his second term was finished. They certainly did not envision the career of politicians ever-present in American government today. And because these career politicians want to win re-election, they are willing to do whatever it takes to achieve that goal, even if it means supporting Trump's unfounded claims of election fraud long after the election if that is what is popular among the Republican base. More likely than not, they know this is a futile effort, but because this is what their constituents want, they are willing to go along with it. They have, in the process, lost all sense of rational behavior that they otherwise would have possessed if they were not slaves to their office. In all fairness, the forefathers' country was much different than the US of the present day. The issues were not as many and complex as the issues the current government has to deal with today. But let there be no mistakes about it; what we are seeing now with how people in Congress are behaving with respect to their irrational support of Trump after he left office are some of the negative aspects connected with career politicians.

These, again, are ways in which Trump has disrupted the way how a former president has behaved through the hold, however irrational it is, that he has on his party even after he has left office.

Chapter 20: Concluding Thoughts

Donald Trump is definitely a freak of nature. His outrageousness knew no bounds, and he behaved like no other president before him. He had no desire to act like his predecessors, nor did he care what people thought about his behavior. He only cared about himself above the national interest. And he stirred a lot of anger towards him from his detractors.

He brought out everything wrong with the American society that was festering under the surface, like the racism and bigotry still present in it, and he showed that there is still a long way to go for the American society to be a truly color-blind society.

He was also the type of president the forefathers feared with his wealth and vast assets both within the US and abroad. All of this wealth can cause the officeholder to blind himself to the national interest. Instead, it can make them use the office's power to pursue their interests in violation of their oath of office. He also lied and didn't care if he didn't tell the truth like no other president before him. He used the present media climate because there would be channels like Fox or even talk radio that would enable his wild machinations. He also openly and publicly admired well-known dictators who are geostrategic adversaries of American interests abroad.

Previous presidents supported dictators, but all this was kept on the down-low so the American public would not be aware that the American government supports dictatorial regimes. And these dictators that previous American administrations supported helped further American interests abroad, while Trump's admiration for Putin or Kim Jong-un serves no purpose in furthering American interests. His isolationist policies would work to the detriment of American interests abroad.

The US has a huge economic presence the world over as well as numerous military bases in various regions of the world. If Trump's isolationist policies were continued long after his administration, it would mean a diminishment of American power overseas, both economically and militarily, as American businesses abroad may suffer if the US retreats back into its isolationist shell. The aura of American power and prestige will diminish in the eyes of the world.

Trump also did not behave in a manner befitting the holder of the office. His wild antics of making fun of others and insulting others did not bode well for the image of the president of the US, both in the eyes of his detractors and in the eyes of those internationally. He also advocated simple solutions to complex problems to get votes. He also held and showed racist and bigoted views that were not in accordance with how presidents before him behaved. And his bigotry is definitely out of date in the twenty-first century, with non-whites showing themselves capable of the achievements of their white counterparts. Nixon's bigotry only came out when the Nixon tapes were made public. He definitely did not show his bigotry to the public as president.

All of these show how Trump has disrupted the narrative of presidential behavior and cheapened the office during his four years as president.

Donald Trump has thus been a disruptor and destroyer of the narrative of how an American president should behave. He has also shown ugly elements within the American social narrative boiling underneath the surface, waiting for their voice. He was so bad that he destroyed many narratives showing the many problems within society and politics today. He did not behave like an American president is expected to behave on many levels. He acted in a way that an American president is not expected to behave. He was tactless and rude. He did not care about the American people in general but only his base. Nor did he even reach out just a little to those who did not vote for him. He was corrupt. He did not seem to be doing what was in America's best interest. He explicitly and implicitly made racist statements that encouraged racist elements in society to behave accordingly as they saw their beliefs and actions backed by the president. As he is brazen, he likes to get 'chummy' with dictators in a way previous presidents have not. He acts clownish and buffoonish. He appeals to voters' basest instincts. And he blurts out what's on his mind on social media, unlike previous presidents whose pronouncements were carefully thought out and crafted for appropriate public consumption. Through all these things, he has broken the mold of how a president should behave and how he is portrayed by Americans domestically and internationally. He has shown that America still has a long way to go to achieve a color-blind society, with all the racists coming out of the woodwork against blacks, illegal immigrants, Asians, etc. He has given them a voice, encouraged them, and made them believe that they can behave the way they want without impunity. He also wants the US to be on a more isolationist track and withdraw from its international responsibilities. The US has come a long way from its isolationist past to the superpower it is today. A giant step forward in American influence worldwide was the fact that it was the big winner in World War II, and it was able to extend its influence all over the world in the initial aftermath of the war through the Marshall Plan when Europe was economically devastated. And American influence has continued to grow ever since. Trump's behavior will only make the US regress and less influential on the world stage. No other president has acted the way he has, and many did not believe that someone like him could be elected president of the world's most powerful country. The American narrative is not perfect.

Though Americans pride themselves on American exceptionalism and how the US has come a long way towards harmonious race relations compared to how it was in the past, the Trump years have shown that the US still has to work to truly achieve a racially harmonious society as Trump has brought to the surface those who have racial prejudices through his fiery rhetoric. It is true that not all Trump supporters are racist. Some are just conservatives who believe in the Republican platform and will vote for the Republican nominee. Still, Trump has given that extreme faction of society a voice and a political party to latch on to where they probably did not feel they previously belonged. Due to his isolationist policies, Trump has also given America's allies food for thought. If someone like Trump can be elected again in the future, they could be left in the cold when faced with an external threat to their safety and security. They now realize that the days of latching on to American power are over, and they need to take on a larger responsibility for the future of their own security.

The Course of Empire: Destruction[107]

Romeo and Juliet[108]

---

[107] Cole, T. (1801-1848). The Course of Empire: Destruction [Painting]. The Met, New York, NY. United States.
[108] Bacon, J (n.d). Romeo and Juliet from Children's Stories from Shakespeare [Painting]. 1st-Art-Gallery.com. Romeo and Juliet from 'Children's Stories from Shakespeare'

Ernest Hemingway[109]

John Hawkwood[110]

[109] Arnold, L. (1940). Ernest Hemingway in Cuba [Photograph].
Radiofrance.
https://www.radiofrance.fr/franceculture/podcasts/la-compagnie-des-
auteurs/l-envers-de-sa-propre-legende-8812790
[110] Uccello, P. (1436). Sir John Hawkwood [Fresco]. Duomo, Florence,
Italy.

Martin Luther[111]

The Parisian Life[112]

[111] Cranach the Elder, L. (1530). Portrait of Martin Luther [Painting]. Private Collection, Geneva, Switzerland.
[112] Luna, J. (1892). The Parisian Life [Painting]. Government Service Insurance System, Pasay, Philippines.

Emilio Aguinaldo[113]

Richard Nixon[114]

[113] Amorsolo, F. (n.d.). Malacañang Presidential Portrait of Emilio Aguinaldo [Painting]. Malacañang, Manila, Metro Manila, Philippines.
[114] Rolls Press. (1969). Portrait of American Republican politician and 37th President of the United States, Richard Nixon (1913-1994). [Painting]. gettyimages.

Napoleon Crossing the Alps[115]

Napoleon Crossing the Alps[116]

---

[115] Delaroche, P. (1850). Bonaparte Crossing the Alps [Painting]. Walker Art Gallery. Liverpool, England.
[116] David, J-L. (1801). Napoleon Crossing the Alps [Painting]. Château de Malmaison, Reuil-Malmaison, France.

Rudi Dutschke[117]

Donald Trump[118]

[117] DW. (n.d.). [Rudi Dutschke, The Leader of the Student Revolt in Germany] Retrieved August 27, 2022.

[118] Craighead, S. (2017). Donald Trump poses for his official portrait at the White House [Photograph]. White House, Washington DC. United States

Section 3 – Narratives and their Flaws

Chapter 1: The Superior Western Narrative

There has been a common belief among Westerners in general in the past and Americans in our present times. The belief is that the Western narrative or the western view of the world will eventually win, and this is what every nation aspires to and how every society will end up as it is the epitome of civilization regardless of background, religion, culture, economy, political environment, etc. It can be argued that one of the holy books of the Western narrative is The White Man's Burden by Rudyard Kipling. He wrote it to encourage the United States to colonize the Philippines as the US was not a traditional colonial power.[119] And Americans at that time were hesitant to control a foreign people since they themselves believed in the equality of man (however flawed it was in practice in the US). Even during the years of American control of the Philippines, many Americans and politicians did not believe colonization was congruent with American values. Throughout the time of the American occupation of the Philippines, American political

---

[119] The White Man's Burden. (2022, July 25). In Wikipedia. https://en.wikipedia.org/wiki/The_White_Man%27s_Burden

commentators and cartoonists abounded, arguing against and satirizing the colonization of other people.

It was because the US was not a country that was accustomed to being in the colonization/imperialism business, nor did its ideals and beliefs counsel such behavior. In these times, many in the US believe that every society must evolve into a Western, Jeffersonian type democracy as the belief goes, especially among certain factions in American politics and culture like neoconservatives. In past centuries, the narrative was different. The European imperial and colonial powers carried the mantel of their narrative. It tried to impose it on the rest of the world through colonization with various objectives and extents depending on the colonial or imperial power. For example, the Spanish tried to completely makeover the people they colonized by Christianizing them. The British were more concerned with trade and commercial exploits and wanted to impose laissez-faire economics. These are all part and parcel of the various threads that combine to make up the narrative. Today Europeans are less adamant about imposing the narrative on the rest of the world or have frankly accepted that the narrative cannot be imposed on the rest of the world. So that mantel has been taken up by the United States.

The problem with the narrative being imposed on the rest of the world or believing that this is how the rest of the world will develop is not possible as different peoples and societies in different areas of the world have experienced different forms of societal organization and development or have gone through a completely different narrative altogether. The Western experience of going through the fall of Civilization in the form of the Roman Empire falling, then the Dark and Middle Ages, the Renaissance and Enlightenment, the Industrial Revolution, and now the fourth Industrial Revolution, as many social pundits are now labeling our times, is a unique narrative to the West and the desire to replicate it in other societies will be a difficult task. There will be unique problems in those societies when a foreign model is imposed on them. These societies may revert to anti-democratic ways or factional infighting, which is antithetical to democratic societies because these behaviors have been deeply ingrained among their people. Even in the West, there are problems and setbacks in the narrative and Western societies do not live up to their narrative's full potential as there are problems beneath the surface. These problems completely contradict the ideals Western societies have set up for themselves, like the anti-immigrant sentiment in Europe or blacks dying at the hands of police which seems to happen regularly now in the US. These undercut the narrative that the West has created for itself. In Section 2 you read about how the American narrative broke down in the person of Donald Trump. He has divided Americans into factions with his race-baiting language, lack of care for the national interest, and shameless self-promotion. We shall now review the different narratives that societies around the world have experienced to show how societies developed differently compared to the stages of development that the West has experienced. This means that trying to impose Western values and the Western narrative on other societies will be difficult and incompatible with those societies' historical experiences. The Western narrative is unique to the West due to the West's unique stages of historical development that other societies did not necessarily experience.

Chapter 2: The Communist Narrative

Communism is all about narratives. The Communists believe that society goes through various stages of development. The belief is that all the world's workers would rise against their bourgeois masters and take over the reins of government to equalize everything for every citizen with no income and wealth discrepancies among its citizens. The Communist narrative dealt purely with economics and cared less about all the other strains of the Western narrative like the Renaissance, Enlightenment, etc. A perfect example of this were the brutal and intensive Five-year plans of the Soviet Union which started in the first half of the twentieth century as part of Communist ideology for the development of the nation's economy.

The Communists then believed that their narrative in the form of uprisings and revolutions would first occur in the industrialized countries. This was a big mistake as the industrialized countries were least affected by the Communist Revolution. Communist uprisings were most successful in the developing world. Communism was most vulnerable in Eastern Europe, where it fared rather poorly compared to its capitalist Western European neighbors. Eastern Europeans would simply look to their more affluent Western European neighbors and see that something wasn't quite right with their own system of social and economic organization as compared to Western Europeans.

The success of Solidarity in Poland is an exemplar of this. Solidarity was a movement that rose against the utter desperate economic circumstances in Poland, including freezes on wages and inflation by the government that triggered massive unrest throughout huge segments of the Polish population. In the early eighties, the Polish leader Jaruzelski cracked down on the movement with clear overtones from the Soviet Union, who had even positioned its military on Poland's eastern border on what they said were military maneuvers. When Gorbachev came to power, he made it clear that the Soviet Union would no longer intervene and that Poland had to solve its own problems. There were talks between the ruling government and Solidarity leaders. The Communists were willing to acknowledge and negotiate with Solidarity, perhaps because they did not think of them as a threat. They did not realize that Lech Walesa would eventually become president due to the dire straits the country was in under their rule.

There was also an event that temporarily opened the Austrian-Hungarian border in 1989, which gave citizens of East Germany a chance to go to the West. Hundreds of them took advantage of the temporary opportunity. This pivotal event signaled that the Iron Curtain was going to fall.

Though East Germany had just celebrated their fortieth anniversary as a nation and everything pointed towards more prosperous years as a country, Hungary had plans to take down the Iron Curtain just to the south. The Hungarian government announced that their barrier with Austria was just too expensive to maintain. Soon after that, soldiers were seen cutting down a portion of the fence on the border with Austria. This was strategic on the part of the government to really bring down or poke a gaping hole (no pun intended) or at least fan the flames of the downfall of communism. Hungarian officials realized that the summer season was coming, and East Germans loved to go to Hungary for the summer activities it offered. It was obvious to Erich Honecker and the higher-ups that this was like a dam with a leak that would result in a deluge. Then a decision was also made to open the border with Austria; no ifs, ands, or buts. When the border was opened, there were thousands upon thousands that poured through. The writing was on the wall, and East Germany knew this was the beginning of the end since their citizens on vacation in Hungary could now escape to the West. The key factor at play was the Soviets and how they would react. And just like in Poland, they would stand down and would not send their military to crackdown on the open border.[120] Nowhere was the embarrassment of the Communist system more visible than in East Berlin early in the Cold War, where their citizens were flowing into the West at an enormous rate. There was a brain drain due to their declining educated population choosing to remain in the East. There were also long waits just for necessities like an apartment or to purchase their rinky-dink car, the Trabant, not to mention a lack of food in stores.[121] Their city was also not in the best shape, with buildings still bearing the scars from World War II like bullets against the walls of buildings years after the end of the war.[122] Thus the Berlin Wall was the solution to this brain drain, though it heightened tensions and would be an instigator of the escalation of the East-West conflict. The solution was acceptable to the West as they did not contest the building of the wall even though there was a tank standoff at Checkpoint Charlie. But the escapes continued, which meant a constant upgrading and reinforcing the wall. And the escapes were very ingenious: secret compartments in a car, tunnels underneath going from

[120] Meyer, M. (2009). The Year That Changed the World. Simon & Schuster.

[121] Trabant. (2022, July 5). In Wikipedia. https://en.wikipedia.org/wiki/Trabant

[122] 75 Years On: Fascinating Photos of the Scars That Still Mark Berlin Today. (2020, May 7). Amateur Photographer. https://www.amateurphotographer.co.uk/latest/75-years-on-photos-of-the-scars-that-still-mark-berlin-137272

East to West, even a glider.[123] And concomitant with this, the fact that the Berlin Wall constantly needed to get upgraded with more and more barriers, including a deadly portion that was known as a no-man's-land, was a sign that communism was not what it was cracked up to be.[124] Even a part of the Berlin Wall, which had numerous layers, was called the death strip. It was filled with gravel, so people trying to escape by going through it could see footprints.[125] Thus the wall was a living symbol of the failures and shortcomings of communism. There was even a Miss Germany that became Miss Universe who had escaped to the West from the East, which was a huge propaganda embarrassment for the East German government.[126] Though the Berlin Wall did succeed in that people fleeing to the West did lessen after building the wall compared to the time before the wall, it was proof that people needed to be caged in and imprisoned for their society not to fall apart.

---

[123] Ubuntu expert tutorial. (2014, November 9). The Berlin Wall 13 August 1961-9 November 1989 [Video].
Youtube. https://www.youtube.com/watch?v=QrWVOVDc14k

[124] DW News. (2009, June 30). Walled in: The inner German border | DW English [Video]. Youtube.
https://www.youtube.com/watch?v=OwQsTzGkbiY

[125] DW News. (2009, June 30). Walled in: The inner German border | DW English [Video]. Youtube.
https://www.youtube.com/watch?v=OwQsTzGkbiY

[126] Marlene Schmidt. (2022, August 5). In Wikipedia.
https://en.wikipedia.org/wiki/Marlene_Schmidt

As we now know, communism did eventually fall, and today there are only a handful of Communist countries in the world. This shows that their narrative was not exactly successful and did not go the way they had hoped. This is an example of a competing narrative to the Western Narrative, which shows that the Western Narrative is not the only historical narrative worth noting and that the Communist narrative failed to achieve its own objectives. This was because certain assumptions were made like all workers, no matter their nationality, would find a common cause to overthrow their capitalist masters and exploiters. The problem was that many other factors at play divide people that are stronger than economics, like race, religion, culture, etc. These groupings that divide people worldwide have been proven stronger and more lasting than the divisions based on class which has not been proven as comparatively important. We still see ourselves based on our nationalities more than our class and find shared common characteristics with those of the same nationality.

Chapter 3: Muslim Narrative

The Muslim narrative was prevalent in the early era after the founding of Islam and is still prevalent among radical Muslim groups today which professes that the whole world will eventually convert to Islam. It started in the sands of the desert of Arabia with the prophet Muhammad. Shortly after his death, his followers spread like wildfire through conquest, conquering much of the ancient Roman world in the Near East and North Africa, finally being stopped in the south of France. They had access to much of the ancient world's knowledge and progressed in science, literature, the arts, etc. when Europe was still mired in the Dark Ages. They were far more advanced in medicine as well, along with the other fields of human knowledge. European medicine at this time was crude and based on superstition. People who were sick were bled to drive out the 'evil spirits from the body. There was also the tried and true method of boring a hole through the center of the skull, which would inevitably lead to death.[127] Arab medicine was more scientific-based, as they practiced techniques that would still hold sway and be practiced centuries later due to their firm scientific foundations.[128] Avicenna, the father of early modern

---

[127] Trepanning. (2022, July 7). In Wikipedia. https://en.wikipedia.org/wiki/Trepanning
[128] Majeed, A. (2011, November 5). Arabic roots of modern medicine. THE LANCET.

medicine, is an example. His practices survived for centuries after his lifetime. His teachings and techniques were studied by medical students and considered the standard.[129] If you wanted to get the best possible education during this time in human history, then you would have wanted to go to a university in Baghdad, Cairo, or Damascus as the Arab world was considered the center of learning at that time.

They looked down on their European neighbors, whom they considered barbaric and had nothing of value to offer mankind. Even though positive and contributing to the fields of human endeavor, the Arabs still frowned upon anything that came out of Europe. They tended to look down on the Europeans, especially when the Crusaders were in the Holy Land with their brutal slaughtering of the inhabitants of Jerusalem after breaching the walls of the city at the end of the First Crusade. The constant belittling of Europeans had drastic consequences down the line when the Europeans were finally catching up and overtaking the Muslim world in later centuries during the Renaissance and Enlightenment and even after that with the Industrial Revolution. The Arabs discounted all these major époques happening in Europe as the Europeans were still considered inferior in their eyes. The height of Muslim power was arguably during the reign

https://www.thelancet.com/article/S0140-6736(11)61701-7/fulltext
[129] The Cannon of Medicine. (n.d). Islam Wiki.
https://islam.fandom.com/wiki/The_Canon_of_Medicine

of Suleiman the Magnificent of the Ottoman Empire. The Ottoman Empire at its height stretched all the way to the lands of Southeastern Europe up to and including Greece which only gained its independence from the empire in the nineteenth century. Though, it was obvious to all including the West that the Ottoman Empire began to decline after the reign of Suleiman the Magnificent. This was obvious especially after the loss of the Ottoman Empire at the Battle of Lepanto, which was followed by the ascendancy of Christian military strength in Europe.

Today the Arab world and Europe have flipped as opposed to their relative positions of strength vis a vis each other during the Dark and Middle Ages in the West which coincided with the Islamic Golden Age in the Muslim world. Thus the dream of the entire world converting to Islam through brute Muslim military strength is no longer viable except in the outrageous dreams of militant Muslims. The Arab or Muslim world is now trying to navigate their way in this world and find where they fit. The rest of the world needs the oil that they produce, but at the same time, they lag in the technological realm, especially when it comes to the industrialized West or even Far-East Asian countries. Oil has been a blessing for them since it has given them a source of wealth, but it is also a curse because it has made them complacent and less willing to innovate due to this vital natural resource they have that the world needs. The Arab world also suffers from Civil Wars like those in Yemen and Syria. The instability in this region of the world has caused mass migrations to places like Europe, which has caused social unrest and political instability in turn in that continent. Although, one has to admit that there is an oasis of wealth and luxury in the Arabian world like the UAE, which has come a long way in the last fifty years. Fifty years ago, it was nothing but desert. Now it is a modern metropolis. However, there is no hiding that their golden age is long gone. And even if the entire region develops on the same level as the UAE, there are still questions about their political development as it is traditionally a region that has not known democracy, with the exception of Iraq, where it was imposed upon them after the defeat of Saddam Hussein. But for the most part, it is a region of the world anathema to the principles of democracy and individual rights.

Chapter 4: The Japanese Narrative

Other societies have also developed differently from the West, like Japan. It was a feudal society for much of its history until the mid-nineteenth century. It was ruled by the shoguns or military dictators who held the real power in Japan for centuries up until Commodore Perry's arrival. The Samurai, warriors known the world over as an integral part of Japanese culture and history, played a key role during these times. They had their code of honor in which they lived by which included their loyalty to their feudal lords.[130] Their code included how they fought in battle, how they behaved in their everyday lives, even what they ate. When Commodore Perry arrived there in the middle of the nineteenth century, Japan was still a feudal society. Due to the expedition, trade and diplomatic relations were established, and Japan was opened up to the West after a long period of isolation. They were hesitant at first when Perry arrived but eventually and reluctantly allowed him to land for negotiations, which resulted in the opening of Japan to the rest of the world.

Shortly after Perry's arrival and diplomatic success, the Treaty of Amity and Commerce between Japan and the

---

[130] Bushido. (2022, August 1). Bushido. https://en.wikipedia.org/wiki/Bushido. In Wikipedia. https://en.wikipedia.org/wiki/Bushido

United States was signed that opened up several ports and granted extraterritoriality to foreign residents and freedom of worship for American nationals within their designated settlements.[131] The treaties were unfavorably unequal in favor of the United States, and Japanese sovereignty was curbed for the first time in its long history. But this was the motivation for the Japanese. So they decided to emulate the West and industrialized, which they were more or less able to do by the latter part of the nineteenth century within a generation of first opening up their ports to outsiders, thus skipping all the steps in between feudalism and industrialization. This period of modernization coincided with the Meiji Era when imperial rule was now in the person of the emperor, Emperor Meiji.[132]

Thus their development had a higher learning curb as they went from feudal to industrial in a little over forty years. By the beginning of the twentieth century, they won a war against the Russians, to the surprise of the international community as an Asian power had defeated a European power for the first time since the days of Genghis Khan. What was more remarkable was that they were able to

---

[131] Treaty of Amity and Commerce (United States - Japan). In Wikipedia. https://en.wikipedia.org/wiki/Treaty_of_Amity_and_Commerce_(United_States–Japan)
[132] Meiji (era). (2022, August 1). In Wikipedia. https://en.wikipedia.org/wiki/Meiji_(era)

rebuild again and become an economic world power within a few decades after the destruction wrought upon them during World War II. The Japanese were able to do this through perseverance and the indomitable Japanese spirit embodied in the word 'gaman,' which has no exact equivalent in English.[133] And of course, the Japanese have always been known for their group discipline to achieve the goals of national success for the common good instead of the individualistic ethic of Westerners, most especially the rugged individualism of Americans. They were able to "endure the unendurable and suffer what is insufferable," as Hirohito told the Japanese people in his speech at the end of the war. Tokyo's hosting of the Olympic Games in 1964 was proof positive that Japan had bounced back and was once again an important player on the world stage. The US also imposed a Western, liberal-democratic government on Japan, similar to Western states. We made the Emperor a symbolic figurehead without any temporal power, similar to European monarchs.

Before World War II, the Japanese Emperor had much more power, as evidenced by the fact that many wanted to see him prosecuted for war crimes committed by the Japanese. It was only MacArthur's vehement stance that

---

[133] Gaman (term). (2022, July 31). In Wikipedia. https://en.wikipedia.org/wiki/Gaman_(term)

Emperor Hirohito not be prosecuted that immunized him from the prosecution that so many wanted. MacArthur's decision was based on the fact that he did not want an uprising among the Japanese people, which he thought would happen if the Emperor were prosecuted, whom they considered to be a god.[134] MacArthur was thinking of the future occupation of Japan, which he desired to be peaceful and smooth.

In any case, all these historical events that Japan has experienced since the war has now made their trajectory and interests parallel to the West. Thus Japan now is rather currently parallel to the West in its development economically and technologically, so it remains to be seen if they will have setbacks or will continue on their progress, economically, technologically, and politically as well. Also, it does not seem like an autocratic form of government will take over Japan any time soon, and it also does not seem like their economic strength will worsen at any time in the near future. All indicators show that their narrative will parallel that of the West even though they skipped some stages in between as they went from a feudal society to an industrial society in a generation during the second half of the nineteenth century. It just needs to be seen whether the

---

[134] Kramer, G. (1989, January 9). MacArthur and Others Resisted Wartime Passions and Spared Emperor. AP. https://apnews.com/article/f7272c57e597fb4d27150feaf954e2f5

rumblings and demonstrations among the Japanese population against the US military bases in Okinawa will grow louder over time though there are no indications whatsoever that this will affect the US-Japanese alliance, which has shown itself to be robust since the end of World War II.[135] Japan, like its World War II ally Germany, has repackaged itself and given itself a facelift as a peaceful, economically powerful nation willing to live in peace and cooperation within the framework of the international community as opposed to its warlike imperialist nature before World War II. No matter how impressive they went from a feudal society to an industrial society and how they rebuilt again from the ashes of World War II, they caused a lot of pain and suffering from the territories they occupied before and during World War II. For instance, Chinese deaths are estimated to be as high as twenty million. And to top it all off, the Japanese do not like discussing the war in order to avoid an embarrassing chapter in their history. Another issue that lingers to this day is those comfort women who are fighting it out with the Japanese government in order to get acknowledgment or compensation. There were also the various holdouts who refused to surrender even

---

[135] Protests of US military presence in Okinawa. (2022, June 21). In Wikipedia.
https://en.wikipedia.org/wiki/Protests_of_US_military_presence_in_Ok inawa

though the war was over, like Onoda in the Philippines, who did not surrender until twenty-nine years after the war was over.[136] These holdouts caused chaos and havoc among the communities which they were targeting. This is a part of their narrative that they refuse to acknowledge. This shows again that there are skeletons in the closet of every narrative. There is horror underneath the facade of technological progress that they show to the world. This is one flaw of their narrative. Another flaw of their narrative is the fact that their development was achieved minus some of the stages of development that the West went through, like the Enlightenment and the Renaissance, which does not seem to have had any negative effects on their development in comparison to the West. But it needs to be seen in the long run if their narrative will diverge from that of the West due to the fact that they did not experience an Enlightenment or a Renaissance. Only time and circumstances will tell.

---

[136] Onoda. (2022, August 3). In Wikipedia. https://en.wikipedia.org/wiki/Hiroo_Onoda

Chapter 5: The Chinese Narrative

The Chinese have their historical narrative and are only catching up to the West now economically and, to a certain extent, technologically as well. Much of Chinese history has shifted between times of peace and political unity and times of war. The Chinese have seen numerous dynasties rule their land like the Tang and the Han just to name two. They fell behind the West in the last few centuries when the West went through the Renaissance, the Enlightenment, and the Industrial Revolution. They are only now catching up to the West since the 1980's industrially and technologically. However, there are issues with this as many say they do not innovate but simply copy technology from the West by stealing it through espionage or through companies like Huawei, which has been believed to have strong government support and connections with the Chinese military. It is believed that China does not innovate due to key factors in Chinese society like the lack of free speech, propaganda from above, and the practice of memorization and rote learning in education.[137] But China is nowhere near the Western liberal democracies regarding democratic values and commitment to civil rights and human rights. The

---

[137] Zhang, R. (2020, August 11). My Experience with Rote Memorization. Blog. https://roy99zh.medium.com/my-experience-with-rote-memorization-f69715f3245e

Tianamen Square massacre is a physical manifestation of the lack of progress when it comes to civil and human rights.

Nor does China pretend that it wants to be on the same level as the Western democracies regarding political development on Western lines. China today, in some ways, is trying to find its lost grandeur from ancient times. Ancient China was responsible for the "Four Great Inventions": the compass, gunpowder, paper making, and printing. All four were important for developing civilizations in other parts of the world. Due to its geographical distance and isolation from the West, it was largely immune to the technological and social developments in the West in the past centuries and fell behind. This had devastating results for the Middle Kingdom as it got "carved up" like Thanksgiving turkey among the imperial powers in the age of imperialism during the nineteenth century due to their lack of development despite the size of their land and their population. In the post-war era, when the Communists took over, they had programs like the Cultural Revolution and the Great Leap Forward that had devastating results, costing untold numbers of deaths. I was watching an interview where the subject was rude Chinese tourists who cut in line and push and shove in public. When the question came up as to why Chinese tourists are like that, the interviewee responded that the Cultural Revolution had done away with a lot of educated

Chinese. This shows the devastating results of the Communist programs imposed on society. Here is a literal example where the narrative is set back even though the objective was to progress forward. China really did not see success until the reforms of the 1980s under Deng Xiaoping. Up until the 70s, Deng's predecessors retained the status quo, which had not born fruit for the nation in terms of progress. Today they are trying to "catch up" to the West economically though not in other aspects like politics and civil and human rights. This is the problem of not going through the other stages of development that the West had to go through, like the Renaissance and the Enlightenment. Though if they really were sincere about development on Western lines, they still have to deal with the problem of pollution by all their industries, whereas the West is already tackling the problems of the environment during the present phase of world history, which many social pundits call the "Fourth Industrial Revolution." But this is understandable as they are still in an earlier industrialization phase similar to what the West went through in previous centuries with all the pollution-causing factories notorious in England during the nineteenth century. In spite of this, no matter what happens or what events are thrown at them, the Chinese have time and patience as they have had a long history as a Civilization. As Bill Clinton once said in a speech, "China has seen more millennia than the US has centuries."[138] However, one needs to see what the future holds for China if there will be a military confrontation with its aggressive maneuvers in the South China Sea at the expense of its neighbors. So their narrative is still questionable as they seem to be bullying their way to get the natural resources in the territories arguably held by their neighbors under international law. The big questions are: will China choose the path of continuing escalation of tensions and possible aggression against their neighbors or other powers? Or will they choose the path of peaceful co-existence on the world stage while using their economic might as leverage when dealing diplomatically with other nation-states?

Their economic and technological progress narrative has its downsides, namely the pollution that their economic development is causing. It is similar to the pollution caused in England during the early stages of the Industrial Revolution. Questions also arise regarding serious deficiencies in human rights and getting along with their neighbors, not to mention their threatening behavior around the South China Sea area. They also have corruption problems with Communist government officials. But if you

---

[138] Transcript: Clinton Speaks Before The National Geographic Society. (1998, June 11). CNN.
https://edition.cnn.com/ALLPOLITICS/1998/06/11/clinton.china/trans cript.html

are waiting for the Chinese to become democratic in the future, you are in for a long wait. China believes that strict authoritarian one-party rule is its strength and will keep it from taking advantage of by other external powers. In the past, it was carved up by the imperial powers when there was no strong central government making it easy prey for outside powers. This is similar to the North Korean attitude embodied in the term "Juche," which basically means they rely only on themselves due to their bad experience in the past when colonized and exploited by outside powers. It is only natural for them to think that if they were to go the route of democracy, the higher-ups in government would lose control of their grip on society which will make them prey to outside powers who would want to see them weakened. This is only reasonable as they experienced this in the past. The Western powers will not understand this as they have not experienced the historical past that China has experienced. So the Western narrative, when being imposed upon the Beijing government, comes off as a new form of imperialism from the West. No matter how good-natured the West thinks it is in forcing them to democratize and encourage them to practice human rights, the Chinese government will always take it negatively as a form of Western bullying and meddling in domestic affairs, just as they did in the past with imperialism. The common theme here is that countries like China and their neighbor North

Korea will not buy into the western narrative of democracy and freedom of speech and all else that the West is known for, as they believe these are not their values. When they adopt these values, they are being overrun by Western values and have thus lost their identities and autonomy. China will develop technologically and economically, but at the same time, it will develop on its terms, and the Chinese have made this clear again and again. As of now, they are economically engaged with their neighbors, but at the same time using their might to take advantage of the situation, like giving out loans on strict terms with exorbitant interest rates.[139] They are also building roads to make access to their neighbors much easier, fueling their economic growth. China is recreating a modern version of the Silk Road with modern transportation links through the Central Asian republics linking to Europe. These include road and rail infrastructures that connect to remote areas like semi-arid deserts and towns in remote areas of western China and the Central Asian republics making these regions more and more economically tied and dependent on Beijing.[140] These are expensive projects, but because China is a one-party state, these

---

[139] Sirimanna, B. (2011, June 19). Chinese project loans at high interest rates. Business Times.
https://www.sundaytimes.lk/110619/BusinessTimes/bt01.html
[140] mustefeez rehman. (2018, August 24). China's New Silk Road |. DW Documentary. [Video]. Youtube.
https://www.youtube.com/watch?v=1qd8juCdTkA

projects can be implemented without any political opposition. The new Silk Road highway will go through Central Asian republics where the Russians were formerly dominant. Now the Chinese have taken over that role. This is a theme of what is going on in the world we live in. Regional powers are trying to carve out their own spheres of influence in certain geographical areas, and the Chinese are doing it with their neighbors in one manner or another, mainly economically. Thus their narrative only takes in some aspects of Western development and not others. This is another example where exporting Western values wholesale to other non-Western societies is incompatible with those societies.

Chapter 6: The Jewish Narrative

It is also impossible to ignore the Jewish historical narrative. The Jews have had a presence in the land of present-day Israel for around 3000 years. Over those initial centuries, they were conquered by outside forces like the Babylonians, the Assyrians, and the Romans. They have experienced diasporas that have forced them away from their homeland. For a great part of their history as a people, they have been living as a minority community within other societies. They have been a visible minority and have been treated differently from the rest of the people. They have suffered from pogroms in Europe where there would be riots among the local population against the Jews in their quarters which would involve destruction and killing, which would usually be triggered by some questionable incident like a Jew defiling the Communion host or someone could be missing like a child.[141] The locals believed that a Jew had taken him or her. In general, when times were bad like if there was a plague, the Jews would typically be the culprits, so the town's inhabitants would go to the Jewish neighborhoods to wreak havoc and massacre some Jews. These were usually perpetrated by the masses who were more often than not ignorant and lacked the knowledge to

---

[141] Netanyahu, B. (2001). The Origins of the Inquisition in Fifteenth-Century Spain. New York Review Books.

know the reasons for why things were happening in their society like plagues, social phenomena like economic downturns, etc., so a scapegoat would be an easy explanation which would be Jews. They were forced to wear clothes that marked them as Jews. They were also relegated to certain quarters in a city or town and to certain professions. For example, Christians were not allowed to charge interest when lending money, but Jews did not have this same limitation, so this was a natural occupation for them to enter. This played a part in the stereotypical image of Jews as greedy. Plus, the fact that they continued these types of professions in future generations even solidified that stereotype. Also contributing to the stereotypes are the way they are portrayed in the Bible as the money lenders and tax collectors etc. This caused a lot of suffering for Jews due to these images of them. In the Muslim world during the Islamic Golden Age there was more tolerance of Jews compared to how Jews were treated in Medieval Europe, though this tolerance had its limits as well. Jews did not have an equal status to Muslims legally under the law, and there were also sporadic outbursts of violence against them.[142] But for the most part, their history can be said to have cycles

---

[142] The "Golden Age" of Jewish-Muslim Relations: Myth and Reality. In J. M. Todd & B. Stora (Eds). The History of Jewish-Muslim Relations: From the Origins to the Present Day (pp. 28-29). Princeton, New Jersey: Princeton University Press.

where they are forced away from their homeland only to return at a later time and fight the inhabitants who are already there inhabiting their homeland. This happened in biblical times when they had no choice but to leave Egypt when things were not going well for them there. They waited for around a generation or so outside their Promised Land until conditions were right and they could enter and be ready to fight the inhabitants already living there.

Then the Jews would be expelled again from their land by the Romans in the early part of the common era. This cycle would be repeated again in the twentieth century when they suffered under Nazi rule via the Holocaust, and in the immediate aftermath of World War II, the international community voted for a Jewish homeland in Palestine. And when the Jews declared a Jewish state in 1948, they had to fight a war of Independence against several of their Arab neighbors. After several wars like the Suez Crisis, the Six-Day War, and the Yom Kippur War, Israel is still standing strong as ever as a viable nation-state. Israel is now a thriving nation that has come a long way since its birth a few years after World War II. This is a narrative that has developed differently from the Western historical narrative due to their unique problems as a people despite living within Western society and other societies as well. And as much as they like to portray their narrative as 'living in their Promised homeland once again, it has come at a cost. The negative side that they would rather not want to talk about or discuss is the fact that they threw out many of the local inhabitants already living there in 1948 when the state was founded. They have also since thrown out Palestinian inhabitants so they can build settlements in contravention of International Law. There have also been accusations by Palestinians of unequal treatment under the law. All this undermines the narrative that Israel is the paradise at the end of the rainbow that the Jews have been searching for their entire existence as a people. It may be so for Jews but not Palestinians living in their midst.

Granted, the Israelis need to be tough as they are surrounded by enemies who are bent on their destruction. Israeli civilians are always on the receiving end of terrorist attacks from suicide bombers, rocket strikes, etc. So the blame can go back and forth for a long time to come as to who is responsible for the violence and who has to take the first steps to stop it, but it still shows the problems with the Jews returning to the homeland that was supposed to be given to them by God. And the Israelis living in Israel always have to be on the alert for terrorist attacks every now and then from suicide bombers, or rocket attacks from Hamas launched from Gaza. This shows that, once again, a narrative is not perfect, and it comes at a cost. Israelis had to be harsh against the Palestinians whom they live among, and they are constantly being threatened, which means Israel is far from a Jewish paradise though it is the best alternative for Jews where they can live without having to worry about being oppressed by an anti-semitic government or an anti-semitic citizenry. The problems Israel has with their democracy with accusations of unequal treatment between Jews and Muslims is completely against the narrative of a fully functioning democracy where every citizen is seen in the eyes of the law as equal. Again these flaws show that Israel falls short of a fully functioning democracy along western lines, as that is an important part of the narrative of a fully- functioning democracy. Jews in other countries also have a different experience from the majority population depending on the degree of anti-semitism in those societies. So when all is said and done, they have a different story of their own to tell from the point of view of a traditionally oppressed minority. And this is how the Jews who have moved to Israel see themselves. They are tough with regards with the Palestinians living in their midst, but they do it out of an instinct to survive as they see their state at the brink of annihilation if they let their guard down. And if they don't have their own state and have to live in other countries, then they are susceptible to oppression from the majority population which is what they have historically experienced.

Chapter 7: The Nazi Narrative

When talking about narratives, the ultimate "ism" of ideologies in the twentieth century cannot be excluded. Nazism was the "ism" that caused much suffering and destruction during the century. Nazism's belief structure was not new. They were a mutation of the beliefs of German Nationalism during the previous century and European anti-semitic stereotypes since time immemorial. In the nineteenth century, when Germany was still not a nation, there was a debate among intellectuals as to how to proceed with a liberal German state.

And herein lies a big part of the problem, which would later morph into Nazism. There was a sense from the beginning that German Nationalism was not natural. It did not flow naturally from historical events but rather had to be intellectualized by intellectual elites within society. The result was a highly racial ethnic nationalism instead of the typical liberal nationalism that nation states fall under. The Nazis would later continue this tradition of intellectualizing and establishing rules about who was German based on German nationalist principles from the nineteenth century of defining who was German along racial lines. Though there were questions on what defined the German nation, whether it was language, culture, or shared history, Romanticism would be the basis of German Nationalism.[143] There would be an emphasis on cultural identity, collective self-determination, and territorial unification of racial elements later on. These were all contributing factors in the impetus to creating the Germany of today in 1871 at the Palace of Versailles in the Hall of Mirrors after two wars, one with Austria and another with France. Nazism picked up where German Nationalism left off in the nineteenth century after the humiliating terms of the Treaty of Versailles after World War I. Yes, the Nazis were angry about how they were treated due to losing the war, but they wanted to create a mythical narrative that included a lot of pagan Germanic mythology.

The German hierarchy, in the person of Heinrich Himmler, wanted to institutionalize their Germanic pagan religion, similar to how the French revolutionists attempted to do away with Christianity by creating a cult of the Goddess of Reason.[144] The Nazi beliefs included how the Germans were once pure but were debased by 'subhuman' Jews. For instance, Himmler was so interested in a book, which belonged to a private individual that he wanted to get his hands on the book, no matter what the cost. It was about

---

[143] German Nationalism. (2022, June 21). In Wikipedia. https://en.wikipedia.org/wiki/German_nationalism
[144] Religious aspects of Nazism. (2022, July 29). In Wikipedia. https://en.wikipedia.org/wiki/Religious_aspects_of_Nazism

the origins of the German people and proof of a pure Germanic tribe in the distant past.[145] The Nazi hierarchy wanted to go back to the mythical pagan Germanic religion of the past since Christianity was an offshoot of Judaism and therefore was not Germanic. They also did not believe in the tenets of Christianity about kindness and turning the other cheek as it did not promote strength but weakness.[146] The idea of the purity of the German people was a reason the Nazis wanted to "purify" their race due to the fact that they believed they were once pure. Still, their blood was "diluted" through the centuries due to the inferior 'subhuman' Jews. And their reference to themselves as the Third Reich connotes that they are the ultimate Reich. There is an implication that the Third Reich is the evolution and perfection of the previous two Reichs with the First Reich being the Holy Roman Empire which started with the coronation of Charlemagne and ended with Napoleon when he defeated the Prussians and walked into Berlin. The Second Reich was the unification of Germany in 1871 orchestrated by Otto Von Bismarck until the November

---

[145] Dirda, M. (2011, July 6). "A Most Dangerous Book'? Online the eye of the reader. The Washington Post. https://www.washingtonpost.com/entertainment/books/a-most-dangerous-book-only-in-the-eye-of-the-reader/2011/07/01/gIQAOrwS1H_story.html
[146] Rosenwald, M. S. (2019, April 20). Hitler hated Judaism. But he loathed Christianity, too. The Washington Post. https://www.washingtonpost.com/history/2019/04/20/hitler-hated-judaism-he-loathed-christianity-too/

Revolution of 1918, when Germany changed from a monarchy to a republic.

The problem with this mythologizing or mythicizing of a narrative is that it is not real and is an alternate story that you want to be told to make you and your people feel extra special. It ignores all the problems and flaws in the narrative when one studies the true history, like how the Germanic tribes which invaded Europe lived, intermarried, and integrated with the local population throughout the centuries, especially during the time immediately after the Roman Empire. It also ignores that Jews were relegated to certain professions like money lending, which lent itself to usury that Christians were not allowed to charge. This is a reason the monarchs highly valued them. The Jews had the finances and expertise, so their knowledge and resources were highly valued and protected by the crown. The masses practiced Anti-Semitism through pogroms, similar to the situation in Spain at the end of the golden age of co-existence among the three Abrahamic religions. So the Nazis continuation of anti-semitic practices by labeling them as sub-human is faulty since the stereotypes of Jews as greedy was a self-fulfilling prophecy due to the fact that they were relegated to certain professions in the past that perpetuated that stereotype.

Thus the flaws of not treating different races equally and the violence practiced by the Nazis are major flaws in the narrative and propaganda that they portray are so superior. And their search for a pure Germanic race as well as purifying the German people is just a mutation of Darwinian evolutionary theories as well as a more virulent form of German Nationalism which started in the nineteenth century run amok.

Chapter 8: Anti-Semitism in General in Connection With Nazism

When it comes to the Nazis and the German people, I will analogize it to the chicken and the egg problem. And I would argue that it is both. Anti-Semitism did not start with the Nazis and has had a long history in the West. The Nazis would not have any firm foothold if it were not for the history of antisemitism in the West. Though the Nazis would take their antisemitism to whole new levels of hate and death. Although when they started their anti-Jewish legislation and propaganda, they also won over Germans to their side, who were probably on the sidelines at best and were ambivalent.

But because of their propaganda, Germans probably thought that the Jews were now taking their jobs. They already had no feelings one way or the other for the Jews, and now according to them, they were the cause of all the problems in German society like the bad economy, loss of jobs, and the defeat in World War I. In the case of the historical past of anti-semitism, take Spain's case, for example. Though there were efforts to convert the Jews to Catholicism to correct the error of their confession, the crown was benefitting a lot from them. There was no push from above. There was a time in Spain when people of the three faiths lived amicably in society. Then the mood changed, and there was pressure on Jews to convert. There were some 'conversos' like Paul of Burgos, who was even hardcore in his Catholicism as he became an archbishop because he was a rabbi in his old faith.[147] But for a majority of conversos, they were not trusted by the Christian majority, who thought they were still secret Jews in private.[148] Motivation for the Inquisition and denouncing one's neighbors as relapsed Jews was that the conversos were gaining success in filling influential posts and getting hired for the most lucrative jobs. Some Jews would be Christians in public but Jews in private. This is a reason, to this day, merchants would hang pork for everyone to see. This practice goes back to the era of the conversos of several centuries before to prove their conversion was genuine by the fact that they were displaying their pork which means they were willing to eat it. During the Middle Ages in Spain, the monarch protected the Jews as they were needed for their skill and expertise, as told by B. Netanyahu in his book "The Origins of the Inquisition" as this was the situation in Spain in the centuries before the Inquisition was created in that country.[149] A parallel example is rich Chinese businessmen

[147] Netanyahu, B. (2001). The Origins of the Inquisition in Fifteenth-Century Spain. New York Review Books.
[148] Marrano. (2022, June 30). In Wikipedia. https://en.wikipedia.org/wiki/Marrano
[149] Netanyahu, B. (2001). The Origins of the Inquisition in Fifteenth-Century Spain. New York Review Books.

in some societies where they were part of the ruling elites or were close to the head of state who needed their money. My grandfather once said the Jews are like the Chinese in the Philippines to analogize how rich and powerful Jews are in the societies of which they were citizens. The Chinese, just like the Jews, are always a prosperous minority in the countries where they happen to migrate. Even far away from the West, the Chinese invest and show off their wealth like high-end luxury properties on the French Riviera and French wineries. This was typical, for example, in Southeast Asian countries like the Philippines, where Marcos had a lot of Chinese cronies who benefited from him and with whom he helped. And Jews of times past were typically segregated into their own ghettos, so there was not much intermixing between the races and intermarriage. Though intermarriage happened, it was not prevalent in society to change the culture and dynamics of the community.

These are ways Jews were treated throughout Europe, so the antisemitism of the Nazis had a very long historical record. And finally, the price that had to be paid to attain the objectives or end point of the Nazi narrative, which was racial purity was simply pure evil in the form of genocide and war against other European countries on the continent. So their history, as they would like to portray it, has a lot of hidden or unmentioned negative characteristics underneath

331

to support the narrative, which is supposed to be so noble on the surface. Nazism is a perfect example of a narrative where the narrative takes pride of place as the Nazis always emphasized where the German people came from, where they are and where they are headed in the future, but at the same time, it is full of flaws with all the killing and destruction. The six million Jews are not the worst for what they did. It is estimated over twenty million Soviets died. Six million Jews are thus very believable for those Holocaust deniers who do not believe in the numbers of Jews killed in the Holocaust due to the fact that the Nazis killed many others like those mentioned above, over twenty million Soviets. Again the narrative is not always perfect, and in the case of the Nazis, it is not just flawed; it was simply pure evil.

And one must also see the problems with the narrative that Nazism was an aberration in the history of the West since there has been a history of antisemitism in Europe since time immemorial. There have been pogroms and massacres of Jews throughout European history. And they have been discriminated upon and hated in the societies in which they lived. And even to this day antisemitism is still prevalent and may even be getting worse. The Nazis took antisemitism to far worse levels, but it cannot be said that they started the phenomenon since it has been a cancer in Western society for a long time.

Chapter 9: Napoleonic Narrative

As I have been living here in France, I cannot help but include Napoleon and his legacy. No painting better encapsulates the aura of his invincibility, which is a part of his narrative as the painting of David of Napoleon crossing the Alps with his horse on its two hind legs. This was propaganda for consumption at home. It was freezing in the Alps, and Napoleon was well covered from the cold. He was not even riding a horse but a mule.[150] Propaganda was everyday life for Napoleon and his government, from rigging elections to making it seem like he had an overwhelming mandate to manipulating the press to make it seem like his victories completely defeated and humiliated France's enemies. This is part of the myth of why we still think of Napoleon as this invincible general today. It was all part of the propaganda that was in effect during his reign, and history today is still eating it up to a certain extent. He is considered a hero in France, and many places here in Paris are connected to him and bear his memory. He lived in Chateau Fontainebleu, where one can see his throne with the big letter 'N.' He is entombed in the Hôtel des Invalides. Even his tomb holds pride of place at the dome of the Hôtel des Invalides. I was just watching the local news, and his two

---

[150] Bonaparte Crossing the Alps. (2022, April 2). In Wikipedia. https://en.wikipedia.org/wiki/Bonaparte_Crossing_the_Alps

hundredth death anniversary was being celebrated with Emmanuel Macron visiting his tomb, among other events. Such is the regard that the French had for this native-born Corsican who grew up to rule an empire that stretched from the Atlantic to the frozen lands of Russia. There are various places with paintings of the battles he fought or events in his life, or even various memorabilia connected to him. His hero status among the French is unquestioned. I have even seen a bust of him in a museum where he was rather muscular as if he was a regular in the gym. I am sure this was an exaggeration of his actual physique. Napoleon was born into a minor noble family in Corsica. His father could get him a scholarship to get educated in France through their nobility. French was not his maternal tongue, and he only learned the language as a child of nine or ten years old. When he started at the military academy, he did not enjoy it at first and was a fervent Corsican nationalist who wanted his homeland independent from France. Peers bullied him due to his birthplace, difficulty speaking French, and accent. Upon graduating, he was still a Corsican nationalist. He went back to his homeland to fight for the cause of Corsican independence even though Paoli, the foremost Corsican patriot, did not trust him and his family. Upon leaving and returning to France, he started to come around to the ideals of the French Revolution, and his ascent to power was sure and swift. He first gained recognition in the Siege of Toulon, where the French were able to expel the British from the harbor through his leadership skills. He would defeat a royalist insurrection in Paris. Then he would serve with distinction in the Italian campaign, followed by the expedition to Egypt. Upon returning to Paris from Egypt, he would take power in a coup helped by his brother. He would then become emperor a few years later, which was the height of his power. He won many battles against opponents with superior numbers than his forces through superior tactics and knowledge of the battlefield. Speed and maneuverability were always key with Napoleon, and his opponents would always be beaten because of their inability to maneuver fast enough. He also always knew the terrain wherein he was about to fight a battle. His best battle, Austerlitz, was his masterpiece as it destroyed the Third Coalition. He was so successful as a commander that numerous Coalitions had to be formed against him. He was not just a great military leader but also codified the law, improved education, reformed property rights, supported meritocracy, etc. The idea of meritocracy was earth-shattering as European society up to that time was very class-based, with the nobles having many rights that others did not have due to their birthright. Such is the legend and narrative of this legendary French Emperor. He also could identify with his men at their level, which made him a beloved commander.

But there are many dents in the armor of his mythical aura of greatness. For instance, his armies were known for their speed and maneuverability. In order for his armies to do this, they were ordered to 'live off the land' to not be bogged down with enormous supplies. The local populations through which his armies moved suffered through this policy of living off the land as food and whatever else was needed was taken from them. The occupied territories were also forced to pay for the cost of the occupation. Elections were also not the most honest. During the plebiscite of the French Consulate, the regime would toy with the numbers to show that the French were very enthusiastic about the regime, with almost 100% approval. This is reminiscent of the Nazis' rallies with all the pomp and pageantry to show that all Germans were supportive of Nazism. Napoleon knew the art of propaganda more than a century before Hitler and his Nazi entourage. The referendum also did not have a secret ballot, so if you were to defy the regime, you were doing so openly, which many were hesitant to do. He was also very brutal at times. For instance, in the campaign in the Near East, he allowed his soldiers to pillage after breaking into Jaffa after a siege. This was motivated in part by the way the ruler of Jaffa treated Napoleon's messenger. The messenger was decapitated, and his head was displayed at the end of a pole for all of the French forces to see.[151] Napoleon was also notorious for looting art treasures. It started in the Egyptian campaign where art treasures were taken to further 'Egyptology' as it was still a mysterious and lost civilization at this point in modern history. This did include the taking of the Rosetta stone, which was key in deciphering Egyptian hieroglyphs (which eventually ended up in the hands of the British). But be not mistaken. He did loot a lot of Egyptian artifacts like many others who visited Egypt before and after him. He took a lot of art from Italy during his campaigns there, and the taking of artworks was legalized and written into the treaties that were signed with the vanquished.[152] Napoleon also took records of the Inquisition from Rome.[153] He also took the Horses of Saint Mark upon conquering Venice. He also confiscated the four-horsed chariot on top of the Brandenburg gate after marching into Berlin after the defeat of the Prussians at Iéna and Auerstädt. He also looted Frederick the Great's tomb despite having great admiration for him and declaring that the French would not have been victorious if Frederick the Great were still alive to lead the Prussians. He also had the Duc d'Enghien executed on

[151] Roberts, A. (2015). Napoleon the Great. Penguin.
[152] Selin, S. (n.d). Napoleon's Looted Art. Imagining the Bounds of History. https://shannonselin.com/2019/04/napoleon-looted-art/
[153] Records of the Roman Inquisitions 1626. (n.d). Trinity College Dublin. https://www.tcd.ie/library/exhibitions/directors-choice/roman-inquisitions/

trumped-up charges, many historians believe. There was the affair he had with an officer's wife. He was interested in an officer's wife during the campaign in Egypt, and he wanted to spend time with her, so he sent the officer on an errand to France. This was Napoleon's opportunity to move in on the officer's wife. With this affair, Napoleon certainly showed himself to be a modern King David, as King David also had an affair with the wife of a soldier in his army. Long story short, David had the soldier killed by ordering the soldier to be positioned on the front lines of a battle where he would be killed. At least the officer with whose wife Napoleon had an affair did not meet such a cruel end as he simply wanted a divorce, and that was that.

The officer's ship was intercepted by the British, and he was sent back to Egypt, where he learned about the affair which caused their divorce.[154] He also had some military disasters, like his inability to breach the walls at Acre during his campaign in the Near East, and he lost a lot of soldiers to his failure. And who can overlook the debacle of the invasion of Russia? The retreat after occupying Moscow was a disaster. His army was no match for the Russian winter, which they were not prepared for. Only a small portion of his forces made it back alive. Though his military feats were

---

[154] Roberts, A. (2015). Napoleon the Great. Penguin.

legendary, this was a debacle that certainly put a dent in the narrative of his legend.

All these are, of course, a blow to the narrative of his mythical status among the French and further proof that not all narratives are perfect. There are always ignored or hidden things that make the narrative less appealing for posterity and historical consumption. As a matter of fact, to this day, not all art stolen by Napoleon has been restituted to the former owners of the art. An example of this is "The Wedding Feast at Cana," which is displayed at the Louvre. It was taken by Napoleon's forces, and it still has not been returned. The fact that not all art looted by Napoleon has been restituted is evidenced by the fact that an Italian worker in the Louvre stole the Mona Lisa in 1911 in the mistaken belief that it was looted by Napoleon when it has actually been legitimately in France since the time of King Francis I when the French King invited Leonardo Da Vinci to live in France in one of his properties. Though the Mona Lisa was not one of the artworks looted by Napoleon, the fact that someone would think it shows that there are still artworks in France taken by Napoleon, and the public does not know exactly what these works are. And the restitution of these works is mired in bureaucratic red tape, French dillydallying, and unwillingness to return them due to the dangers of what could happen in the journey and the costs of having them returned.

Chapter 10: The Narrative of the Conquered and Colonized Peoples

Another narrative that needs to be considered is the narrative of the colonized peoples whose culture, history, or development has been entwined with the influence of the colonizing power that has colonized them. The different colonizing powers had different priorities and objectives for their colonies. Spain was motivated by God, gold, and glory. One sees this with Spain's history in the Americas. The Spanish conquistadors under Hernan Cortes conquered the Aztecs while Francisco Pizarro conquered the Incas. This gained those two Spanish commanders and their men the glory of conquering overseas empires. They could also convert the natives to Catholicism as they were now in control. And they were also to take a lot of the gold that these native empires possessed with them, as they did not value the precious metal as the Westerners did. The natives considered gold sacred as the tears or sweat of the sun and not for its monetary value.[155] Of course, all the gold the conquistadors were able to amass and bring back to Europe caused runaway inflation which was the flip side of amassing a lot of wealth for the mother country.[156] Thus the

---

[155] Sweat of the Sun. (n.d). American Museum of Natural History. https://www.amnh.org/exhibitions/gold/golden-ages/sweat-of-the-sun
[156] Price revolution. (2022, March 23). In Wikipedia. https://en.wikipedia.org/wiki/Price_revolution

people who the Spanish were colonizing were not getting the whole narrative of Western culture and progress since the primary concern was converting souls to the one true faith. Thus the societies in the Americas turned out to be pious Catholics but were political dictatorships either through the military or through a ruling oligarchy, and they did not industrialize like the Western nations and have remained primarily agriculture producing societies. To be fair, they were kept in this state so that they would be dependent on the mother country for their needs. The colonizers typically saw the colonies as regions where they could get raw products that the mother country needed to create manufactured goods.

The Americans always believed in their form of government and the enduring qualities of their democracy which they believe makes them stand out compared to all other peoples. Due to the success of the American Revolution, the Americans instituted a democratic form of government when it was still unknown in a great portion of the world at that time. Due to this, Americans have tried to instill their form of government on the peoples they have conquered due to the fact that theirs was one of the first in the modern world, so they believe they are experts at making it work. This was done to the Philippines after gaining the islands from Spain, Japan, and Germany after their defeat during World War II and to Iraq after the victory in the war against Iraq in 2003.

The problem here is that if the foundations for democracy are not present, then there will be underlying problems that will not let the democracy develop on the Western model. There is a reason why successful democracies are few and far between and are primarily found among the industrialized nations of the West. There needs to exist a strong middle class whose interests are not opposed to the elites by leaps and bounds and who are willing to play along with the rules if they lose power. These are not present in developing societies. When democracies are imposed on them, there is a small wealthy elite, and the majority of the masses live in poverty. One class's interests are very much the opposite of the other, and when there is a government that favors one class over another, it is as though the other class' voice is being drowned out, and the only way to have their voices heard is through revolution.

I will give the example of the Philippines as Spain colonized it for hundreds of years and the US for just under half a century, and each colonizer has left its imprint on the country. Not only did Spain enforce Catholicism among the Filipino people, but Filipinos have inherited a lot of their culture from Spain. This includes food, customs, and behavior. The Spanish also let Filipinos adopt Spanish surnames.

Because of all the Spanish influence on Filipinos and the way they behave, Filipinos tend to be a culture where land is at a premium and wealthy elites tend to use and employ the cheap labor readily available all around them. And a typical comment one will hear Filipinos say is that "Well, we got this from Spain. This is just how we are." And the national hero Jose Rizal has warned the Filipinos about this.[157] The Filipinos acquired not only the cultural influences of Spain but also the bad traits. So when one sees Filipinos nailing themselves to the cross on Holy Week, it is because they inherited the intense, hard-core Catholicism of the Spaniards. So these are some aspects of the Western narrative that Spain gave, which is religion and the social, class structure.

Then the Americans took over the Philippines after winning the Spanish American War and paying Spain $20 million and then winning the subsequent Philippine-American War. Once firmly in control as the colonizing power, they had a different set of values they wanted to instill into the Filipinos, primarily government and specifically the tenets of democracy. Thus the Commonwealth was created in the mid-1930s, subsequently

---

[157] Rizal, J. (1913). The indolence of the Filipino. Manila.

suspended by World War II. The purpose of the Commonwealth was specifically to get the Philippines ready for democratic self-government. After regaining the Philippines from Japan at the end of World War II, there was only one year left of American rule before granting the Philippines independence. When the Philippines became an independent country in 1946, it learned democracy from its American masters. However, it still had the societal development and structure inherited from Spain, which controlled the Philippines for several hundred years. Thus it was still an agricultural country with a small wealthy elite and the majority of the masses living in poverty or just above it. There was not a large enough middle class similar to industrialized countries to have a solid foundation for the tenets of democracy to work. Thus, you had an elite who controlled government levers and could assure that the people elected into office maintained the status quo. This ensured that though there may be overtures and actions towards land reform, this would not be sufficient to overturn the overall structure of society and who was in charge, which was the entrenched elites. Thus democracy did not really give the masses more power but actually, in a way, kept them in their place. Plus, corruption is rampant in the Philippines, where bureaucratic red tape is filled with corrupt individuals. This means that if you need to deal with someone, you always need to shell out a bribe with each person you deal with in each step of the process as you go up the bureaucratic ladder. Suppose you want something done, whether it is paperwork for an infrastructure project or even, selling property or getting an ID like a Social Security card, bribing is a way of life in the Philippines in order for these tasks to be accomplished. When my mom and I talk about it, she says that corruption is so pervasive because people need the money. In a way, this is true.

Filipinos are always migrating to other countries or working abroad as overseas workers because there are no jobs or jobs that pay sufficient wages in the Philippines. Overseas workers play a huge part in the overall Philippine economy, and it is their wages. They are spent in the Philippines, which is the fuel of the Philippine economy. This is evidence that the Philippine economy is not large enough to accommodate the entire workforce of its citizenry which is essential in developing the local economy which is in turn good for a stable democracy to take hold. Filipino Americans are a large group among Asian Americans in American society. Filipinos are also prevalent in all areas of the world, especially in the Middle East, where many Filipinos are domestic workers or, in the case of males, construction workers. Depending on the country, Filipinos in particular countries are either in the medical field or domestic workers. Even though Filipinos need money in the

Philippines, which fuels or motivates corruption, it is not fair to paint all Filipinos with such a broad brush. Government officials usually abuse their power and live it up to the hilt. For instance, my grandfather, an appointed government official, was an upright and honest man. Still, my grandfather would take the bus sometimes to his office and was commended for it in the media. He was also offered a bribe by one of the companies regulated by the board that he belonged to, and he declined it. The money was offered to him in an envelope from how I heard the story and that it was for his' spending money when he traveled overseas. And it is not just in the Philippines, where corruption is prevalent but in many countries as well. Although there are upstanding citizens in the Philippines, there is no question that graft and corruption are pervasive. In the developing world where earning a decent wage is difficult, when people attain positions of power, they tend to abuse it by being corrupt so they can live a lavish lifestyle that they otherwise would not be able to achieve if they were not in positions of power in the government. If not for their position, they would be living miserable lives. In these regions of the world, the difference between a government position and one in the private sector could be between extravagant wealth and abject poverty. All of these societal problems do not bode well for a true, stable, Western style democracy to take shape in the mode of how the Americans would have wanted for the Philippines.

Under the Duterte administration, the Philippines has practiced a culture of impunity when it comes to the police killing individuals, like what is going on in the drug war by President Duterte, or when it comes to political assassinations perpetrated by political rivals, which seem to happen more so than normal with what you would think would be a fully functioning democracy where everybody accepts the rules of the game. All of these 'extrajudicial killings,' the term used by the media in the Philippines, are still happening despite the Philippines adopting many of the legal protections in the American legal system. For example, the Exclusionary Rule or even the Miranda warnings are given in Filipino (Tagalog) to suspects arrested for a crime. These rules protect citizens from the disproportionate power and overreach that the government can practice toward its citizens. The Exclusionary Rule does not allow evidence collected in violation of the citizen's constitutional rights. The police cannot enter houses without a warrant. They also cannot search citizens at will without probable cause. The Miranda warnings protect citizens from the abuse that police can use against a suspect to get a confession. These have been violated not only by Duterte with the killings of drug addicts but also during Martial Law in the 1970's when the constitution was suspended and the right of Habeas Corpus along with it. These are essential foundations for a fully functioning democracy where people do indeed rule and where the government cannot use its overbearing power to oppress its citizens and keep them in a constant state of fear. Thus one can conclude from all of this that though the Americans tried to mold Filipinos in their image legally and politically, Filipinos still revert to ways of doing things outside of the way Americans would have wanted them to behave due to the fact that Americans gave them their legal system.

Things also move very slowly in the Philippines, which is typical of a Hispanicized country that was cradled under the Spanish yoke. "Philippine time" is a common excuse for people being late for appointments or meetings. And bureaucratic red tape is notorious for being slow and cumbersome, which lends itself to corruption since people will want to bribe civil servants in order for their documents to move faster. This is why Duterte signed a law cutting down on red tape for businesses that need to get permits or even other things like licenses and passports.[158] Duterte realized that efficiency in government is a public service that

---

[158] Cabato, R. (2018, May 29). Duterte signs law cutting down red tape for business permits. CNN Philippines. https://www.cnnphilippines.com/news/2018/5/29/duterte-signs-zubiri-law-ease-of-doing-business-anti-red-tape-business-permits.html

cuts down on the ugly aspects of government. This is to assure that people got their documents when they needed and they can move on to other things and also to cut down on corruption. Filipinos also always tend to blame the government for all the ills in society and, in many ways, take a lack of responsibility for their own actions in order to improve their circumstances.

This is the opposite of the American mentality, where many Americans believe the government is the problem, and they want as little government as possible in their lives as they know how to best live and run their lives. This is why American democracy has a strong foundation. It is built from the ground up. The school board council meetings and town hall forums are where democracy is in action, and it is where regular citizens get their voices heard, and the American president is a distant potentate at best when it comes to the lives of ordinary citizens. Filipinos tend to blame the government for all the problems without doing anything about it themselves at the lower levels. Add to this the huge chasms in class and the divergent interests of the rich and the poor. All these class differences will further the divide among citizens, which is why Filipinos tend to look to the government to heal all these divisions, which it cannot do. All these things show that the Philippines has a long way to go to be a fully functioning democracy along Western lines,

351

let alone a Jeffersonian-style democracy despite it being groomed along the American paradigm. And due to the intense type of Catholicism that the Philippines has inherited from Spain, separation of Church and state does not exist in reality, although this is the case on paper due to the American principles of democracy that the Philippines has inherited. The church's influence in government is very strong. For instance, divorce is still illegal in the country, whereas every other nation-state has a law allowing it. There is no other reason for the law against divorce in the Philippines but for the strong Catholicism of the Filipinos and the church's influence on society and, more specifically, on government. Filipinos are also infamous for the "crab mentality" and cannot stand it when they see fellow Filipinos doing well. I have heard this term used by Filipinos to describe the relationships of Filipinos among themselves. It is called crab mentality because if you have a pile of crabs, each crab will use the other crabs to climb to the top of the pile. This basically says that Filipinos will use their fellow Filipinos to make it to the top at the expense of those Filipinos that they used. Arguably this "crab mentality" among Filipinos had an 'original sin' of sorts during the Revolutionary war against Spain. At a time when the Filipino revolutionary forces needed to be unified against the Spanish, there was a power struggle within the leadership. In short, Emilio Aguinaldo (whose descendants are our family's cousins) ended up in control of the government. When Andres Bonifacio, another important player in the revolution, refused to recognize the validity of Aguinaldo's ascendancy to the leadership, he was executed. The Filipinos, at the time, could not lose their leaders to intrigue and infighting due to the fact that Spain was already a more powerful military power as it was, and the Filipinos needed all the unity that they could muster. Then in the subsequent Philippine-American War, Filipino general Antonio Luna was assassinated under mysterious circumstances by Filipino soldiers who were supposedly under orders from Emilio Aguinaldo. This was not the best move as Antonio Luna was a very competent commander, albeit a harsh one. An American general even considered Luna the only real general that the Filipinos had.[159] The crab mentality is such a cultural problem among Filipinos that it is a problem not just among regular Filipinos but also in the higher-ups of leadership who are supposed to be above such trivial intrigues and more responsible for carrying the mantle for the national good at a time when unity was badly needed among a people who practiced so little of it. On top of this, Filipinos also had strong regional identities, which worked

[159] Szczepanski, K. (2019, August. 18). Biography of Antonio Luna, Hero of the Philippine-American War. ThoughtCo.
https://www.thoughtco.com/antonio-luna-philippine-american-war-hero-195644

against national unity against more powerful invaders even though leaders tried to forge unity as best as they could. All this spelled doom for the Filipino cause, which ended with the Philippines' surrender to the US. To make things clear, the Filipinos did not stand a chance against the superior American forces. But the infighting and intriguing within the Filipino leadership certainly did not help. This type of attitude cannot work in a fully functioning democracy where factions in government need to negotiate and "reach out across the aisle" to take the American phrase in order for things to get done and for government to function smoothly. Thus we see here that though the Philippines has adopted elements of the Western narrative from its colonizers, it is imperfect or incomplete due to the existing conditions in the country that pit one strand of the narrative against the other. The Philippines has a long way to go to have a sizable and robust middle class that can lay the foundations of a successful democracy along Western lines though this is improving as the Philippines is a place where foreign investors invest in call center agents as well as India due to the English proficiency of these societies. If the call center industry keeps growing, it may be the foundation of a pivotal middle class that can make the transition to a properly functioning democracy on Western lines. There is also the cultural jealousy Filipinos have toward fellow Filipinos that work against the forging of a successful democracy on

Western lines. Jealousy will eat one up and want the destruction of the other, which works against the proper functioning of democracy where one wins but does not then go out to destroy his or her adversary. The Duterte administration has also turned toward China and forged stronger economic ties with China and away from the traditional ally of the Philippines, the US. Maybe one can read from this not just stronger economic ties with China but also a repudiation of the rule of law that the US has given the Philippines by how Duterte acted while in office.

Once Duterte is no longer president, Philippine foreign policy may shift back again in favor of its traditional ally, the US. But the damage has already been done.

Duterte broke the narrative that the Philippines would be a democracy with the rule of law and the respect for the civil liberties of its citizens. And this can happen again with a future president should he or she decide to re-assess Philippine foreign policy and realign it again away from the West.

Another way the Philippines follows its own beat and creates its own narrative is with the election of Bongbong Marcos in a landslide victory (une victorie écrasante) to replace Rodrigo Duterte. He is, of course, the son of former dictator Ferdinand Marcos who ended democracy in the Philippines when he declared Martial Law. Let's face it. He won because of his name. He lied about his educational credentials and wasn't exactly a remarkable senator. What his voters remember is his father. Many in the West, especially the US, don't understand that many Filipinos admired Ferdinand Marcos during his twenty-year presidency because of all the accomplishments in his administration. It included all the infrastructure built like highways and such and the law and order he brought down to bear in the Philippines. Americans automatically believe that dictators in other countries are detested by their citizens. This is not always the case. A strong and efficient dictator who brings law and order and discipline to society can be an admired leader. This is incomprehensible in the West or the US, specifically because of the undemocratic nature of their rule. But many in other countries would rather have an effective and efficient leader, even if it has to exist at the expense of doing away with democratic values. This is another way the narrative in the Philippines differs from that of the US, its former colonial master. Democracy has not exactly brought about an efficient government in the Philippines because the social foundations for a fully functioning democracy like that present in the successful democracies of the West (a robust middle class) are not as strong in the Philippines, which means a dictator who can bring about progress, law, and order, and discipline will be much admired in a developing country like the Philippines because he can bring about much-needed leadership qualities that were lacking in previous administrations who were democratic. This is what they see in the election of Bongbong Marcos. Western-style democracy has not always worked well in the Philippines, which means Filipinos are willing to elect the son of a dictator in the hopes that he can bring about law and order and efficiency just like his father while at the same time turning a blind eye on all the corruption and stolen money by the Marcoses as well as all the Filipinos tortured and killed during the Martial Law years. This shows another way the narrative in the Philippines has diverged from the direction the US would have wanted the Philippines to go.

Iraq is another case where the democracy imposed upon them by the US has not worked according to script with all the factional fighting among various groups and the tendencies similar to all other Arab countries to include Islam into political discourse. There has been no history of democracy in Iraq or any other Arab country so the various factions in society do not know how to adhere to the "rules of the game" especially when it comes to politics, as there has not been a history of "reaching out across the aisles" in that region of the world. When one faction or party comes to power, it is a system wherein all other societal factions and interests have to suffer the consequences as there is no give and take, which is a hallmark of American Jeffersonian democracy and absent in other areas of the world.

Afghanistan is a perfect example where Western invaders have not had much success from the British to the Soviets and the Americans. Often called "The Graveyard of Empires," it has been a place where invaders have been bogged down and mired going back centuries to the era of "The Great Game," which were confrontations between the British and the Russians over Afghanistan to define their respective spheres of influence in and around the area. And recently, the fall of Kabul in quick fashion to the Taliban after twenty years of being ousted from power was rather shocking despite pronouncements to the contrary by the US government that such an event would not happen once American forces pulled out of the country. The speed at which the Taliban became victorious was even faster than the Nazi defeat of Poland in 1939, which took five weeks, or the defeat of France the following year, which took six weeks. Afghanistan has been a fiercely tribal society and incompatible with Western ways of a national organization. No matter how much the US wants to impose a strong central government in Kabul that exercises power over every corner of Afghanistan, the tribal nature of Afghanistan and its strong regional affiliation will always work against such a government to end its effectiveness in the long term. The problem is that conventional armies like the American military are accustomed to fighting conventional enemies with defined objectives. The goal of a military is to engage the enemy's military with a formal top-down structure; capture the government, capital city, or leader, then make them surrender at a negotiating table. This will end hostilities because these individuals with whom the winning side is negotiating have command and control over everyone underneath their command, which ends any hostility. This is the objective of any military force. In a very tribal society like Afghanistan with no top-down structure, a conventional military force will be bogged down and mired in endless fighting because there will be nobody to negotiate with that has complete control of all enemy combatants due to their tribal nature and diffused command structure. Afghanistan is a perfect example of a society that lacks a top-down central government similar to other conventional nation-states since warlords rule their strongholds throughout the country.

Japan and Germany are very good examples of the success of democracy being imposed upon them by an outside power. This is so because Japan and Germany or West Germany at that time were able to rebuild from the ashes of World War II (even though East Germany was not able to; their infrastructure still bearing the destruction of

World War II years after it ended) within a short period in the post-war period.

They were able to industrialize once again to their former selves and build a robust middle class which is the foundation of a successful democracy. Due to their understanding of the principles of democracy and the fact that their interests are not that drastically divergent from the ruling class, they can accept the rules of the game of democratic fair play. And because democracy was imposed upon them, they rebranded themselves and were able to look at their society during and shortly before World War II with a more critical lens. They now have the outlook of the victors who have imposed democracy upon them. An example of this is when stations like Deutsche Welle and Nikkei World create documentaries about the war; they are impartial documentaries and critical of their Nazi and imperial Japanese ancestors. This is evidence that they have come a long way from their former autocratic organization and world view during World War II.

Chapter 11: Bumps in the Road with Narratives

History is filled with narratives that have problems on different levels. For example, Western history is filled with narratives that are not always what they seem to be at face value. The narratives can be debunked or revealed to be flawed. The narratives are not always progressive but can be regressive, meaning society is taken a few steps back instead of improving from its former state. Narratives also always have a dark side underneath the sanitized version of the narrative. And when the Western narrative is imposed on other peoples in the form of colonization, it does not always come out as expected as the colonized peoples have their own cultures and experiences. Inspired by these great men who were connected to Paris at one time, I, too, want to contribute some intellectual theories towards this great end of learning. I intend to show in this chapter how Western Civilization is not necessarily leading to some end point where the entire world lives in liberal democracies, practices laissez-faire economics, respects human rights, and escapes their current state of poverty to become industrialized states. The Western model is not exactly a universal model that all states seek to aspire to and is not the 'natural endpoint' of all societies. There have always been bumps and setbacks throughout history, and Western history and development have not always been a natural, linear progression of development culturally and technologically. For instance, 1974 was a sort of crisis year for some of the world's leading and established democracies. Richard Nixon resigned due to the Watergate scandal and was subsequently and controversially pardoned by Gerald Ford. Chancellor Willie Brandt of West Germany resigned due to the Guillaume Affaire. In the Guillaume Affaire, Brandt's assistant Günter Guillaume was revealed to be a Stasi agent, symbolizing how entrenched East German Stasi spies were in West Germany. And though not in the same crisis level as the aforementioned two, Georges Pompidou died while in office in France. He spent his time in office on modernization efforts which were interrupted by his death in office.[160] These are examples of how democracies can also have problems and experience crisis points. And suppose established industrial democracies can experience problems. What more newly-established democracies who have not yet mastered the rules of the game and tend to go back to undemocratic ways of behavior which they had previously known before becoming democracies when faced with pivotal crisis points in their national development. An example of this would be the Philippines in 1972 when

---

[160] Georges Pompidou. (2022, July 24). In Wikipedia.
https://en.wikipedia.org/wiki/Georges_Pompidou

Marcos declared Martial Law when faced with what he claimed was a Communist insurgency about to engulf the Philippines. Some states break down after the death or removal from office of a strong or competent leader as no leader is strong enough to bring the state together and mediate between all the various factions present within society. We see this with the weakening and breakdown of the former Yugoslavia after Marshall Tito died while in power and Iraq when Saddam Hussein was ousted from power. People are accustomed to reading novels and watching movies where there is a happy ending and resolution to the storyline. We, here in the West and in the US in particular, tend to look at world history and current events that way. We like to think that all the world will be like the West someday and live in harmony where all nation-states become democratic, economically developed, wealthy, respectful of human rights, and practice laissez-faire free trade economics. Even the way nation-states are classified as developing and developed implies that all states are working toward achieving the end point of being developed like the core states in the West. Frankly, I believe this is just a pipe dream, and we just need to think of world history and current events like a soap opera or professional wrestling, where the storyline just continues, and new plots are created continuously without any happy ending or resolution. In other words, there is no utopia at the end of the tunnel where the whole world is living in peace and harmony as wealthy, technologically advanced, industrial states in accordance with the Western model. States, for example, switch sides and make friends of former enemies and enemies of former friends. This has happened throughout history. In the drama between the various Italian city-states during the Renaissance, for example, the Italian cities would switch sides and befriend the French one day, Venice another day, or the Pope, or the Holy Roman Empire based on their interests and what kept them alive from one day to the next. The American colonists fought on the side of the mother country against the French and the Indians in the French and Indian War. The French were seen as a rival power on the continent who blocked the expansion of the continent to the West by controlling the vital Mississippi River Valley. The Indians sided with the French against the English and colonists because the colonists were encroaching on their lands. In contrast, the French were more interested in trade and had no such desires on the Indian lands as the colonists. Then shortly after, during the American War of Independence, the colonists seeing their interests were different from the English mother country, fought a war of independence against them with the aid of the French, who wanted to avenge their embarrassment against the English in the French and Indian War which happened not that long ago in order to weaken the English power and influence on the continent. Then just a few decades later, during the events leading up to the War of 1812, the US seeing their interests in maritime trade as paramount, followed a policy of neutrality towards the British and French, who were engaged in their own titanic struggle in Europe. Napoleon imposed the Continental System in order to block and strangle British maritime trade by blocking it from landing at any port in Europe. And the British responded with their own counter-blockade called the Orders in Council. Though they initially genuinely tried to be neutral, the US could not help but be sucked into the conflict as the British were practicing impressment, which they asserted as a right to board American vessels and take back British nationals who were deserters. Napoleon also slyly manipulated the situation for the Madison administration to be hostile toward the British, just like how he was famous for manipulating battlefield movements to route the enemy forces in his more masterful battles.[161] The policy of impressment, though in practice, was far more sinister as the British were actually also taking Americans who had no allegiance whatsoever with Britain. Add to this the fact that the British were allies with Indian tribes who were fighting Americans and the fact that certain factions in

---

[161] Napoleon And Napoleonic Rule. (n.d). Encyclopedia.com. https://www.encyclopedia.com/history/encyclopedias-almanacs-transcripts-and-maps/napoleon-and-napoleonic-rule

American politics coveted conquering Canada, and you have a recipe for a war against Britain. This war obviously gave the US the self-confidence it needed since it did not end in disaster for the young republic, even though its power was nowhere near the level of the great powers in Europe. For most of the nineteenth century, the relationship that the US had with either the French or the British was rather cold and distant as the US was a rising power and trying to challenge the status of the established powers like Britain and France. During the US Civil War, for instance, the British and the French practiced a policy of neutrality as best as they could. In reality, there was a need for the raw goods that the South produced, like Cotton, so the French and the British were able to make some trade of this commodity in exchange for arms which the South needed against the North, which had an industrial economy and was, therefore, more capable of producing weapons for their troops. Then a generation later, the US engaged in the Spanish-American War because it wanted to play with the great powers and be seated at the table, so to speak of the Imperialist powers. The US wanted to be seen as an equal of the old world European powers. The alliance between the US, the British, and the French did not solidify until the early part of the twentieth century during the First World War, which continued into the Second World War. The point here is that there are no BFFs (Best Friends Forever) when it comes to national self-interests in world affairs. It is much more akin to a dog-eat-dog world. Yesterday's enemies could be today's friends. There is no linear narrative where everyone just becomes good friends, and it will stay that way happily ever after.

A good example of this principle would be the complex relationship of the Israelis with their Arab neighbors. Basically, when Israel declared itself a state in 1948, it had only enemies among its neighbors. As time went on and as the Arab states kept losing war after war, one Arab state after another slowly if reluctantly, became friends with Israel as they saw it in their best self-interests in accordance with the principles of realpolitik. And even though these Arab countries have officially made friends with Israel and are no longer hostile toward the Jewish state, there are still huge segments of their population that are anti- Israel and Pro-Palestine. The governments of these countries thus have to do a balancing act on how they speak to their people about Israel and how they treat Israel in their bilateral relations. The way the international community sees Israel is also in flux. It is now seen negatively by many internationally for the way they treat the Palestinians in the occupied territories and how they build settlements arguably illegally under international law in the territories. In times past, they were seen in a more positive light. This was especially true after the Six-Day War, when Israel was on the brink of defeat by a coalition of Arab countries who were bent on doing away with Israel. It was seen as the underdog during that war in 1967. When it surprisingly defeated its Arab enemies in six days, Israel was cheered by much of the world for beating insurmountable odds.[162] One would also think that the world learned a lot from the Holocaust and improved its treatment of Jews. However, this is not the case as there is still a lot of anti-semitism today. There is no improvement or progression in how Jews are treated. One would think we would all be aware of how Jews were treated in the past and learn from history, which is what we are supposed to do, which is a major reason why we study history. We see anti-semitism today in violent acts against Jews or anti-semitic slurs. It is important to compartmentalize anti-Israeli sentiment and anti- semitism as they are not one and the same. One is standing up against the policies of Israel vis-a-vis the Palestinians. The other is hatred of Jews because of who they are.

However, some elements of the anti-Israeli crowd are also anti-semitic. This cannot be denied. These examples show the changing nature of politics and history with shifting alliances which I have mentioned is akin to a mid-day soap opera or professional wrestling with its changing

---

[162] Six-Day War. (2022, July 29). In Wikipedia. https://en.wikipedia.org/wiki/Six-Day_War

storylines, and those who are good guys one day can be heels the next. And citizens may act and behave differently from their government's policies. And just because a group has been treated badly in the past, like the Jews, does not mean that the world has learned from it, and the treatment of said people will now improve, and they will live happily ever after. It just is not so in the real world. This is another reason for the need for a Jewish state in Israel. When things go bad for Jews somewhere, they have a state they can migrate to that they can call their own, where they will not be oppressed for being who they are. A perfect example of the changing status and reputation of states is Japan and Germany. Clearly, in the West and in much of the world, these two nations were seen as 'bad guys' during World War II with all the atrocities they committed, but in the aftermath of World War II, they have remade themselves into peace-loving nations which is a perfect example of the changing nature of history and politics with its plotlines constantly in flux. They were heels before, but now they are 'good guys' to use the parlance of professional wrestling. Japan does not even have offensive military capabilities, only self-defense capabilities. Germans today also have a phobia of having a substantial military. They are also cynical of too much government interference permeating their lives. Both Japan and Germany today are concentrating on their manufactured exports like cars and electronics. This is one of the reasons why the US has a high military expenditure, so states like Japan and Germany do not have to shell out military costs on their own. In the case of Japan, they are power players in the realm of video games and electronics in general. Germany exports high-quality luxury cars among its many exports.

That said, there is also no historical progression toward world peace in how nations behave despite making all efforts with that objective in mind. In our present day, there are all the international organizations of nation-states like the EU, ASEAN, the AU (African Union), UNASUR (Union of South American Nations), and of course, the all-encompassing one that includes most if not all of the world, the UN.

These international organizations, whose goal is to cooperate economically and peacefully, have not stopped social conflicts around the globe, which still plague humanity. The Civil War in Syria is a major one that has caused mass migrations of Syrians to other regions like Europe, which has caused social tension in European countries in turn. Thus the linear progression of development is extremely flawed as states, superstates, and international organizations often face setbacks and regressions. The expression one step forward, two steps back is a very apt analogy in politics and international affairs. In the present day, we see this in the Arab Spring, where things are still in flux a decade after the events and are still nowhere near the stage of linear development along western lines (i.e., liberal democracies).   Even events in Hong Kong where they experienced Western-style freedoms under British rule are now slowly but surely falling under the grip of Beijing, which has resulted in widespread and sometimes violent protests. And in Myanmar, the citizens experienced a certain amount of freedom but have had their democracy taken away under a crackdown of military rule when the military did not like the election results. Thus the result was bloody riots as the citizens of Myanmar were not willing to give up the freedoms that they had won. Thus this is another example of a setback or regression, if you will, from a society of hard-won freedoms moving backward and returning under repressive military rule. And in the Philippines, the masses elected a crude-speaking man who was perceived to be 'one of them' who then commenced a brutal crackdown on drug users and traffickers. He has also not afforded them a lot of their rights under the law, to the ire of some groups in the Philippines and too much of the international community, including international tribunals. And who could forget the Marcos dictatorship when Marcos, a democratically elected president, declared Martial Law before his second term was about to end, turning the only democratic country in Asia into a dictatorship. All this happened decades into Philippine self-rule when the Philippines was groomed to be a Western-style democracy similar to the US during the commonwealth period of the mid-1930s and after independence was granted shortly after World War II in 1946. It had problems early on in the post-war years immediately after World War II with Communist rebels in the countryside in the form of the Hukbalahap, but the Philippines was able to pull through these trials with American help in the person of Edward Lansdale, who helped the Filipinos against these Communist rebels and who certainly had a hand in the election of Ramon Magsaysay to the presidency.[163] This democracy was tested under the Marcos administration with his declaration of Martial Law and then again during the Duterte administration with his flaunting of human rights and civil rights against drug users and dealers. And obviously, the US, a nation that has a long-established history of democracy with a line of presidents who were willing to accept the rules of the game and knew how to behave in a proper presidential manner, elected someone who flaunted all those norms openly to the anger of many of the American left and center and much of the world at large who looked up to the United States as a model of a fully functioning democracy and as 'the shining city upon a hill" as Reagan described it. Who

[163] Edward Lansdale. (2022, August 4). In Wikipedia. https://en.wikipedia.org/wiki/Edward_Lansdale

would think that in 2016 someone who was so crude and outspoken as Donald Trump and who would outright say racist and other tactless and outrageous things would be elected as President? This definitely does not go along with the narrative that the US has become less racist and more open to other ethnic and religious groups as American history would suggest or imply through the teaching of its historical narrative to school students and the larger public by such factions as the media or the school curriculum. There is no end point in American society where we all work and achieve a utopia where every race, creed, and sexual orientation will live in perfect harmony and happily ever after. The law may no longer support racist laws like Jim Crow or immigration quotas based on race which means that there is indeed legal improvement when it comes to discrimination. However, there is still prejudice boiling below the surface, like apprehensive feelings towards immigrants or companies not hiring based on race or sexual orientation. We as a society need to shine a light on it and combat it in all its forms whenever it rears its ugly head.

Another perfect example of the regression of the narrative in recent years is how Vladimir Putin has tried to divide the West and create chaos within and among the nation-states of the West, thus trying to make his own mark in tearing to shred the progress the West has made, and thus he is trying to create cracks and fissures in the Western historical narrative. Europe has always been mired in war (quite a number of which were on a massive scale) for centuries upon centuries, and so it is only natural that Europe works together and find common cause in a union where all European states are working together peacefully and harmoniously toward economic prosperity on the continent. They are states that need to interact with each other, whether it be peacefully or through war. They have already experienced the ravages of war throughout the centuries through numerous wars like the Thirty Years' War which laid waste to the Holy Roman Empire (present-day Germany for the most part), and the Napoleonic Wars, which left scars on the entire continent. Naturally, the progression towards peaceful relations and peaceful co-existence is how the narrative should progress in theory and what Europe, through the EU, is working towards. Putin, however, has other designs. He wants the various European nation-states going on just like always and advancing their own self-interests at the expense of their neighbors. Putin did this by supporting Trump as Trump is seen as trying to weaken the Western Alliance by forcing fellow NATO members to increase their share of defense expenditure. Putin realizes that the West is more unified today than it has been in the past, which does not bode well for Russian interests as the Russians no longer have the Communist East and the 'Iron

Curtain' as a buffer against an 'imperialist' West that the Soviets, the Russians' predecessors, had. So he has to fight back with the twenty-first-century tools embodied by the internet and social media via hackers and trolls. Some Russian hackers did the government's bidding by creating fake user accounts and spreading 'fake news' in favor of Trump and against his opponent Hillary Clinton. It was also in his best interest that Brexit happened as it has weakened the EU as an important member has left it. One need only look back to Russia's history to find the explanation of why it behaves the way it does. Russia has not always developed at the same pace as its European neighbors especially Western European states. Russia was one of the last holdouts to serfdom and the feudal structure when Western Europe had already firmly done away with the system. The Russian Revolution in the early twentieth century also happened rather late compared to other revolutions. The Western European powers were already industrial imperialist powers at this time when Russia was still getting its act together. And today even though most of the European states are democracies, Russia is still one of the last holdouts in Europe to have an autocratic government. One sees here the slow progress of Russia compared to its other continental neighbors which explains why Putin behaves the way he does. These are some examples of how the Western model or narrative has flaws and has not ideally worked out how the West wants to portray its history or narrative.

The bottom line is that there are always problems with narratives, whether it is a Western or non-Western society. There will be setbacks, ugly sub-narratives hidden under the surface, and problems when imposing one's narrative on other societies that have their own. Instead of thinking of societies as having a storyline with a happy ending, one needs to just see them as continuous plots with twists and turns without really any firm and happy resolution at the end. One just has to continue and move on from one plot line to the next. It does not matter how good the narrative is supposed to be like that of the US with its tale of democracy and equal rights for all; there are still flaws in it like racism and such, and the huge flaws in the American image with the Trump presidency. All of this will be shown with the various narratives of the various societies and time periods throughout history. This is similar to marketing. We use marketing to create something desirable for others, whether it be hiding or masking whatever flaws something being marketed might have. It is the same with history and narratives. People, cultures, or prominent figures would want to market themselves to make them seem extraordinary or flawless to posterity. And it is the narrative that needs to be unraveled to see the reality hiding underneath.

Chapter 12: Narratives and Their Flaws

There are many historical narratives apart from the Western historical narrative due to people's unique circumstances and experiences in a geographical area and their encounters and behaviors towards others and their environment. Their narratives are their own and, when judged compared to the Western way of development, would be unjust and illogical, especially if a Western way of life or narrative is taken as a whole in all its aspects: economic, social, political, cultural. Some other non-Western societies may absorb one or two strands of the Western narrative to the detriment of the others. The reason for this is the way the West developed throughout the centuries. This has positioned the West to develop the way it did economically, politically, technologically, and culturally, etc., basically due to its unique circumstances geographically and socially, which was fertile ground for its development from the Dark Ages to the advanced developed societies of today.

When the West has tried to impose its narrative or its way of life on other societies through colonization, the colonized people only get one strand of the narrative and not the whole, whether it is religion or free trade (though this was done for the benefit of the colonizer) or through a liberal democratic government. And even when they receive this from their Western colonizers, there are usually problems. The colonized do not develop the Western narrative imposed on them as well as their colonizers in the colonizers' societies due to the different circumstances between the various societies. And even in the West like the United States, there are problems with the narrative that they have imposed upon themselves with its lofty goals and ideals. We see this in recent years with the presidency of Donald Trump as he has race-baited and flouted all the presidential norms through his speeches and behavior. It has been said that Trump was a disruptor. He disrupted not only the political establishment; he was also a disruptor of the narrative. Since he has sparked the anger of certain racist factions of society, he has set race relations a few steps back with his rhetoric. And problems with the American narrative can also be seen in society with the police killing of black men and the resulting Black Lives Matter movement in response to these racially divisive killings, as well as problems with systemic racism with blacks still living to an extent in racially segregated neighborhoods and their standard of living lower than their white counterparts. This can be seen in the busing controversy in decades past and the racial protests that accompanied it. In Boston, for example, blacks have a median net worth of $8 while their white Bostonian neighbors are worth around $250000.[164] This shows that racial problems have no geographical limitations, with Northern liberal 'blue' states having as many racial problems as any other area of the country. One would not normally associate racism and racial problems with those 'left leaning' states. When I was younger, I, too, thought that perhaps racism was related to geography, with some areas of the country being racist or more racist while other parts were not. I lived in New Orleans, which is still a rather racially segregated city. Metairie is a predominantly white suburb, while downtown and New Orleans East is predominantly black.

I also lived in the San Francisco Bay Area, the Twin Cities, and LA. In these three areas where there is more racial diversity, I always thought that there was less racism or none at all since the neighborhoods as I saw them were more racially diverse. Of course, there are also racial problems in these urban areas with police and blacks. Racial tensions abound, Rodney King, George Floyd; the list goes on and on. There were also historically restrictive covenants based on race in California, including liberal, progressive areas within the state like the San Francisco Bay Area, with language in

[164] Brown, A. (2021, March 5). Boston Federal Reserve: Black Boston Families Have Net Worth of $8 And White Families $250k. The Moguldom Nation. https://moguldom.com/344217/boston-federal-reserve-black-boston-families-have-net-worth-of-8-and-white-families-250k/

covenants that stated that real estate could only be sold to whites. Many Filipinos immigrated to towns in California like Stockton, where they had their own little community called "Little Manila." These Filipinos experienced a lot of hostility, violence, and discrimination from the majority white population. Businesses had "No Filipinos" signs.[165] The Filipino club was even bombed in Stockton in 1930.[166] All this is proof that discrimination has no borders and has had a history as well in what today are left-leaning "blue states." In Europe, I also thought the Germanic countries were probably more racist than the Latin countries, where racial purity was not a big issue compared to the premium on racial purity that the northern peoples of Europe believed in, which I also believed. Of course, there is racism in France, Italy, Spain, and other countries as well besides the Germanic countries. Now that I am older, I no longer believe these theories that I had when I was younger. I now realize that racism does not have geographic boundaries. Germany can also be a good example where the narrative does not work and has run into problems. Germans would like to think that racism died with the defeat of Hitler and the Nazis in

[165] Owed, M.T. (n.d). 'Positively No Filipinos Allowed'. POSITIVELY FILIPINO. http://www.positivelyfilipino.com/magazine/positively-no-filipinos-allowed
[166] Mardo, P. (2018, April 11). Why We Need To Remember Stockton, California's Filipino American Legacy. BuzzFeed. https://www.buzzfeed.com/paolamardo/stockton-california-little-manila-center-vandalism-history

World War II and that today Germany is a multi-racial/cultural society that has learned from its Nazi past and has made a better society out of it. But if one were to look closely at German society today, this is not the case. Anti-semitism is on the rise, as well as right-wing ultra-nationalism that is anti-semitic as well as anti-immigrant.[167] Protests by these far-right groups all over the country are broadcast on the news. Even in the post-World War II period immediately after the war, with the intense de-Nazification program in Germany, not all Nazis were purged. Many escaped to other countries and continents like South America and were never brought to justice. Otto Skorzeny, according to the Israeli Mossad, was located by them in Spain and recruited to work for them to weed out German scientists working for the Egyptian missile program.[168] In West Germany, many former Nazis made it into the post-war government. An example was Hans Globke. Globke supported the discrimination of Jews during the Nazi regime, which was a precursor to the Holocaust. After the war, he was one of the most influential figures in the government of Konrad Adenauer. East Germany used the fact that West

---

[167] Germany sees spike in anti-Semitic crimes-reports. (n.d). DW. https://www.dw.com/en/germany-sees-spike-in-anti-semitic-crimes-reports/a-56537178

[168] Prateek, D. (July 21). The Strange Case of Hitler's Bodyguard Who Became an Agent for Mossad. History of Yesterday. https://historyofyesterday.com/the-strange-case-of-hitlers-bodyguard-who-became-an-agent-for-mossad-87086a765320

Germany had former Nazis in their government as propaganda against West Germany that it was simply a continuation of Nazi Germany. There was a strong left-wing student movement in West Germany motivated by the sins of their parents' generation and galvanized by the death of student Benno Ohnesorg who was shot to death during a protest by a police officer (a Stasi agent, as was revealed only recently many decades after the fact) and the shooting of political activist Rudi Dutschke.[169] Rudi Dutschke put fuel to the fire of anti-establishment sentiment with rallies on University campuses where students chanted slogans like "Ho Ho Ho Chi Minh" against what they saw was American imperialism. The killing of Ohnesorg and the shooting of Dutschke morphed elements of the left-wing student movement into a more violent movement. The Communist terrorists in West Germany in the 1960s and 1970s, embodied by the Baader-Meinhof gang, were motivated by these unrepentant Nazis who were prominent in West German society, along with what they saw as government hostility toward the left. Their killing and destruction put West German society on edge during those decades. An example of this was the kidnapping and subsequent murder of German industrialist and former SS officer Hanns Martin

---

[169] Leicht, J. (2009, June 3). 1967 police murder of West German student was committed by a Stasi agent. (ICFI). World Socialist Web Site. https://www.wsws.org/en/articles/2009/06/stas-j03.html

Schleyer.[170] These are examples of how Germany did not become a shining light of tolerance after the war but still had racial and other social problems which continued throughout the decades after World War II, and they did not completely eradicate all culpable Nazis after the war, thus shattering the myth that they may want to believe about themselves in connection to their historical narrative. Even other developed countries had formidable left wing/Communist movements. In Italy the Red Brigades kidnapped and eventually killed Aldo Moro, leaving his body in the trunk of a car that was found on a street in Rome. In Japan there was the infamous Asama-Sansō incident where the United Red Army engaged in a bloody purge of its members and broke into a holiday lodge taking a woman hostage. The standoff which lasted ten days ended in a police assault of the lodge where two officers were killed before the URA radicals were taken into custody. This incident caused a decline in popularity toward leftist movements in Japan.[171] All this shows how other countries also had social problems in the post World War II era especially with regards to the flaring up of left wing/Communist movements and that not everything was smooth sailing in these democracies. Though it cannot be

[170] Edel, U. (Director). (2008). Der Baader Meinhof Komplex [Film]. Constantin Film Produktion.
[171] Asama-Sansō incident. (2022, August 3). In Wikipedia. https://en.wikipedia.org/wiki/Asama-Sansō_incident

denied that Communist movements were much stronger in developing countries where there was a much stronger base of support among the impoverished masses who probably saw communism as their way out of their miserable lives.

Even other European countries, who suffered under the Nazis and would argue that they were forced by the Nazis to give up the Jews in their countries are now experiencing a rise in antisemitism masking as right-wing nationalism. One can see this in right-wing ultranationalist rallies in various countries all over Europe on the overarching issue of immigration into Europe. Even in 1960s Poland, under Communist rule, Jews were discriminated against and pressured to leave. This was especially virulent in the wake of the Six-Day War when the ruling regime considered Israel the aggressor and thought Jews in the country were not really loyal citizens and therefore traitors to Socialism.[172] There were thousands upon thousands of Jews who left the country and renounced their Polish citizenship. This is an example of anti-semitism even after all the horrors that Jews suffered after World War II, just a little over two decades after the war. Today, immigration into Europe from the Middle East from places like Syria has increased due to war and social upheaval. Pegida is making headlines and making their

---

[172] Bala, A. (n.d). Anti-Semitism in Poland after the Six-Day War, 1967-1969. NOT EVEN PAST. https://notevenpast.org/anti-semitism-in-poland-after-the-six-day-war-1967-1969/

voices heard to be a veritable political force to be reckoned with to counter the establishment by the immigration-friendly Angela Merkel. Even in everyday life, Jewish schoolchildren sometimes face bullying from classmates for being Jewish.[173] As the horrors of World War II are fading from memory and the Germans who were alive to experience the horrors of what happened to the Jews are dying, a new generation of Germans is growing. They are the ones who have not experienced how their forefathers treated the Jews during the Holocaust and are now thus more insensitive toward Jews in their midst. Their numbers are growing more and more prevalent in society, resulting in incidents against Jews in schools and in public. From a psychological standpoint, this makes sense since in the decades after World War II, many of the Germans who were alive and experienced the horrors against the Jews had a sense of collective guilt that this was done in their name. So they had to make up for it by being more sensitive against anti-semitism in their midst due to the extremes that could result from such behavior. This is borne out by the fact that we have heard stories of the war from our grandparents or parents, which means they are first-hand accounts and not second-hand accounts that one reads in books. I have personally

---

[173] DW News. (2018, January 25). Living in fear: How anti-Semitic is Germany? | DW English [Video]. Youtube. https://www.youtube.com/watch?v=QiEeFNqMAOc.

heard stories of my grandparents about what happened during the war. In the future, when the people who were alive die out, then the force of the emotions that come through in their stories will no longer be present. We cannot hear stories about the Napoleonic Wars first-hand from someone who experienced it.

We have to read it in books, and the force just is not the same. We do not feel the pain that the storyteller felt from being there. This is a reason why we usually hear of the glories of the French during the Napoleonic Wars, and the pain that their occupation forces have caused usually gets drowned out in the narratives about Napoleon. But be not mistaken, Napoleon and his armies were brutal and cruel when they had to be.

They lived off the land to the detriment of the civilian populations of the areas they were occupying, and they extracted as much money as they could from the occupied peoples to pay the costs of the occupation. Since World War II, Holocaust survivors that are still alive can still relay their stories to those who were not alive during World War II and, along with it, the pain and suffering they felt with how they tell the stories. As future generations who did not experience the suffering first-hand tell the stories, the pain that the Holocaust survivors felt cannot be passed on to the recipients of the stories. This is why anti-semitism is very likely to come back when the stories of the Holocaust fade into memory. In post-World War II Germany, except for die-hard, unrepentant Nazis, most Germans who did not support such extremist behavior felt guilt and wanted to make amends for what happened during the Nazi regime that was done in their name. Some of this collective guilt showed itself in policies towards Israel, like secret arms shipments that were being sent to Israel up until the 1960s.[174] Many Germans did not support Nazi policies. However, they had no choice due to the brutal nature of the regime, so they just kept quiet, and some may have supported some of the Nazi grievances like the humiliating way the Germans were treated under the Treaty of Versailles. Some may have supported some anti-semitic measures against the Jews but in no way envisioned the horrors of the death camps. Not all were ardent, passionate, and unrepentant Nazis, and the majority of guilt-ridden Germans were used to build the foundations of a new post-war Germany. The current generation of Germans does not have that same sensitivity as they were not alive during the war. And if they did not live it, then they would have no idea of the cruelty that certain people experienced during that historical time period. And

---

[174] Aderet, O. (2014, February 27). How Israel Tried to Conceal Its Biggest Arms Deal With Germany. Haaretz.
https://www.haaretz.com/2014-02-27/ty-article/.premium/israels-secret-arms-deal-with-germany/0000017f-f6c8-d887-a7ff-feecf4e80000

the reason General Eisenhower ordered his men to film the brutalities in the camps was so that it could not be denied by anyone who did not witness it or by future generations that it did not happen.[175] German civilians were even made to walk through the camps to see the dead bodies in order to show them what was done in the name of their government. Mothers were covering the eyes of their children as they were passing through in order to spare them the carnage. These civilians had to bury the corpses and do whatever else needed to be done to somehow rectify the horrific scenes of depravity. Footage of the dead bodies in the camps was shown during the Nuremberg trials as evidence against the accused. The Dachau Massacre was a reprisal committed by American soldiers against the Germans in the camp due to the horrors that the Americans had witnessed committed in the name of the Third Reich.[176] For the American soldiers to be so worked up as to commit what were arguably war crimes against the Germans in the camp shows the brutality and the depravity that happened at Dachau, just like many other camps. As all of this fades into memory, the less sensitive present-day Germans and everybody else will be toward anti-semitic acts, no matter how minor or major. This

---

[175] You Kwang-On. (2019, August 9). General Eisenhower Ordered to Film Nazi Concentration Camps [Video]. Youtube. https://www.youtube.com/watch?v=hC6XLt6SnA4
[176] Dachau liberation reprisals. (2022, August 6). In Wikipedia. https://en.wikipedia.org/wiki/Dachau_liberation_reprisals

problem of present-day anti-semitism is not just relegated to Germany. This can be seen in Eastern European countries as well, which do not have the economic power to absorb immigrants that Germany has. Even in France, for example, with the most number of Jews in any European country, anti-semitism is alarmingly on the rise, and an increasing number of them are leaving France and immigrating to Israel. Though the French may not want to admit it, nor do they like to categorize themselves on stats by race, it is rather evident that many of these crimes are committed by citizens of Muslim backgrounds. Those French Jews leaving France and migrating to Israel are moving to Netanya, which is considered a sort of French Riviera in Israel.[177] These are still problems in Germany and Europe in general, even though the horrors of the Holocaust are long past.

---

[177] DW Documentary. (2018, November 8). Antisemitism in Europe | DW Documentary [Video]. Youtube. https://www.youtube.com/watch?v=CD1LuZtBAZo

Epilogue

Narratives are not perfect. There are always problems with narratives, no matter how the society relaying their narrative wants to portray them. There is not always a linear progression of improvement in society as there will always be problems and setbacks. And narratives, no matter how ideal and perfect they are made out to be, have problems underneath that are either overlooked, brushed aside, or intentionally hidden. Although the Roman Empire portrayed itself as civilized and militarily powerful, it had an ugly dark side to its greatness. Their civilization was built on the backs of exploited slave labor which came boiling to the surface in the slave revolt of Spartacus. And even though they had great leaders like the Caesars, they had some bad ones as well, like Caligula, who had acted insane when he was emperor. We see this with the Napoleonic narrative. The French put Napoleon on a pedestal and saw him as the greatest Frenchman to ever live who, in some eyes, had attained a godlike status.

However, his narrative is not perfect. He was responsible for grave atrocities, manipulated elections, massacres, looted art, etc. The Nazis wanted to portray their society as the perfection of the German race and the final Reich of the German people, the previous two Reichs simply improving on their way to the third and final Reich.

But their narrative is filled with violence towards Jews, the Soviets, and all the countries they invaded who came across their path. They believed in mysticism and the occult and thought this would have magical powers that would carry them to victory even though they were very scientific with their advanced weapons. They also were the beneficiaries of the German mantle of scientific excellence among the European peoples. The narratives of non-Western societies are incompatible with the Western narrative or did not go through the same historical progression as the West. These societies will not absorb the Western narrative in the same way they have had their own historical experiences, which will be incompatible with Western ways. They may reject the Western narrative wholeheartedly, or if they do accept it, they will make it their own different from how the West adopted it. Or they could revert to their old ways of doing things when the going gets tough when it comes to obstacles in continuing with the Western narrative like going back to despotism etc. This can happen when a democratically elected leader is seen as incompetent or weak, which precipitates a military coup d'etat. This is seen in Chile when Salvador Allende was ousted by the military led by Pinochet or, more recently, when the military overthrew the democratically elected government of Ann San Suu Kyi in Myanmar because they claimed the election was not fair.

And there are the societies that just did not develop the modern nation-state system like Afghanistan, where the West will be hard-pressed to impose anything seeing as Afghanistan is a very tribal society ruled by local warlords who will have more sway with their people than any central government that the US can impose in Kabul. However, there have also been problems even with the West and their own narrative of progression going back to the Dark Ages all the way to the Fourth Industrial Revolution. It has not been clean, as there have been setbacks and problems with the narrative throughout its history. First of all, the Roman Empire, with its high civilization and immense knowledge, gave way to the Dark Ages, where Western Civilization regressed in its progression toward advancement. And the various ages like the Age of Faith and the Renaissance had ugly sides to their narratives as the Age of Faith was marked with rigorous enforcement of belief toward orthodoxy and the one true faith, and the Renaissance also was a time of violence between the Italian city-states, the bastions of all this new-found knowledge that was lost for so long. The Enlightenment with the French Revolution took things too far as they wanted to do away with the Catholic Church all together in society and replace it with a state religion. Even the Industrial Revolution, which was a tremendous technological leap forward, was marked by massive pollution in cities and dangerous conditions for factory workers. The US, with its narrative of democracy and American exceptionalism, has had problems with its narrative from the nation's very founding. Slaves were not considered people during the negotiations for the Constitution. And the North was not free from blame as they exploited their factory workers in less than safe conditions in the factories. These dueling narratives between the North and the South leading up to the Civil War were founded on exploiting those marginalized in society and not seen as important in the social order. These were the ugly underbellies of the Northern narrative, which was based on economic and technological progress with their factory-based economy, and the Southern narrative with their leisurely southern way of life and chivalric behavior. And throughout American history, there has always been a nativist and anti-immigrant strain that has reared its ugly head. We see this with the Know-Nothing Party in the mid-nineteenth century and in our times today with Trump and the illegal immigration problem that he always repeated in his pronouncements. Then the gains made for blacks during Reconstruction were erased after Reconstruction ended and Union troops left the South. The advances made for different groups during the 1960s came at a price, as all the protests and violence made it seem like the fabric of American society

393

was getting torn apart. And just when we thought Jim Crow and racism were far behind us, we have someone like Trump elected who showed that there are still many nativist and racist elements in society waiting to float to the surface if given the proper encouragement. The US Supreme Court has also recently overturned Roe v. Wade which legalized abortion in 1973. This shows social regression in the historical narrative as a right that women had for almost fifty years has now been taken away. Depending on where you are in the political spectrum, if you are a social progressive this smacks of authoritarianism since the state can now control what a woman can do with her body. Thus the US, which is supposed to have its act together and is this great democracy where everybody gets treated equally regardless of race, gender, religion, sexual orientation, etc., still has some major flaws if one were to look at American society just underneath the surface of its tremendous rhetoric. Thus I have shown in this book that all eras and societies have their faults and are not perfect no matter how they make themselves out to be, and in the US, we saw all the social problems come up to the surface during the Trump years. And finally, it is not even a sure-fire thing that all of the world will eventually be democracies as the West, especially the US, believes all nations will eventually evolve to become. In a town hall meeting, Biden said that Xi Jinping and Putin did not believe that democracy was the form of government that would win out in the twenty-first century. This is certainly against the Western narrative that their form of government can and will be exported to all corners of the earth and that it will eventually be the type of government that all the world is working towards. All this shows that narratives can be dissected, destroyed, and revealed with all their flaws laid bare.

Index

Abe, Shinzo, 271
Acqua Alta, 34
Adams, John, 14
Aguinaldo, Emilio, 199, 289, 352, 353
Alaric, 32, 118
Alfred the Great, 65
Allende, Salvador, 181, 391
al-Sahhaf, Mohamed Saïd, 165
Ancien Regime, 120, 141
anti-semitic, 71, 140, 323, 324, 327, 368, 381, 387
Anti-Semitism, 327, 329, 384
Antony, Mark, 30
Arab Spring, 116, 371
Archduke Ferdinand, 97
Armas, Carlos Castillo, 180
Arminius, 27, 28
Asama-Sansō incident, 383
Attila, 32, 33, 86
Auschwitz, 144
Austerlitz, 336
Avicenna, 302
Avignon Papacy, 43
Aztecs, 342
Baader-Meinhof gang, 382
Babylonian Captivity, 43
Baghdad Bob, 165

Balangiga Bells, 198, 199
Barka, Mehdi Ben, 21
Batista, 178, 179
Battle of Actium, 30
Battle of Lepanto, 304
Battle of Port Arthur, 260
Battle of the Teutoburg Forest, 28
Belle Epoque, 19
Berlin crisis, 188
Berlin Wall, 188, 195, 215, 248, 249, 299, 300
Biden, Hunter, 210, 214, 271
Biden, Joe, 4, 7, 150, 167, 201, 202, 210, 232, 271, 274, 277, 395
Big Lie, 168, 231
Bismarck, Otto Von, 326
Black Death, 53, 56
Black Lives Matter, 131, 378
Blinken, Antony, 20
Boebert, Lauren, 276
Bonifacio, Andres, 353
Bourbon Restoration, 120, 138, 141
Bourbons, 122, 123, 139
Brandt, Willie, 362
Brexit, 91, 93, 94, 195, 375
Brooke, Sir Alan, 190, 192

Brown v. Board of
Education, 148
Brutus, 53
Burisma, 210
Bush, George W., 221
Caesar, Augustus, 30
Caligula, 390
Calvinists, 73
Capetian Dynasty, 65
Capitol Insurrection, 111,
114, 117, 150, 231, 238
Cardinal Richelieu, 74
Carlos the Jackal, 20, 21
Carlson, Tucker, 173
Carter, Jimmy, 166
Cassius, 53
Catharism, 40
Cawthorn, Madison, 276
Charlemagne, 37, 50, 326
Charles X, 122
Charlie Hebdo, 125, 127
Charney, Geoffrey de, 43
Checkpoint Charlie, 299
Chicago Democratic
Convention, 240
Christmas Carol, 79
Churchill, Winston, 9, 10
Cid, El, 64
Civil Rights Act, 119,
140
Clark Air Base, 194
Clash of Civilizations,
189, 190
Cleopatra, 30
Cleveland, Grover, 274
Clinton, Bill, 168, 212,
314

Clinton, Hillary, 6, 270,
375
Clinton, Roger, 212
Colby, William, 188
Cole, Thomas, 117
Commodore Perry, 306
communism, 81, 178,
188, 215, 216, 219, 220,
221, 223, 296, 298, 300,
301, 384
Communists, 81, 182,
198, 223, 296, 297, 313
Concert of Vienna, 121
Continental System, 365
Copernicus, 45
Cortes, Hernan, 342
COVID, 7, 145, 163, 166,
167, 231, 270
Crimea, 97, 99, 105, 193,
196, 214
Crimean War, 97, 214
crusades, 40, 41, 42, 80,
264
Cuban Missile Crisis, 188
Cult of Reason, 121
Cultural Revolution, 261,
313
Dachau Massacre, 388
Dali, Salvador, 18, 19
Daniels, Stormy, 209, 210
Dante, 52, 53
Dark Ages, 23, 36, 37,
47, 48, 56, 58, 86, 87, 94,
112, 263, 302, 377, 392
Dauger, Eustache, 21
D-Day, 19, 190, 191
De Goya, 46

Declaration of Independence, 145, 153

Declaration of the Rights of Man, 14

Diamond, Jared, 262, 263

Diem, Ngo Dinh, 180

Duc d'Enghien, 338

Duterte, 176, 197, 199, 349, 350, 355, 372

Dutschke, Rudi, 291, 382

East Berlin, 299

Eastman, Max, 20

Ebert, Fredrich, 256

Edward the Confessor, 39

Edwards, Edwin, 208

Eisenhower, Dwight, 104, 191, 388

El Filibusterismo, 17

Electoral College, 10, 239, 241, 271

Emoluments Clause, 203, 204

Emperor Meiji, 307

Engels, 20

Enlightenment, 24, 45, 264, 294, 296, 303, 311, 312, 314, 392

Era of Good Feelings, 275

European Coal and Steel Community, 90

European Economic Community, 90

European Union, 84

Exclusionary Rule, 349

Facebook, 227

feminicide, 129

Ferdinand II, 73

feudalism, 51, 53, 56, 57, 77, 88, 307

First Crusade, 41, 65, 303

Floyd, George, 126, 379

Ford, Gerald, 166, 212, 362

Four Great Inventions, 313

Franklin, Benjamin, 14

Frederick the Great, 338

French and Indian War, 364

French Revolution, 15, 24, 40, 67, 120, 121, 122, 123, 138, 141, 335, 392

Gaddafi, Mommar, 235

gatekeepers, 171

Gaye, Marvin, 136

General Assembly, 99

German Nationalism, 324, 325, 328

Ghibellines, 52

Globke, Hans, 381

Goddess of Reason, 121, 325

Godwinson, Harold, 39

Gorbachev, 248, 249, 297

Gravel, Mike, 219, 220

Great Leap Forward, 313

Great Society, 142

Green, Marjorie Taylor, 276

Guelphs, 52

Guillaume Affaire, 362

Guillaume, Günter, 362

Guns, Germs, and Steel, 262, 263

H-1B visa, 253

Haidt, Jonathan, 12
Haldeman, 154
Hamas, 322
Hannibal, 30
Hannity, Sean, 173
Hawkwood, John, 61, 287
Hemings, Sally, 14, 272
Hemingway, Ernest, 19, 20, 287
Heston, Charleton, 64
Himmler, Heinrich, 325
Hitler, 6, 76, 140, 143, 158, 159, 160, 326, 337, 380, 381
Holocaust, 321, 332, 368, 381, 385, 386
Hôtel des Invalides, 334
Hugo, Victor, 21
Hukbalahap, 372
Hunchback of Notre Dame, 21
Huntington, Samuel P., 189
Hussein, Saddam, 177, 305, 363
Hydroxychloroquine, 163, 167
Iéna and Auerstädt, 338
Incas, 342
Industrial Revolution, 24, 77, 78, 112, 294, 303, 312, 314, 315, 392
Inquisition, 39, 40, 41, 45, 330, 338
Iron Curtain, 196, 215, 297, 375
ISIS, 222

Islamic Golden Age, 304, 320
Jackson, Andrew, 213, 272
Jefferson, Thomas, 6, 14, 272
Jeffersonian democracy, 151, 358
Jesus, 38, 42, 46
Jim Crow, 150, 153, 254, 373, 394
Jinping, Xi, 270, 395
Johnson, Lyndon, 142, 221
Jong-un, Kim, 176, 183, 216, 282
Joyce, James, 20
Juche, 316
Judas, 53
Julius II, 62
Justinian, 50
Kardashian, Kim, 236
Kelly, John, 5
Kennedy, John F., 209, 230
Kennedy, Robert, 209, 240
Kenzo, 20
Khan, Genghis, 260, 307
Khan, Sadiq, 129, 130
King David, 339
King Francis I, 340
King, Rodney, 379
Kipling, Rudyard, 133, 292
Knights Templar, 42
Know-Nothing Party, 267, 393

Korean War, 222, 223
Kurds, 217, 222
Lagerfeld, Karl, 20
Lansdale, Edward, 372
Lansky, Meyer, 179
Las Damas Romanas, 16
League of Nations, 96, 98, 187
Leroux, Gaston, 21
Les Miserables, 21
Les Trente Glorieuses, 123
Levée en Masse, 67
Lewinsky, Monica, 169
Lodge, Henry Cabot, Jr., 181
Lorenzo the Magnificent, 60, 264
Louis XIV, 21
Louis XVIII, 122
Louisiana Purchase, 185
Louvre, 19, 340
Luna, Antonio, 15, 16, 18, 353
Luna, Juan, 15, 16, 18
Luther, Martin, 68, 72, 288
Lutheranism, 68, 70, 170
MacArthur, 308, 309
Machiavelli, 59
Macron, Emmanuel, 93, 335
Madison, James, 243
Magsaysay, Ramon, 372
Make America Great Again, 158
Mar-a-Lago, 270, 271, 276, 277

Marcos, Bongbong, 355, 357
Marcos, Ferdinand, 355, 356
Marshal Tito, 104
Marshall Plan, 200, 201, 224, 284
Martel, Charles, 50
Martial law, 178
Martial Law, 178, 349, 355, 357, 363, 371, 372
Marx, Karl, 20
Marxists, 81
Matthiole, Ercole, 21
McCain, John, 234
McCarthy, Eugene, 240
McCarthy, Kevin, 276
McConaughey, Matthew, 114
Medici, Contessina de, 264
Meiji Era, 260, 307
Merkel, Angela, 385
Mexican War, 185
Michelangelo, 57, 58, 62, 264
Miranda warnings, 349
Molay, Jacques de, 43
Mona Lisa, 19, 57, 340
Moro, Aldo, 383
Morrison, Jim, 21
Mosaddegh, 182
Muhammad, 302
Müller, Michael, 249
Napoleon, 40, 67, 76, 97, 121, 122, 138, 141, 290, 326, 334, 335, 336, 337,

338, 339, 340, 365, 386, 390
Napoleonic Empire, 120
Napoleonic Wars, 97, 121, 374, 386
NATO, 75, 76, 83, 185, 188, 196, 197, 215, 374
Nazi Germany, 92, 255, 382
Nazism, 324, 325, 329, 332, 337
Netanyahu, B., 330
Newton, 138
Newton, Helmut, 20
Night of the Long Knives, 143
Nixon, Richard, 137, 154, 156, 211, 212, 237, 240, 259, 283, 289, 362
Noli me Tangere, 17
Obama, 119, 142, 153, 156, 204, 237, 252, 270
Odoacer, 48
Ohnesorg, Benno, 382
Onoda, 311
Orders in Council, 365
Ottoman Empire, 304
Paoli, 335
Parks, Rosa, 148
Paul of Burgos, 330
Paul von Hindenburg, 143
Peace of Westphalia, 74
Pearl Harbor, 187, 260
Peasant's War, 70
Pegida, 384
Pen, Marine le, 93
Pen, Marine Le, 195

Phantom of the Opera, 21
Philby, Kim, 182
Philip the Fair, 42
Philippe, Louis, 122
Philippine-American War, 15, 186, 199, 345, 353
Picasso, Pablo, 18, 19
Pizarro, Francisco, 342
Plato, 26
Plessy v. Ferguson, 147, 148
Pompidou, Georges, 362
Pope Urban II, 41
Pound, Ezra, 20
Prince Harry, 130
Princess Meghan, 130
Protestant Reformation, 45, 68
Proud Boys, 150
Putin, 75, 83, 91, 94, 97, 176, 183, 195, 196, 214, 215, 216, 217, 222, 282, 373, 395
Queen Elizabeth, 233, 234
Reagan, 177, 248, 268, 372
Reconquista, 64
Reconstruction, 147, 186, 393
Red Brigades, 383
Richard the Lionheart, 41
Rizal, Jose, (aka Rizal, José), 15, 16, 17, 18, 345
Robespierre, Maximilian, 121
Roe v. Wade, 137, 394

Rohm, Ernst, 143
Roman Empire, 26, 29, 32, 34, 36, 47, 50, 51, 54, 66, 68, 70, 73, 80, 85, 86, 87, 94, 96, 112, 117, 118, 119, 294, 326, 327, 364, 374, 390, 392
Romanticism, 324
Romeo and Juliet, 60, 286
Romney, Mitt, 271
Roosevelt, Franklin, 166
Roxas, Manuel, 198
Russian Revolution, 375
Sack of Rome, 32, 118
Saint Mark, 38, 338
Saint Mark's Cathedral, 39
SCHENGEN, 92
Schleyer, Hanns Martin, 383
Scipio, 30
Scott, Dred, 147
Scrooge, Ebenezer, 79
Second Punic Wars, 30
Shah, 182
Sharia Law, 135
Siege of Toulon, 335
Silk Road, 317, 318
Sistene Chapel, 62
Six-Day War, 98, 321, 367, 368, 384
Socrates, 26
Solidarity, 297
Spartacus, 29, 390
Stein, Gertrude, 20
Subic Naval Base, 194
Suez Crisis, 98, 321

Suleiman the Magnificent, 304
Supreme Court, 146, 147, 148, 238, 394
Système International d'Unities, 121
Taliban, 47, 192, 215, 358
Tammany Hall, 208
Temple Mount, 42
The Agony and the Ecstasy, 264
The Apprentice, 174
The Blood Compact, 16
The Count of Monte Cristo, 121, 122
The Drama of Pergolèse Street, 17
The Graveyard of Empires, 358
The Great Game, 358
The Origins of the Inquisition, 319, 330
The Parisian Life, 16, 288
The Prince, 59
The Three Musketeers, 74
The Wedding Feast at Cana, 340
Thiers, Adolphe, 123
Third Coalition, 336
Third Crusade, 41
Third Reich, 326, 388
Thirty Years War, 51, 73, 88
Tianamen Square massacre, 313
Traoré, Adama, 126

Treaty of Amity and Commerce, 306, 307
Treaty of Guadalupe Hidalgo, 254, 255
Treaty of Versailles, 325, 387
Treaty of Westphalia, 76
Trump Foundation, 271
Trump University, 174, 271
Trump, Donald, 3, 4, 5, 6, 7, 8, 9, 10, 91, 94, 111, 113, 114, 115, 117, 119, 120, 131, 136, 138, 139, 141, 142, 150, 151, 153, 154, 156, 157, 158, 159, 160, 161, 162, 163, 164, 165, 166, 167, 168, 169, 170, 172, 173, 174, 175, 176, 183, 185, 188, 189, 190, 192, 193, 195, 196, 197, 198, 199, 200, 201, 203, 204, 205, 206, 209, 210, 211, 213, 214, 215, 216, 217, 222, 224, 228, 229, 230, 231, 232, 233, 234, 235, 236, 237, 238, 239, 241, 242, 243, 245, 246, 247, 248, 249, 250, 252, 253, 255, 257, 258, 259, 261, 265, 267, 268, 269, 270, 271, 273, 274, 275, 276, 277, 278, 279, 281, 282, 283, 284, 285, 291, 294, 373, 374, 375, 376, 378, 393, 394
Trumpism, 267, 274, 277
Twitch, 227

Twitter, 156, 236, 237, 238
Uccello, Paolo, 62
United Fruit Company, 180, 219
United Nations, 96, 106
United Red Army, 383
US AID, 229
Vietnam War, 136, 188, 194, 219, 221, 222, 223
Vinci, Leonardo Da, 57, 58, 340
Walesa, Lech, 297
Wallace, George, 155, 156, 268
War of 1812, 118, 185, 365
Wartburg Castle, 69
Washington Monument, 267
Washington, George, 212, 213, 279
Weimar Republic, 139, 140
Westphalian sovereignty, 90
Whiskey Rebellion, 212, 213
Whitmer, Gretchen, 270
Whore of Babylon, 71
William, the Conqueror, 39
Wilson, 187, 213
World War I, 96, 97, 256, 325, 329
World War II, 80, 88, 91, 96, 98, 102, 103, 119, 125, 135, 138, 141, 148,

179, 185, 187, 188, 190,
191, 192, 200, 201, 224,
260, 261, 284, 299, 308,
310, 321, 344, 346, 359,

360, 369, 372, 381, 383,
384, 385, 386
Xiaoping, Deng, 261, 314
Yom Kippur War, 321